DAVID SEYFORT RUEGG

THE SYMBIOSIS OF BUDDHISM WITH BRAHMANISM/HINDUISM IN SOUTH ASIA AND OF BUDDHISM WITH 'LOCAL CULTS' IN TIBET AND THE HIMALAYAN REGION

ÖSTERREICHISCHE AKADEMIE DER WISSENSCHAFTEN
PHILOSOPHISCH-HISTORISCHE KLASSE
SITZUNGSBERICHTE, 774. BAND

BEITRÄGE ZUR KULTUR- UND GEISTESGESCHICHTE ASIENS

Nr. 58

ÖSTERREICHISCHE AKADEMIE DER WISSENSCHAFTEN
PHILOSOPHISCH-HISTORISCHE KLASSE
SITZUNGSBERICHTE, 774. BAND

David Seyfort Ruegg

The symbiosis of Buddhism with Brahmanism/Hinduism in South Asia and of Buddhism with 'local cults' in Tibet and the Himalayan region

Verlag der
Österreichischen Akademie
der Wissenschaften

ÖAW

Wien 2008

Vorgelegt von w. M. Ernst Steinkellner
in der Sitzung am 14. Dezember 2007

British Library Cataloguing in Publication data.
A Catalogue record of this book is available from the British Library.

Die verwendete Papiersorte ist aus chlorfrei gebleichtem Zellstoff hergestellt, frei von säurebildenden Bestandteilen und alterungsbeständig.

ISBN 978-3-7001-6057-1

Druck und Bindung: Börsedruck Ges.m.b.H., A-1230 Wien

Printed and bound in Austria

http://hw.oeaw.ac.at/6057-1
http://verlag.oeaw.ac.at

Foreword

It has long been observed that at certain levels in Buddhist thought and religion there appear divine beings, celestial and daemonic, that do not belong strictly and exclusively to Buddhism alone because their counterparts or namesakes are to be found also in what we now term 'Hinduism' or 'Brahmanism' (and eventually in Jainism too). In this connexion there are two questions at least that arise: What are the status and significance of these entities within what we call 'Buddhism'?, and how exactly do they relate to their Brahmanical/Hindu namesakes and counterparts?

An answer that has often been given is that these entities have been borrowed by Buddhists from Brahmanism/Hinduism. This explanation, however, raises the further question as to why Buddhists would have wished to borrow entities that are alien to the religion they follow. For a borrower borrows from an *other*, thus raising the issue of alterity and the alien. What then could it have been that motivated Buddhists to borrow so long as Buddhism and Brahmanism/Hinduism are *ex hypothesi* regarded as separate religious systems alien to each other? Was it confusion of mind, or perhaps the laziness of habit of new converts to Buddhism? Or was this borrowing motivated by Buddhists' desire to emulate or compete with Brahmanism/Hinduism? But why should supposed converts from Brahmanism/Hinduism have wished to vie with what they had converted from by borrowing from it? Trying to answer such questions may lead to endless speculation perhaps more revealing about the speculator than about what actually happened at some time in ancient and mediaeval India. More fundamental is the question whether one can even properly speak of borrowing where a civilization and religious culture are known to be in large part shared by both Buddhists and Brahmanists/Hindus, at least at certain significant levels. Seldom have advocates of the borrowing hypothesis adequately examined this crucial question.

Another way of explaining the presence within Buddhism of the namesakes and counterparts of Brahmanical/Hindu divinities is then to hypothesize that they belonged to a common ground, a 'substratum' shared by both Buddhism and the ambient religions in the land of its birth. The expression 'substratum' was employed, between inverted commas, in our article 'Sur les rapports entre le bouddhisme et le "substrat religieux" indien et tibétain', *Journal asiatique* 1964, pp. 77–95.

Here 'substratum' is to be understood in a sense different from its meaning in linguistics, where a language's substratum will often be of a type different from, and genetically unrelated to, that language. In the 'substratum model' under discussion in the present study, however, the religious substratum is not allogenic, or exogenous, in relation to the form of Buddhism incorporating it. (Such an interpretation based on the 'substratum model' is of course not reducible to a version of the modern idea of 'Hindutva'.) This observation is in its turn related to one of the great problems arising in the history of India, the question of the circumstances in which Buddhism largely disappeared as a distinct entity from the land of its birth.

Why then did the Buddhists not all engage in good housekeeping and clear out everything that was shared with Brahmanism/Hinduism, and which might seem alien and exogenous to Buddhism? By thinking in terms of borrowing, advocates of the 'borrowing model', and in particular those opposed to the 'substratum model', have presupposed that Buddhism and Brahmanism/Hinduism are two separate and different religious systems requiring to be kept neatly apart at all levels of analysis. However, even though many of their basic texts clearly show that they were very well aware of the differences separating them from Brahmanists/Hindus, it appears that Buddhists did not necessarily wish always to engage in such tidy housekeeping. And, evidently, this was because the entities belonging to the shared Indian substratum had a role or function within Buddhism. A brief, and still preliminary, statement concerning this function is that, within the Buddhist world view, it was not unusual to conceive of such entities as occupying its 'mundane' storey. This storey is what is known in Sanskrit terminology as the *laukika*, the 'worldly' or 'mundane', as opposed to the *lokottara*, the 'supramundane' or 'transmundane'. (See our 'Note on the relationship between Buddhist and "Hindu" divinities in Buddhist literature and iconology: The *laukika/lokottara* contrast and the notion of an Indian "religious substratum"', in R. Torella [ed.] *Le parole e i marmi* [R. Gnoli Felicitation Volume, Serie Orientale Roma, vol. xcii, Rome, 2001], pp. 735–742.)

What is the significance of this *laukika* level for a Buddhist? Concisely stated, this level is inhabited by 'worldly' divinities and numina that occupied the minds of Buddhists as well as of other Indians. In Buddhist thought, the position of these entities was an inferior and subordinate one relatively to that of beings representing the supramundane level of the cosmos, namely the Buddha and the higher Bodhisattvas including the higher protectors of the Dharma (*dharmapāla*, Tib. *chos skyoṅ*), who have been classified as *lokottara*. (It is important to observe that the *lokottara* level is not here identical with the *pāramārthika*, the level described as being 'of ultimate meaning'; for this *lokottara* contrasted with the *laukika* is still conceptualized as being intra-cosmic, even if beings classified as *lokottara* in the structure under discussion in the present study may relate or point to the acosmic *paramārtha*.)

Now, in the frame of the *laukika* : *lokottara* contrastive opposition, the mundane and transmundane levels were not necessarily and invariably thought of as frozen and as hermetically sealed off from each other in an immutable vertical layering. Because the Buddha and Bodhisattvas (both peaceful and wrathful ones) act compassionately for the benefit and the ultimate liberation of all sentient beings (*sattva*), a mundane divinity or daemon occupying the *laukika* level may finally be raised – i.e. transfigured or trans-valued – to the *lokottara* level of the *ārya* or 'Noble (of the spirit)', thus becoming even a higher protector of the Dharma. In our sources, the process of perfectionment undergone by ordinary, mundane, beings, regarded as 'trainees' (*vineya*, Tib. *gdul bya*), may be referred to as a process of training (Skt. *vi-nī-*, Tib. *'dul ba* 'tame'), a concept that is only inadequately rendered by the term 'conversion'. This is a salvific act of liberation characterized, from the point of view of both trainer and trainee, as compassionate, even when it is represented as being not totally peaceful but highly energetic and even forceful. Just as ordinary beings or worldlings (*pṛthagjana*) – however much they may still be mired in defilements (*kleśa*) – may benefit from this compassionate liberating activity of the Buddha and Bodhisattvas and thus, in the perspective of the Mahāyāna and Vajrayāna, themselves eventually accede to 'noble' (*ārya*) bodhisattvahood (and onwards to buddhahood), so may divinities and numina of the worldly level be 'trained' and transformed into Ārya-Bodhisattvas, thus finally becoming integrated into the *lokottara* level.

The contrastive *laukika* : *lokottara* structure, as thus understood in its connexion with the 'substratum model', is antithetical to the view according to which the schema where the *lokottara* is superordinate to the *laukika* level was intended by Buddhists to express in agonistic and secular-historicist fashion the victory of Buddhism over Brahmanism/Hinduism. This has been a widely spread view, and it seems to have been maintained by modern writers on the basis of iconographical depictions of a superordinate Buddhist deity, classified as *lokottara*, dancing, or treading, on a putatively 'Hindu' one. (This view may have been influenced by an icon such as the *śarabheśvaramūrti*, on which see p. 60 with notes 68, 70 and 138, and perhaps by the theme of *brahmahatyā*, on which see p. 59 with note 87.) But this interpretation of the Buddhist icons in question is by no means necessary, and it is not supported by the way such figures have been understood in a large number of relevant Buddhist texts where, iconologically, the schema represents rather the superordination of the transmundane over the mundane and subordinate level.

We thus encounter three distinct interpretations of the relation between Buddhism and Brahmanism/Hinduism, and of entities of the *lokottara* level in relation to those of the *laukika* level: (i) the 'substratum model', (ii) the 'borrowing model', and (iii) a more or less secular and historicist interpretation of the schema as representing the agonistic or hostile relation 'Buddhism *vs.* Hinduism' in the world, i.e. in history. Although interpretations (i) and (ii) are theoretically opposable, they are not entirely exclusive of each other: in the practice of historical analysis of individual cases in Indian (and Tibetan, etc.) religion the former model will be most appropriate in certain instances, while in other historically and philologically defined cases the second model may be relevant. It does not seem that both models will normally be applicable simultaneously to a single individual case; but it does appear that a given historically verifiable borrowing can best be explained against the background of a common ground, the 'substratum' shared between Buddhism and Brahmanism/Hinduism. As for the agonistic view (iii), it is of course possible that the structured contrastive opposition *laukika*: *lokottara* relating to two levels, one superordinate to the other, has on occasion been understood (or misunderstood) in terms of a historical-secular hostility 'Buddhism *vs.* Brahmanism/Hinduism', or *vice versa*, as has indeed happened in modern India where icons depicting a divine being dancing, or treading, on another entity are sometimes being explained in just this fashion. Such a 'Buddhism *vs.* Hinduism' view of the relevant icons has been adopted uncritically also by some workers in the fields of art history and iconography, who speak of 'Hindu' gods being trampled upon and humiliated. But such subordinate entities seem better described as 'mundane' and pan-Indian – i.e. as belonging to a shared religious substratum – rather than as strictly Brahmanical/Hindu alone. Here the expression 'pan-Indian' is not to be understood to imply that a given entity or feature is to be found in the same form in each and every Indian religion without exception, but rather to signal that it is widely represented both in what is called Brahmanism/Hinduism and in Buddhism. (Concerning an icon depicting the victory of the Buddha over heterodox *tīrthika*s, compare pp. 75–76 below.)

With regard to the 'borrowing model' (BM), in one version of it (see below, p. 105 ff. with p. 150 note 202) examples of material held by both Śaivas and Buddhists have been indifferently termed Śivaism, notably in the case of Yoginī or 'Mother' Tantras. Two analytically distinct things – namely Śaiva material in the strictest sense and material common to both religious groups – are thus grouped together as a single entity labelled Śivaism. For the 'substratum model' (SM), on the other hand, what was held in common and shared would remain unspecified and unlabelled as to sectarian affiliation (except of course in a case of historically characterized and verified borrowing by one religion from the other), while when expressed in Śaiva or Vaiṣṇava scriptures it might no doubt be referred to as Śivaist or Viṣṇuite, and when expressed in a Buddhist text it might be no less appropriately called Buddhist. In other words, in one version of the BM, materials distinguishable from the viewpoints of both religious history and psychology have received the selfsame appellation. But for the SM the telescoping together of what are after all two analytically distinct levels is something to be carefully avoided whenever possible. And the SM seeks to take due account of the two different levels within Buddhism known as the *laukika* – i.e., *inter alia*, what is held in common between Buddhists and Hindus, etc., and does not require to be identified in sectarian terms – and the *lokottara* which, for the Buddhist, is strictly speaking Buddhist.

Of course, as already mentioned, in the course of Indian religious history it may well be that a Buddhist living, and perhaps also educated, in a Śaiva or Vaiṣṇava milieu might take over into his ideas and practices certain matter acceptable to Buddhism but still identifiable as of Śaiva or Vaiṣṇava origin. Once this transfer has been accomplished in time, however, the material would become integrated into a new synchronic whole, a Buddhist one. Under the appellation of *laukika* such an adopted component would be contrastively opposed in Buddhist thought to the properly Buddhist *lokottara*. To label it as Śivaism or Viṣṇuism, as Śaiva or Vaiṣṇava, once it has been incorporated within the Buddhist system seems methodologically problematic inasmuch as it collapses the diachronic and synchronic axes. To do so is also questionable; for, from the religio-philosophic viewpoint of at least an informed and educated Buddhist, such specification and labelling would tend to render it ritually and doctrinally devoid of meaning and hence unauthentic and inoperative. It may be recalled that Buddhists have themselves been aware of, and have indeed confronted, the possibility of infiltration into Buddhism of non-Buddhist elements. An example, usually regarded by Buddhist tradition as a contamination, were ideas and practices that Buddhist sources have attributed to the so-called Red-Ācārya and the Blue-clad ones who were active at the turn of the second millennium in the western Himalayan area (see below, pp. 127–129). Numerous other examples of various kinds regarded in Buddhist traditions not as cases of contamination but rather as 'mundane' or 'worldly' – i.e., explicitly or implicitly, as *laukika* – components are discussed in this book.

The 'emic' *laukika* : *lokottara* structure – well attested as it is through the history of Buddhism – merits close attention because it yields a highly useful interpretative schema or template, one that often turns out to be at least as pertinent as the concepts of interreligious borrowing, syncretism, fusion, relativism, indifferentism, or inclusivism (i.e. Paul Hacker's Inklusivismus). The *laukika* : *lokottara* schema corresponds to a vertical, two-layered, symbiosis of Buddhism and ambient Indian (or Tibetan, etc.) religion, with Buddhism in its *lokottara* aspect constituting the upper, superordinate, level. In view of the fact that communication and a passage between the two levels are open (see above), it is possible to speak of an intercommunicating bi-level symbiosis and transfigurative accommodation.

Evidence is also collected here showing that the schema of the *laukika* : *lokottara* – known in Tibetan as the *'jig rten pa* : *'jig rten las 'das pa* – has been employed not only in India but also in Tibet (and other Buddhist lands) in order to structure and represent the relationship between so-called 'local' divinities and cults and the great figures of a universalist (but imported) Buddhism. In this connexion, attention may also be drawn to the East Asian concept of a 'true ground' and its 'trace', known in Japanese Buddhism as *honji suijaku*.

It is not to be supposed that the *laukika* : *lokottara* schema, meaningful and productive though it has been in Buddhist thought, provides the single and sole key for interpreting all relevant texts and iconographic depictions. Especially pertinent already in Indian Buddhist thought have been the concepts of transformation (*vikurvaṇa/vikurvāṇa*, Tib. *rnam par 'phrul ba*) and (docetic) manifestation (*nirmāṇa*, Tib. *sprul pa*). Beside the vertical and hierarchical schema of the mundane : supramundane levels, Buddhist versions of docetism thus occupy a central place in some of the structures and processes considered in the present study.

This study thus offers materials and interpretations concerning the 'emic' contrastive opposition mundane : supramundane and related topics, the substratum and borrowing models for religious symbiosis, and the question of the confrontation between Buddhism and Hinduism. Rather than with attempting a linear historical treatment of the materials over a period of a couple of millennia, this study is concerned in the first place with themes, motifs and structures. In our sources the application of the *laukika* : *lokottara* schema is sometimes made explicitly, and sometimes it is more implicit or latent.

It is hardly necessary then to state that the following pages are not intended to provide a complete and exhaustive account either of the relationship between Buddhism and Brahmanism/Hinduism and between it and local divinities and cults in Tibet, or of all the various aspects of the *laukika* : *lokottara* contrastive opposition in the history of Buddhist thought. (A few further aspects have been touched on in our *Ordre spirituel et ordre temporel dans la pensée bouddhique de l'Inde et du Tibet* [Publications de l'Institut de Civilisation Indienne, fasc. 64, Paris, 1995].) In the present study attention is given in particular to the pertinence of the 'substratum model' beside the 'borrowing model' in analysing certain highly important features in the history of Buddhist thought and religion. Whilst (as already mentioned) the 'borrowing model' may no doubt be applicable in certain historically and philologically defined instances, the 'substratum model' retains its significance and usefulness – one being to provide the necessary cultural-historical conditions for borrowing of any sort to have taken place from Brahmanism/Hinduism to Buddhism, or indeed *vice versa*. An effort has also been made to show how the processes of religious integration investigated here differ from those that are explainable in terms of Paul Hacker's often-discussed concept of inclusivism.

The primary sources and the secondary literature relating to the topics investigated here are of course very abundant. Concerning the original

Indian, Tibetan and other Buddhist sources, for reasons of space it has been possible to consider here only a limited, but nevertheless significant, selection of textual and iconographic evidence where the *laukika* : *lokottara* schema is found to be applicable to Buddhist religious, ritual and philosophical thought in connexion with the incorporation of the 'mundane' level, along with its pan-Indian divinities and numina, in the Buddhist world view. As regards the secondary literature, because of its abundance and variety references to it could not be exhaustive. But with a view to furnishing at least an indication as to the discussions that have appeared over the years, bibliographical notes refer to earlier treatments of the problems as well as to more recent examinations of them; unavoidably, some intervening contributions have had to be left unnoticed.

*

My most sincere thanks go to Ernst Steinkellner for his valuable comments and for submitting this work to the Austrian Academy of Sciences for the Beiträge zur Kultur- und Geistesgeschichte Asiens, and to Cristina Scherrer-Schaub with whom I have been able to discuss this work and who has also provided valuable comments. I recall that many years ago I had the opportunity to discuss several topics addressed in this book with the late Jean Filliozat. Responsibility for whatever shortcomings and errors remain rests of course with the author. I wish also to thank Helmut Krasser for his generous and indeed essential help through the publication process, and Markus Viehbeck who has formatted this book in conformity with the style used in publications of the Austria Academy. My warmest gratitude goes too to Ulrich Pagel and Burkhard Quessel who have most generously given time to resolving many a problem.

D.S.R.

March 2007

Table of contents

Introduction

That there was no sharp and radical break, no unbridgeable gulf, between many of the religious and cultural representations of Buddhism and the other religions of India seems sufficiently clear, even if their respective ideas and practices have very often been treated as if they were not only distinguishable but quite separate and even opposed entities. Their separate treatment is of course justifiable for many practical purposes, but not genetically or theoretically. This situation of religious and cultural relationship, and of polythetic family resemblance, on the two axes of the diachronic and the synchronic – which might, at least tentatively, be described as a CONTINUITY and SYMBIOSIS of what have been distinct but historically related traditions – is rooted not only in a common civilization but in matters of religious and philosophical ideas and practices: the Buddhists of India were after all Indians, even if we do not wish to reify these names. To say this is, after all, merely to state what should be obvious, namely that the ambient culture of India was the matrix from which, historically, sprang Buddhism as well as Brahmanism/Hinduism and Jainism and in which they developed and flourished over the centuries.[1]

---

[1] As is well known, in the history of the Indo-Aryan languages the words *hindu/hindū* (not to speak of *hindutva/hindūtva*) are attested relatively late. In this study the term 'Hinduism' is being used simply as a convenient, and somewhat conventional, designation for the later periods of what – in particular in relation to the earlier period – is known to modern scholars as Brahmanism. Some scholars have employed the designations Hindu and Hinduism to denote respectively a person and a religious system excluding (and possibly opposed to) the Buddhist and Buddhism, the Jain and Jainism, the 'tribals' and their religions, etc. Others have on the contrary used the two words inclusively as cover terms to refer in general to the inhabitants and the ('higher') religion(s) of South Asia. Modern uses of the term 'Hinduism' have been surveyed by D. Lorenzen, 'Who invented Hinduism?', *Comparative studies in society and history* 41 (1999), pp. 630–59. As for 'Brahmanism', in the following the expression will often be used in a wide sense, the more eastern regions of India in which Buddhism arose not having originally been part of the area (the original Āryāvarta) in which Brahmanism in the stricter sense was centred. The expression as used in this study may thus cover also the religion and culture of those designated as *brāhmaṇa* in the compound *śramaṇa-brāhmaṇa* (cf. n. 3 below). It is not a main thesis of this study

Nevertheless, by some modern writers on the subject including Indian ones, the relationship between Hinduism and Buddhism has not seldom been described in agonistic (and occasionally polemical) terms as one of confrontation and struggle. Alternatively, by a second group of writers, Buddhism has been subsumed under, or inclusivistically incorporated within, Hinduism. This second view sometimes even turns up not so much as an alternative to the first one but rather as a sort of free variant or alternate of it (for instance in the case of modern 'Hindutva'). Very remarkably, these views seem sometimes to have been adopted against the background of a fairly secularist understanding of the situation, including even when they were propounded in an ostensibly religious context. Confrontation and struggle – even antagonism or forceful incorporation – and much of what goes with them there have no doubt been aplenty. And, evidently, many a Brahmanical/Hindu authority has felt that his tradition was being attacked, perhaps even threatened, by Buddhists; whilst many a Buddhist did not spare certain ideas and practices of the Brahmans/Hindus. Yet the description of this relationship as predominantly one of struggle and antagonism appears one-sided. The relation has, rather, consisted in a complex historical and religious SYMBIOTIC INTERACTION that might, on occasion, also involve critical engagement, struggle (for social, secular, intellectual and religious dominance), and antagonism. This view of the matter that operates with the idea of a common GROUND OF SUBSTRATUM underlying much of Brahmanism/Hinduism and Buddhism has been adopted by a third group of writers on the subject and is in part that of the present writer.[2]

---

that Buddhism was a development of late Vedic Brahmanism (whatever may in fact have been its links with it; see pp. 5–6 below).

[2] In part – but no doubt only in part – the problem has probably to do with the circumstance that, in practice, the terms of the familiar oppositions religious/secular (including political) and sacred/profane have been less markedly exclusive, and confined each to its own separate domain, in Indian (and Buddhist) thought than is now the case in the West. With respect to Indian culture and history, then, they are perhaps 'etic' more than 'emic' categories. And it could, then, seem that the understanding of the relationship between Buddhism and Brahmanism/Hinduism, and of certain of their religious narratives and icons, in a decidedly secularist-profane and historical-polemical sense – i.e. as Hinduism *vs.* Buddhism or Buddhism *vs.* Hinduism as represented for example by Benoytosh Bhattacharyya's interpretation of certain Buddhist icons (see below, pp. 45 n. 68, 60) – was a 'modernist' view due to Western influence

It is to an examination of certain aspects of this multi-layered and highly complex religious and cultural constellation (or nebula) that the following pages are devoted. Clearly, in view of the vast extent of the relevant materials, no claim can be made here to a full and comprehensive coverage of the primary sources or to exhaustiveness with regard to the secondary literature.

---

on Indian thinking in the nineteenth and twentieth centuries rather than to a searching analysis of the Buddhist sources. See, however, the Tibetan source cited below, pp. 75–76.

Yet, even in earlier Sanskrit works, secularist, social, (quasi-)historical, and polemical understandings of their relationship are not without precedent. G. Verardi has collected a number of Purāṇic passages indicating that narratives concerning the contest between the *deva*s and *asura*s, and icons relatable to these struggles, were directed against Buddhists or Jains; see his article 'Images of destruction: An enquiry into Hindu icons in their relation to Buddhism', in: G. Verardi and S. Vita (ed.), *Buddhist Asia 1* (Kyōto, 2003), pp. 1–36. Now this situation raises the interesting question as to whether 'orthodox' Brahmanism/Hinduism – socially 'lay' with only a very limited monastic component – has been not only more socially and 'orthopractically' exclusive (both within itself and in relation to the 'non-orthodox' in India), but also, at least on occasion, markedly more secularist, even euhemerist, in its outlook than Buddhism has usually been. In the materials reviewed by Verardi, a concrete historical interpretation of narratives and icons seems to be present. A solution to the problem considered by Verardi might possibly lie in the direction of distinguishing between the ahistorical and universal value or significance of a narrative or icon in terms of atemporal archetypes – such as the structural opposition *laukika* : *lokottara* to be considered in the present study –, and the concrete, indeed euhemeristic, interpretation of which such a narrative or icon became susceptible with reference to a particular historical circumstance. However, such an assessment of course involves generalizations; and by its very nature generalization may require qualification and restriction in specific individual cases. (When the narrative or icon in question is ambiguous – that is, when it lends itself to interpretation either as an ahistorical and atemporal archetypal structure or as reflecting a historical event/process – the question may still remain open as to which interpretation is primary and which secondary. Perhaps the narrative or icon is to be considered atemporal and universal in its value and significance, but temporal and historical in its particular reference?)

1. Śramaṇas and Brāhmaṇas: Some aspects of the relation between Hindus, Buddhists and Jainas

The continuity and the symbiosis between Buddhism and the ambient religions have been rather diversely perceived and accounted for over the years by various writers on the subject. And some appear to have been quite astonished by the phenomenon because they apparently expected, *a priori*, to find a clear line of demarcation between the religious representations of the Buddhists, the Brahmans/Hindus, and the Jains. Still, that Buddhism sprang from an Indian matrix and milieu has, nevertheless, been generally acknowledged, if perhaps sometimes only half-heartedly. The precise modalities of the relationship between Buddhism and Brahmanism/Hinduism have, however, never been comprehensively and exhaustively investigated, something which is scarcely surprising in view of the overwhelming mass of relevant materials. On the one hand, there is clearly a continuity between the two; but equally clearly there have also existed many significant tensions and points of difference and of discontinuity.

Continuity and symbiotic co-ordination or complementarity appear in fact to be what is expressed by the compound *śramaṇa-brāhmaṇa-* (Pali *samaṇa-brāhmaṇā*) 'ascetic and Brahman' in Buddhist texts from the time of the canon onwards.[3]

---

[3] In Aśoka's inscriptions, in addition to *samanabaṃbhana*, etc., the compounds *bambhaṇasamaṇa/brahmaṇaśramaṇa*, etc., are also found. (For the phonology of words for 'Brāhmaṇa' see O. v. Hinüber, *Das ältere Mittelindisch im Überblick* [²Vienna, 2001], § 284.)

Sometimes the relation between these two categories has been represented as a more or less straightforward opposition. This view is reflected in Patañjali's explanation for the singular number of the copulative compound *śramaṇabrāhmaṇam*, which is said by him to be accounted for by the fact that there is a *virodha* 'opposition' between the two referents of the two members of the compound; see *Vyākaraṇa-Mahābhāṣya* ad Pāṇini II.iv.12 *vārtt.* 2: *yeṣāṃ ca virodha ity* [cf. II.iv.9] *asya avakāśaḥ/ śramaṇabrāhmaṇam/*). This usage may then be contrasted with the dual number of the *dvandva* compound *brāhmaṇakṣatriyau* (see comm. ad II.iv.6).

Whether the groups, or traditions, of the *śramaṇas* and *brāhmaṇas* are in fact opposed depends of course on the circumstances of each case; many Buddhists are indeed

A further noteworthy piece of evidence for continuity between Buddhism and Brahmanism is the provision made in the Buddhist Vinaya according to which one who has the Brāhman's long locks of hair and keeps the sacred ritual fire (*aggika jaṭilaka*) – i.e. one who has instituted his ritual fire (*āhitāgni*) – may be given ordination as a Buddhist monk (*upasampadā*) without being obliged first to undergo a probationary period (*parivāsa*). The reason given in this canonical source is that such persons accept the doctrine of acts (*kammavādi[n]*, *kiriyavādi[n]*), that is, they hold that actions bear fruit and so have their consequences.[4]

---

known to have been of Brāhman origin. Abhinavagupta has alluded to a *brāhmaṇa-śramaṇanyāya* in his *Dhvanyālokalocana* i.4 (KSS ed., p. 51); here the reference is to a temporal succession of two different states, the latter substituting for the former but the former designation of Brāhman still being applied to the ascetic (this has been rendered as 'much as a *śramaṇa* (Buddhist monk) who was once a brahmin is called a brahmin *śramaṇa*' in D. H. H. Ingalls, J. M. Masson and M. V. Patwardhan, *The Dhvanyāloka of Ānandavardhana with the Locana of Abhinavagupta* [Cambridge, Mass., 1990], p. 81).

Compare the two terms *brāhmaṇa* and *parivrājaka*. In Ardhamāgadhī, we have the expression *māhaṇa-parivvāyaya* (etc.). See e.g. W. Schubring, *Isibhāsiyāiṃ* (Hamburg, 1969), p. 536; and H. Nakamura, 'Common elements in early Jain and Buddhist literature', *IT* 11 (1983), pp. 316–7. There exists, moreover, a *vipraparivrājakanyāya*, namely 'the principle of the Brahman and Wandering Ascetic' according to which *parivrājaka*s are a subset of the set denominated *vipra*s; see, e.g., Sāyaṇa's introduction to his commentary on the *Ṛgveda* (p. 12.31 f.).

Concerning Śramaṇa traditions and so-called 'Śramaṇism' see, e.g., P. S. Jaini, 'Śramaṇas: Their conflict with Brāhmaṇical society', in *Collected papers on Buddhist studies* (Delhi, 2001), pp. 47–96; G. C. Pande, *Śramaṇa tradition: Its history and contribution to Indian culture* (L[albhai] D[alpatbhai] Series no. 66, Ahmedabad, 1978); B. G. Gokhale, 'Early Buddhism and the Brahmanas', in: A. K. Narain (ed.), *Studies in history of Buddhism* (Delhi, 1980), pp. 67–77; J. Bronkhorst, *The two sources of Indian asceticism* (Bern, 1993). And on the use of the terms *bhikkhu* and *samaṇa* see R. O. Franke, *Dīghanikāya* (Göttingen-Leipzig, 1913), pp. 304–7. See also K. R. Norman, 'Theravāda Buddhism and Brahmanical Hinduism: Brahmanical terms in a Buddhist guise', *Buddhist Forum* 2 (1991), pp. 193–200 (= *Collected papers*, iv [Oxford, 1993], pp. 271–80). For the use of the expression Brahmanism in this study, see n. 1 above.

4 See Vinaya (*Mahāvagga*) I 71: *ye te bhikkhave aggikā jaṭilakā te āgatā upasampādetabbā, na tesaṃ parivāso dātabbo/ taṃ kissa hetu/ kammavādino ete bhikkhave kiriyavādino*. For *kammavādi*(*n*) see also Dīghanikāya I 115, II 339. In Aṅguttaranikāya I 62, the Buddha describes himself as both a *kiriyāvādi*(*n*)and an *akiriyā-*

As for non-theism, historically it does not seem to constitute strictly speaking a criterial factor between Buddhism and Brahmanism since in both Brāhmanical thought – in particular in its earlier periods as in the (Karma-) Mīmāṃsā – and in Buddhism traditions are found that do not posit a Creator God or a God that presides over the destiny of individuals.[5]

---

vādi(n), i.e. he accepts, according to context, either the *kiriyāvāda* and the *akiriyāvāda* (compare Vinaya I 234). In Pali the word *āhitaggi*, the equivalent of Skt. *āhitāgni* 'having "instituted" the fire', is attested in Aggavaṃsa's *Saddanīti*, p. 414. 22.

Compare the story of Uruvela-Kassapa – one of the three Brāhmaṇa Jaṭila-brothers (*tebhātika-jaṭila*) all named Kassapa (Kāśyapa) – in the *Mahāvagga* (Vinaya I 24 f.), where this personage's earlier life and practices are contrasted with his life as a disciple of the Buddha. For verses ascribed to Uruvela-Kassapa see *Theragāthā* 375–80. The Buddha's first disciples – the *pañcavaggīyā* – are said to have been Brāhmaṇas. Further examples of Brāhmaṇas having become Buddhists are given in G. P. Malalasekera's *Dictionary of Pāli proper names*, p. 341 ff. (It is noteworthy that Pali has used the spelling *brāhmaṇa*, which phonetically is not a Middle Indo-Aryan form and is considered a Sanskritism, i.e. an Old Indo-Aryan form; but a Pali hermeneutical etymology (< *bāheti*) of the word presupposes a Middle Indo-Aryan form, such as **bāhaṇa*. See O. von Hinüber, *Das ältere Mittelindisch im Überblick* § 284; id., 'Linguistic considerations on the date of the Buddha', in: H. Bechert (ed.), *The dating of the historical Buddha*, Part 1 [Göttingen, 1991], p. 186.) In the later history of Buddhism, Brāhmaṇas have very often figured in important roles.

Another interesting link between early Buddhist practice and Brahmanical culture is that between the late Brahmanic *upavasatha* 'fasting day' and the Buddhist *uposatha*/*poṣadha* (the adoption in Buddhism of the *uposatha* has been attributed by some to the needs of the laity, but this is speculative). Cf. Haiyan Hu-von Hinüber, *Das Poṣadhavastu* (Reinbek, 1994), p. 2 ff.

In the opinion of H. Oldenberg the elaborate code of *Pāṭimokkha* rules were a substitute in Buddhism for the old and short late Vedic vrata formulae; see his *Zur Geschichte der altindischen Prosa*, *AGWG*, Philol.-hist, Kl. 16/6 (Berlin, 1917), p. 40. For a discussion of Buddhist Vinaya rules against the Indian background, see T. Oberlies, 'Neuer Wein in alten Schläuchen?', *BEI* 15 (1997), pp. 171–204. – On the Brahmanical sacrifice according to Buddhism, see H. Falk, 'Vedische Opfer im Pali-Kanon', *BEI* 6 (1988), pp. 225–54; and O. Freiberger, 'The ideal sacrifice: Patterns of reinterpreting Brahmin sacrifice in early Buddhism', *BEI* 16 (1998), pp. 39–49.]

[5] For some references see below, n. 62, where mention is also made of the quasi-theistic figure of Avalokiteśvara in the *Kāraṇḍavyūha*.

In addition, a continuity between Buddhist civilization and Indian civilization in general is clearly reflected in the domain of the secular, 'worldly' (*laukika*), arts and sciences (*vidyāsthāna*) comprising grammar, medicine, logic, and arts and crafts, where this continuity pertains to both form and content. This is why these four major *vidyāsthāna*s, together with some minor oncs, have often been described as common to the two traditions. In respect to form and method (if no longer to content), continuity extends even to the 'supramundane/transmundane' (*lokottara*) domain of the 'inner science' (*adhyātmavidyā*), that is, to what characterizes Buddhism as doctrine.[6] It is well known also that Buddhist

---

[6] On the *vidyāsthāna*s (Tib. *rig [pa'i] gnas*) as common (Tib. *thun moṅ ba*) to Buddhism and the ambient Hindu civilization, see D. Seyfort Ruegg, *Ordre spirituel et ordre temporel dans la pensée bouddhique de l'Inde et du Tibet* (Paris, 1995), p. 101 ff.; id., 'Notes sur la transmission et la réception des traités de grammaire et de lexicographie sanskrites dans les traditions indo-tibétaines', in: N. Balbir *et al.* (ed.), *Langue, style et structure dans le monde indien*: *Centenaire de Louis Renou* (Paris, 1996), pp. 213–32. – K. Bhattacharya has discerned a grammatical basis to some of Nāgārjuna's reasonings and to Candrakīrti's comments thereon; see his 'Back to Nāgārjuna and grammar', *ALB* 59 (1995), p. 178–89, and 'Sur la base grammaticale de la pensée indienne', in N. Balbir *et al.* (ed.), *op. cit.*, pp. 171–85. Concerning the role of grammar in Buddhist thought see also D. Seyfort Ruegg, 'Mathematical and linguistic models in Indian thought: The case of zero and *śūnyatā*', *WZKS* 22 (1978), pp. 171–81. It may be recalled too that there exist certain grammatical links between the Pali language (especially that of the Jātakas) and Pāṇinean grammar; see F. Kielhorn, 'The Jātakas and Sanskrit grammarians' (1898), *Kleine Schriften*, pp. 294–8, and 'A peculiar use of the causative in Sanskrit and Pali' (1904), *ibid.*, pp. 1012 f., with O. von Hinüber, *Untersuchungen zur Mündlichkeit früher mittelindischer Texte der Buddhisten* (AWL, Abh. der Geistes- und Sozialwissenschaftlichen Kl., Mainz, 1994), p. 32.

As for the parallel between the canonical Pali formula (in rhythmic prose) *diṭṭhaṃ sutaṃ mutaṃ viññātaṃ* and *dṛṣṭe śrute mate vijñāte* in *Bṛhadāraṇyakopaniṣad* IV.v.6, it has been pointed out by K. Bhattacharya in S. Balasooriya *et al.* (ed.), *Buddhist studies in honour of Walpola Rahula* (London, 1980), pp. 10–15; cf. O. v. Hinüber, *op. cit.*, p. 34.

Links and continuities between Brahmaṇical thought and Buddhism have been investigated by, e.g., H. Oldenberg, *Die Lehre der Upanishaden und die Anfänge des Buddhismus* (Göttingen, 1923), E. Windisch, 'Brahmanischer Einfluss im Buddhismus', in: *Aufsätze zur Kultur- und Sprachgeschichte vornehmlich des Orients* (Festschrift E. Kuhn, Breslau, 1916), pp. 1–13, and P. Mus, *Barabuḍur* (Hanoi, 1935), Introduction; M. Falk, *Nāma-rūpa and Dharma-rūpa* (Calcutta, 1943); L. Silburn, *In-*

literature has made use of elements of the Rāma legend in works as different as the Jātakas (the *Dasarathajātaka*)[7] and the *Buddhacarita* by Aśvaghoṣa.[8] Materials from the *Mahābhārata* and the Purāṇas have also been made use of extensively.[9] The connexions between Buddhism and the Yoga school (despite the fact that the latter has its special idea of an *īśvara*) are no less well known.

The concept of *lokottara* is of course distinct from the idea of *paraloka* (Tib. *'jig rten pha rol*) 'other world' (as in rebirth in a further form of existence). It is only a partial synonym of *alaukika* 'non-mundane, out of the ordinary, marvellous' (as e.g. a description of a theatrical representation).

For the term *laukika*, beside the usual translation 'worldly, mundane', the rendering 'pagan' (< Lat. *paganus* < *pagus* 'country district') would probably not be entirely inappropriate in certain contexts in so far as it refers to a diffuse and undifferentiated religious ground. Indeed, the idea

---

stant et cause: *Le discontinu dans la pensée philosophique de l'Inde* (Paris, 1955) (who also considers the later period in Indian Buddhist thought); P. Horsch, *Die vedische Gāthā- und Śloka-Literatur* (Bern, 1966); id., 'Buddhismus und Upaniṣaden', in: *Pratidānam* (F. B. J. Kuiper Festschrift, The Hague, 1968), pp. 462–77; K. Bhattacharya, 'The criterion of orthodoxy in India and the case of Jainism and Buddhism', in: N. H. Samtani (ed.), *Śramaṇa Vidyā*: *Studies in Buddhism* (Prof. Jagannath Upadhyaya Commemoration Volume, Sarnath, 1987), pp. 101–9; M. Tokunaga, 'Buddhacarita and Mahābhārata', *J. of Indological Studies* (Kyoto), 18 (2006), pp. 135–44; A. Hiltebeitel, 'Aśvaghoṣa's *Buddhacarita*', *JIP* 34 (2006), pp. 229–86 (with a bibliography of recent publications). For Kashmir, see T. Funayama, 'Remarks on religious predominance in Kashmir: Hindu or Buddhist?', in: Y. Ikari (ed.), *A study of the Nīlamata* (Kyoto, 1994), pp. 367–75. This theme has of course been touched on in countless other studies (such as, concerning Buddhist influence on Yoga, L. de La Vallée Poussin, 'Le bouddhisme et le Yoga de Patañjali', *MCB* 5 [1936-7], pp. 223–42; E. Frauwallner. *Geschichte der indischen Philosophie*, i (Salzburg, 1953), p. 411 ff.; and, more recently, by A. Wezler (see below, n. 187). For links between Brahmanism and early Buddhist practice and ritual, see above, n. 4.

7 See, e.g., H. Lüders, 'Die Sage von R̥śyaśr̥ṅga', *NAWG* 1897, and 'Zur Sage von R̥śyaśr̥ṅga', *NAWG* 1901. For the Kr̥ṣṇa legend see H. Lüders, 'Die Jātakas und die Epik: die Kr̥ṣṇa-Sage', *ZDMG* 58 (1904), pp. 687–714.

8 See E. H. Johnston, *The Buddhacarita or Acts of the Buddha*, ii (Lahore, 1936), p. xlvii f.

9 For some references, see D. Seyfort Ruegg, *Ordre spirituel et ordre temporel dans la pensée bouddhique de l'Inde et du Tibet*, p. 114 f.

of the *laukika* – as opposed in Buddhist thought to the *lokottara* 'supramundane, transmundane' – is not altogether unrelated to that of the *grāmya* 'common, vulgar' (literally 'of the village' < *grāma* 'village', in contrast e.g. to *vanya* 'of the forest or jungle'), and of the *deśī* 'rustic, popular, vernacular, vulgar (in style)' (a form of speech, singing, dancing, etc., contrasted with the *mārga* or cultivated, classical, style and the *nāgara* or polished, urban style). Terms opposed to *grāmya* or *deśī* are, however, not automatically equivalent to *lokottara* in the sense under consideration here.

In Indian linguistic, literary and cultural history, furthermore, the contrast between *mārga* and *deśī* – between the classical (i.e. Sanskritic) on the one hand and the regional, provincial or vernacular (i.e. Prakritic, Apabhraṃśa, Deśa-Bhāṣā, etc.) on the other – is a familar one. Now, just as Sanskritic linguistic forms might be incorporated into compositions in the regional languages of India, so *deśī/deśya* linguistic forms could on occasion be accommodated in Sanskrit compositions. Linguistically, *deśī* forms are distinguished from those that are either *tatsama* 'identical to the Sanskrit' or *tadbhava* 'derived regularly from Sanskrit' in terms of the analysis of the indigenous Indian etymologists. For lexicographical purposes, (putatively) *deśī* forms were collected together in Hemacandra's *Deśīnāmamālā* (twelfth century).[10] Even though this linguistic opposition is of course not strictly isomorphic with or reducible to the *laukika* : *lokottara* opposition which is at issue here, there nevertheless appears to exist a parallelism between the two in so far as *laukika* elements incorporated into Buddhism are parallel to *deśī* components found in Sanskrit: for Buddhist thought, the worldly, and 'pagan', divinities of the Indian *laukika* substratum are as it were 'regional' and 'vernacular' components within the system of Buddhist thinking. (For the historian of Indian religion, of course, such divinities in Buddhism may rather resemble so to say *tadbhava* or perhaps even *tatsama* entities.)

In certain contexts, furthermore, one might compare the Pali notion of the *tiracchāna* 'horizontal (as of an animal, i.e.), low, inferior', as found for instance in the compound *tiracchānavijjā* 'low, vulgar art' decried (alongside *micchājīva*) in the *Brahmajālasutta* of the Dīghanikāya.

---

[10] See R. Pischel, *Grammatik der Prakrit-Sprachen* (Strassburg, 1900), pp. 6–7, 39.

In terms of cultural anthropology, the opposition *laukika* : *lokottara* might recall the distinction that has been drawn between 'Little Traditions' and 'Great Traditions'.[11]

It is from such a lower – and so to speak 'pagan' and 'vernacular' – level that CONVERSION to a higher religious level – the *lokottara* – would take place.[12] In terms of DOCETISM, moreover, the 'pagan' and 'vernacular' divinities of the *laukika* level may be regarded as ectypes of Buddhist archetypes belonging to the *lokottara* level and represented by Buddhas, Bodhisattvas and Protective Deities (see below, pp. 33, 35, 118, 125, 135, 160).

In the *Sigālovādasutta*, a Dīghanikāya text containing instructions destined for laymen, use has been made of Brahmanical ideas, as has long been recognized. And reference can be made for example to the Buddhist use of *tevijja* 'possessed of the threefold knowledge', representing a transformation of the Vedic Triple Science (*trayī vidyā*, *trividyā*; see below).

The historical links between Buddhism and Brahmanism/Hinduism just listed have assumed a mythologized guise in the tradition – preserved in the bsTan 'gyur as well as by Bu ston and Tāranātha – that the Sūtras of the *Aṣṭādhyāyī* were revealed to the great grammarian Pāṇini by Lokeśvara ('Jig rten dbaṅ phyug, i.e. Avalokiteśvara),[13] a Brahman-

---

[11] For the so-called Little and Great Traditions, see below, pp. 95, 134.

[12] On different ideas of conversion see below, pp. 51–53 with n. 76; and also pp. 36, 53, 58 f., 65.

The Indian *laukika* level would seem to be comparable, at least in part, with the idea of a 'nameless religion' as posited for Tibet by R. A. Stein, *La civilisation tibétaine* (Paris, 1987). Stein has, however, defined this 'religion sans nom' in close connexion with the Tibetan *mi chos*, which is of course not isomorphic with the *'jig rten pa* = *laukika*, any more than its opposite *lha chos* is coterminous with *'jig rten las 'das pa* = *lokottara* (for a few remarks on *mi chos/lha chos*, see D. Seyfort Ruegg, *Ordre spirituel et ordre temporel dans la pensée bouddhique de l'Inde et du Tibet*, p. 26). (The opposition *grāma/araṇya* as defining two ways of religious life would not appear to be relevant here.)

The different idea of an anonymous Hinduism, and of an anonymous paganism, has been considered by P. Hacker; see his *Kleine Schriften* (Wiesbaden, 1978), pp. 799–800.

[13] See P. Cordier, *Catalogue du fonds tibétain de la Bibliothèque Nationale*, Troisième

ical tradition being rather that Pāṇini received this revelation from Śiva.[14] The Tibetan translations of the *'Pāṇinivyākaraṇasūtra'* along with Rāmacandra's *Prakriyākaumudī* appeared under the patronage of Dalai Lama V, regarded as the embodiment of Padmapāṇi (Avalokiteśvara/-Lokeśvara, the Buddhist reflex of Śiva).[15]

Nevertheless – and notwithstanding the above-mentioned provision concerning the *āhitāgni* as a candidate for ordination – Buddhist thought has turned away from the old Brahmanical ritual and tended to reinterpret ethically or philosophically – and so to interiorize – some of the old values of Brahmanism. An example of this is the Buddhist view of the *brāhmaṇa* as a person to be defined by good moral qualities rather than simply by birth.[16] The reinterpretation in the *Tevijjāsutta* of the Brāhmaṇical Triple Science (*trividyā, trayī*) as constituted by perfections rather than by the three Vedas is another case in point.[17] Even on the level of mundane affairs, Buddhists have adopted a highly critical stance regarding the Hindu social order, as shown by (amongst a number of other texts) the *Vajrasūci*,[18] a work ascribed to Aśvaghoṣa criticizing

---

Partie (Paris, 1915), p. 518; Bu ston, *Chos 'byuṅ*, f. 116a; and Tāranātha, *rGya gar chos 'byuṅ* (ed. Schiefner), pp. 42–43. Both Bu ston and Tāranātha cite the *Mañjuśrīmūlakalpa* liii.404–5 (where we find the form *lokīśa*).

[14] This matter has been discussed by M. Deshpande, 'Who inspired Pāṇini?', *JAOS* 117 (1997), p. 444–65.

[15] See our *Ordre spirituel et ordre temporel*, pp. 123–4.

[16] See, e.g., the Brāhmaṇavagga of the *Dhammapada* and the Brāhmaṇavarga of the *Udānavarga*. Concerning non-Buddhist parallels to the *Dhammapada*, see W. Rau, 'Bemerkungen und nicht-buddhistische Sanskrit-Parallelen zum Pali-Dhammapada', in C. Vogel (ed.), *Jñānamuktāvalī* (J. Nobel Commemoration Volume, New Delhi, 1959), pp. 159–75.

[17] See Dīghanikāya 13. See also the *Alagaddūpamasutta* (Majjhimanikāya I 130 f.); and the *Aggikasutta* (Saṃyuttanikāya I 166 f.) preached to Aggika-Bhāradvāja and containing a reinterpretation of the three *vijjās* as *pubbanivāsānussatiñāṇa*, *cutūpapattiñāṇa* and *āsavānaṃ khayañāṇam*, whereby a true *brāhmaṇa* (i.e. not just one by birth) becomes *tevijjo vijjācaraṇasampanno*.

[18] Cf. M. Hara, 'Vajrasūci 3–4', *Nakagawa Zenkyō Sensei shōtoku kinenronshū* (Kyoto, 1983), pp. 221–41; and J. W. de Jong, 'Buddhism and the equality of the four castes', in: *A green leaf* (J. Asmussen Felicitation Volume, Leiden, 1988), pp. 426–8.

inter alia the Indian caste system.[19] Yet attention has been called to a Buddhist concept in the *Manusmṛti*;[20] and in connexion with not teaching Dharma to a Śūdra, Avalokitavrata, the commentator on Bhā(va)viveka's (Bhavya's) *Prajñāpradīpa*, has in his turn quoted the *Manusmṛti* (iv.80).[21]

A very remarkable expression on the Buddhist side of the CONCORD existing between Buddhists and the Brahmanical tradition is in fact to be found in Bhā(va)viveka's *Madhyamakahṛdayakārikās*. In Chapter iii of this work devoted to the quest for knowledge of reality (*tattvajñāna*), this sixth-century Mādhyamika master has written that the supreme *brahman* not grasped even by the god Brahmā and other divinities is the supreme reality (*satya*) that the Buddha has proclaimed, and which great sages such as Ārya-Avalokiteśa and Ārya-Maitreya revere through the device of non-reverence.[22] Other chapters of this treatise deal with the Sāṃkhya and Vaiśeṣika, while Chapter viii is devoted to the Vedānta (and seems to contain the earliest reference in Madhyamaka literature to the term *vedānta*).

An idea comparable to the one found in Chapter iii of the *Madhyamakahṛdayakārikās* – and a possible source for it – is found in the *Laṅkāvatārasūtra* (iii, pp. 192–3), where different divinities – and even various expressions for reality such as *śūnyatā*, *tathatā*, *nirvāṇa*, *advaya*, etc. – are treated as equivalent names (*nāmaparyāya*), as alternating denomina-

---

[19] Compare already the *Ambaṭṭhasuttanta* and the *Aggaññasuttanta* of the Dīghanikāya.

[20] See E. W. Hopkins, 'A Buddhist passage in Manu', *JAOS* 43 (1923), pp. 244–6.

[21] Bhā(va)viveka/Bhavya, *Prajñāpradīpa* i. See J. W. de Jong, 'Buddhism and the equality of the four castes', *A green leaf* ..., pp. 429–30, who invokes the theme of 'Buddhist Brahmanization' following L. Renou.

[22] *Madhyamakahṛdayakārikā* iii. 289–90:

idaṃ tat paramaṃ brahma brahmādyair yan na gṛhyate/
idaṃ tat paramaṃ satyaṃ satyavādī jagau muniḥ//
āryāvalokiteśāryamaitreyādyāś ca sūrayaḥ/
anupāsanayogena munayo yad upāsate//

Cf. V. V. Gokhale, 'Masters of Buddhism adore the Brahman through non-adoration', *IIJ* 5 (1961–2), pp. 271–5.

tions (*saṃ-jñā-*), for the Tathāgata of whom they are as it were reflexes, like an image of the moon reflected in water (*udakacandra*).[23]

By way of contrast, whilst the Buddha has been counted as one of the ten *avatāra*s of Viṣṇu, this incarnation of the great Hindu god (in his aspect of *māyāmoha*) is represented by some sources as the teacher of a *mohanaśāstra* calculated to delude enemies of the true eternal Dharma.[24]

On the side of the Buddhists too there could be resistance to simple assimilation and syncretism with Brahmanism/Hinduism. Throughout the history of Buddhism in India, a sense of identity and distinctness grounded in the possession of an identifiable set of traditions has manifested itself in many ways that have been documented in previous work on the subject.[25] For instance, in the North West of India, an area often marked by a tendency to syncretism, the desire to maintain the distinctness of Buddhist tradition came to a head in later times in a confrontation with particular forms of Tantrism, and ('popular'?) Śaivism, on the matter of ritual sexual practices and mactation.[26]

Amongst Buddhists then – and notwithstanding the idea of religio-philosophical CONCORD as expressed by Bhāviveka in the passage just cited – awareness of a common matrix and milieu shared with the ambient society, religions and ways of thinking of India did not lead to the loss of a sense of identity and distinctiveness in respect to religion, or to

---

[23] This is not the place to consider what link may exist between such a statement and the Vedic idea that the 'one' receives the various names of Indra, Mitra, Varuṇa, etc. (*Ṛgveda* i.164.46): *índraṃ mitráṃ váruṇam agním āhur átho divyáḥ sa suparṇó garútmān/ ékaṃ sad víprā bahudhā vadanty agníṃ yamáṃ mātaríśvānam āhuḥ//.*

[24] Cf. R. S. Bhattacharya, 'Buddha as depicted in the Purāṇas', *Purāṇa* 24/2 (1982), pp. 384–404; and M. Saindon, 'Le Buddha comme Avatāra de Viṣṇu et le mythe de Raji', *IIJ* 47 (2004), pp. 17–44.

[25] See the works listed below in this study.

[26] On this question of *sbyor sgrol*, and on the problem of the so-called *nīlāmbaravrata*, see D. Seyfort Ruegg, 'Deux problèmes d'exégèse et de pratique tantriques' in: M. Strickmann (ed.), *Tantric and Taoist studies* (R.-A. Stein Felicitation Volume, *MCB* 20 [1981]), pp. 212–26, and 'Problems in the transmission of Vajrayāna Buddhism in the Western Himalaya about the year 1000', in: *Studies of mysticism in honor of the 1150th anniversary of Kobo-Daishi's Nirvāṇam* (*Acta Indologica* 6 [1984]), pp. 369–81. Compare also the *saṃsāramocaka*, on which see below, n. 187.

indifferentism in respect to philosophy, as the present study will seek to show. An attempt will also be made to define and demarcate the ideas of SYMBIOSIS and CONCORD – as well as the fact of the background of a partly shared cultural (if not creedal) ground or SUBSTRATUM and MILIEU – from religious ENCULTURATION and SYNCRETISM and philosophical RELATIVISM or INDIFFERENTISM properly speaking.

In short, then, the question is not, as has sometimes been argued, whether the Kṣatriya prince Gautama the Śākyamuni – and many of the other great figures in the history of Indian Buddhism – were Hindus (whatever this might be thought to mean precisely[27]): this question is in any case meaningless at least in relation to the Buddha himself in so far as the designation 'Hinduism' is anachronistic for the Brahmanical religion known from earlier Indian sources assignable to the time of the Buddha. Rather, the crucial question concerns the precise relationship, over many centuries, of Buddhism with the Indian cultural matrix and milieu, that is, with the ambient religions of India including of course Brahmanism.

*

Concerning the relation in Pali sources between Buddhism and Jainism – i.e. the Nigaṇṭhas/Nirgranthas with their great teacher Nātaputta or Mahāvīra at their head –, several studies already exist on the subject even though it has not yet been investigated comprehensively and exhaustively.[28]

---

[27] That many leading figures in the history of Indian Buddhism were by birth and education Brahmans is of course well known.

[28] Beginning with the Introductions to H. Jacobi, *Gaina Sûtras*, Parts i and ii (SBE volumes xxii [Oxford, 1884] and xlv [Oxford, 1895]); E. Leumann, 'Beziehungen der Jaina-Literatur zu anderen Literaturkreisen Indiens', in: *Actes du Sixième Congrès International des Orientalistes, tenu en 1883 à Leide*, Troisième partie, Section 2: Aryenne (Leiden, 1885), pp. 469–564; id. *Buddha und Mahāvīra* (Munich, 1922); F. O. Schrader, *Über den Stand der indischen Philosophie zur Zeit Mahāvīras und Buddhas* (Leipzig, 1902); H. von Glasenapp, 'Die Stellung des Jainismus in der indischen Religionsgeschichte und sein Verhältnis zu anderen Glaubsenslehren', *ZfB* 6 (1924–5), pp. 313–30; id., 'Die Polemik der Buddhisten und Brahmanen gegen die Jainas', *Beiträge zur indischen Philologie und Altertumskunde* (W. Schubring Felicitation Volume, Hamburg, 1951), pp. 74–83; A. B. Keith, 'Mahāvīra and the Buddha', *BSOS*

6 (1932), pp. 859–66; G. C. Pande, *Studies in the origins of Buddhism* (Allahabad, 1957), pp. 541–7; K. Fischer, *Schöpfungen indischer Kunst* (Cologne, 1959), p. 368 (bibliography on Hinduism and Buddhism); G. Roth, '"A Saint like that" and "A Saviour" in Prakrit, Pali, Sanskrit and Tibetan literature', in: *Shri Mahavira Jaina Vidyalaya Golden Jubilee Volume* (Bombay, 1968), pp. 46–62 (= *Indian studies*, Selected papers, ed. H. Bechert *et al.* [Delhi, 1986], pp. 91–107); W. Bollée, 'Anmerkungen zum buddhistischen Häretikerbild', *ZDMG* 121 (1971), pp. 70–92; id., 'Buddhists and Buddhism in the earlier literature of the Śvetāmbara Jains', in: *Buddhist studies in honour of I. B. Horner* (Dordrecht, 1974), pp. 27–39; Bhag Chandra Jain, *Jainism in Buddhist literature* (Nagpur, 1972); C. Caillat, *Expiations dans le rituel ancien des religieux jaina* ([2]Paris, 1975), Introduction; id., 'Gleanings from a comparative reading of early canonical Buddhist and Jain texts', *JIABS* 26 (2003), pp. 25–50; N. Tatia, 'The interaction of Jainism and Buddhism and its impact on the history of Buddhist monasticism', in: A. K. Narain, *Studies in history of Buddhism* (Delhi, 1980), pp. 321–38; id., 'Parallel developments in the meaning of *parijñā* (Prakrit *pariṇṇā*, Pāli *pariññā*) in the canonical literature of the Jainas and Buddhists', *IT* 11 (1983), pp. 293–302; P. S. Jaini, 'The disappearance of Buddhism and the survival of Jainism: A study in contrast', in: A. K. Narain (ed.), *Studies in the history of Buddhism*, pp. 81–91 (reprinted in *Collected papers on Buddhist studies*, pp. 139–53); H. Nakamura, 'Common elements in early Jain and Buddhist literature' *IT* 11 (1983), pp. 303–30; K. Watanabe, 'Some notes on the expression *sabba-vārī-/savva-vāram*', *BEI* 5 (1987), pp. 375–86; J. Bronkhorst, *The two traditions of meditation in ancient India* (Stuttgart, 1986) (with R. Gombrich, 'The Buddha and the Jains: A reply to Professor Bronkhorst', *AS/EA* 48 [1994], pp. 1069–96); J. Bronkhorst, 'The Buddha and the Jainas reconsidered', *AS/EA* 49 (1995), pp. 330–50; *The two sources of Indian asceticism* (Delhi, 1998); K. R. Norman, 'Common terminology in early Buddhist and Jaina texts', *Collected papers*, iv (Oxford, 1993), pp. 264–70; id. 'Early Buddhism and Jainism – A comparison', *Memoirs of the Chūō Academic Research Institute*, No. 28 (1999) (with bibliography); S. Ohira, 'The twenty-four *Buddhas* and the twenty-four *Tīrthaṅkaras*', in: N. Balbir *et al.* (ed.), *Festschrift Klaus Bruhn* (Reinbek, 1994), pp. 475–88; N. Balbir, 'A new instance of common terminology in Jaina and Buddhist texts' in: *Facets of Indian culture*: *Gustav Roth felicitation volume* (Patna, 1998), pp. 424–44; id., 'Jain-Buddhist dialogue: Material from the Pāli scriptures', *JPTS* 26 (2000), pp. 1–42. See also the papers collected in the section 'Buddhism and Jainism' in P. S. Jaini, *Collected papers on Buddhist studies* (Delhi, 2001).

In his *The pādas of the Suttanipāta with parallels from the Āyāraṅga, Sūyagaḍa, Uttarajjhāyā, Dasaveyāliya and Isibhāsiyāiṃ* (Reinbek, 1980) and *Reverse index of the Dhammapada, Suttanipāta, Thera- and Therī-gāthā pādas with parallels ...* (Reinbek, 1983), W. Bollée has made a valuable contribution to the study of old Indian 'ascetic poetry'. The notion of an 'Asketendichtung' common to Buddhism, Jainism and Hinduism is found in M. Winternitz, *Geschichte der indischen Literatur*, i (Leipzig, 1908), pp. 267, 403. G. Roth has published '*Dhammapada* verses in *Uttarajjhāyā*', *Saṃbodhi* 5 (1976, Dr. A. N. Upadhye Commemoration issue), pp. 166–9. See also

In his *Samayasāra* (i.8) the Digambara Jaina philosopher Kundakunda (second century, or perhaps rather eighth century?) has connected the doctrine of two 'truths' (*satya*, to the development of which Nāgārjuna and his Mādhyamika followers contributed so much) with the perspectivist doctrine of the Jaina *nayas*.[29] And Jainas engaged actively in the study and criticism of Buddhist logic and epistemology, to the preservation of which tradition they also contributed so significantly.

There exists a quite well-known later work on ethics entitled in Sanskrit the *Vimala-Praśnottararatnamālā* which has been regarded as belonging to both Buddhist and Jaina literature.[30]

But from the outset there have undoubtedly been very considerable points of difference between the two 'Śramaṇa traditions' of Buddhism and Jainism. Thus, during much of the history of Buddhism, there existed a major disagreement with the Jains concerning the sentiency of plants.[31] And although the ideal of non-harming (*ahiṃsā*) was held in common between the two traditions, it has been somewhat differently understood and put into practice by them. There are also significant differences between them concerning whether *karman* is represented as primarily mental (with the Buddhists) or as more or less material (*paudgalika*, with

---

the article by W. Rau cited above, n. 16; P. Horsch, *Die vedische Gāthā- und Śloka-Literatur* (Bern, 1966); and J. W. de Jong, 'The Buddha and his teachings', in: J. Silk (ed.), *Wisdom, compassion, and the search for understanding* (G. M. Nagao Felicitation Vol., Honolulu, 2000), p. 173.

[29] See S. M. Shaha, 'Kundakunda's concept of vyavahāra naya and niścaya naya', *ABORI* 56 (1975), pp. 105–28; and W. Halbfass, *India and Europe* (Albany, 1988), p. 355. See also P. Dundas, *The Jainas* (London, 2002), pp. 107–09.

[30] The Sanskrit version of this work was published in the Kāvyamālā series, Part vii, p. 121 ff.; and a Prakrit version was published by P. Pavolini, *GSAI* 1, pp. 153–63. The Sanskrit and the Tibetan translation from the bsTan 'gyur were published by Ph. É. Foucaux (Paris, 1867), and the Tibetan alone was published with a German translation by A. Schiefner (St Petersburg, 1858). Cf. A. Weber, 'Über die Praśnottararatnamālā', *Indische Streifen* 1 (1868), pp. 210–27; V. Bhattacharya, *IHQ* 5 (1929), p. 143 f.; M. Winternitz, *History of Indian literature*, ii (Delhi, 1972), pp. 559–60; S. K. Pathak, *Vimalapraśnottararatnamālā* (Greater India Society, Calcutta, 1959).

[31] cf. L. Schmithausen, *The problem of the sentience of plants in Earliest Buddhism* (Tokyo, 1991); id., *Buddhism and nature* (Tokyo, 1991).

the Jainas).[32] In philosophy, Jainism adopted a multi-valued logic and elaborated its doctrine of Non-Absolutism (*anekāntavāda* 'relativism'), Perspectivism or Aspectualism (*nayavāda*) and Conditionalism or the 'Quodammodo Doctrine' (*syādvāda*), while the Buddhists have generally kept to a two-valued logic.[33] Although they appreciated the virtues of philosophical eirenicism, the Buddhist tradition did not advocate Perspectivism or philosophical relativism.[34] Examples of points of difference between Buddhism and Jainism could of course be multiplied.

---

[32] See, e.g., H. von Glasenapp, *Die Lehre von Karma in der Philosophie der Jainas* (Leipzig, 1915); N. Tatia, *Studies in Jaina philosophy* (Banaras, 1951); E. Frauwallner, *Geschichte der indischen Philosophie*, ii (Salzburg, 1956), p. 279 ff.; J. McDermott, *Development in the early Buddhist concept of kamma/karma* (New Delhi, 1984); F. Enomoto, 'On the annihilation of Karman in Early Buddhism', in: *Transactions of the International Conference of Orientalists in Japan*, no. 34 (1989), pp. 43–55. On an interesting effect of this difference between the Buddhist and other 'Śramaṇa' views of *karman*, see D. Seyfort Ruegg, *Buddha-nature, Mind and the problem of Gradualism in a comparative perspective* (London, 1989), p. 143.

[33] For the Jaina *anekāntavāda*, Modalism or Aspectualism (*nayavāda*), and Conditionalism (the 'Quodammodo' or *syādvāda*) and for its theory of seven-fold predication (*saptabhaṅgī*), see S. Mookerjee, *The Jaina philosophy of Non-Absolutism* (Calcutta, 1944); K. N. Jayatilleke, *Early Buddhist theory of knowledge* (London, 1963); and B. K. Matilal, *The central philosophy of Jainism* (*Anekānta-vāda*) (Ahmedabad, 1981). – According to part of the Hindu tradition, Viṣṇu in his aspect of *māyāmoha* appeared as a Digambara and taught the *anekāntavāda* to the demons in order to bring about their destruction; see *Viṣṇupurāṇa* iii.18, and H. v. Glasenapp, *Festschrift W. Schubring* (Hamburg, 1951), pp. 78–79.

[34] See D. Seyfort Ruegg, *Three studies in the history of Indian and Tibetan Madhyamaka philosophy* (Studies in Indian and Tibetan Madhyamaka thought, Part 1, Vienna, 2000), Section II (p. 108 ff.).

2. On common ('pan-Indian') divinities within Buddhism

Buddhist traditions have assigned a significant place in both the canonical and extra-canonical literature to divine beings such as Brahmā and Śakra/Indra, as well as to Sūrya, Candra and a multitude of lesser divinities or celestials, *genii*, and *daimons*. Brahmā and Śakra in particular have both been represented in traditional biographies of the Buddha as playing a prominent rôle in his life. The first, having observed the Buddha's Awakening (*bodhi*), pleaded with him to teach what he had realized for the sake of living beings in the world despite the fact that it was difficult to understand; this celestial is sometimes specified as Brahmā Sa(b)hā(ṃ)pati and he figures as a sort of guardian of the world.[35] And in the *Mahāparinirvāṇasūtra* of the Dīrghāgama Brahmā proclaims the Buddha to be an *etādiso satthā/evaṃvidhaḥ śāstā* and a *tathāgata.*[36] As for Śakra, he acted as a witness to many events in the Buddha's life, acting as his companion and acolyte. And in the 'Miracle of Sāṃkāśya' both Brahmā and Śakra are shown accompanying the Buddha on his descent from the heaven of the Trāyastriṃśa gods.[37] Maheśvara (Śaṃkara/Śiva) also appears as an assistant, interlocutor or devotee of

---

[35] See A. Bareau, *Recherches sur la biographie du Buddha dans les Sūtrapiṭaka et les Vinayapiṭaka anciens: Depuis la quête de l'Éveil à la conversion de Śāriputra et Maudgalyāyana* (Paris, 1963), p. 135 f. Cf. *Catuṣpariṣatsūtra* (ed. Waldschmidt), p. 74 f., where the reference is to a pair of *brahmakāyikā devatās*; and E. Waldschmidt, 'Vergleichende Analyse des Catuṣpariṣatsūtra', in: *Festschrift W. Schubring* (Hamburg, 1951), p. 87, 93–94. For a survey of the place of Brahmā in Buddhist traditions, in addition to the general works on divinities in Buddhist literature (see n. 63), see G. P. Malalasekera's *Dictionary of Pali proper names* (*DPPN*), p. 331 ff., and the encyclopaedic article 'Bon' in *Hōbōgirin*, pp. 112–21. Cf. P. Hacker, 'Zur Geschichte und Beurteilung des Hinduismus', *OLZ* 59 (1964), col. 232–5.

[36] See E. Waldschmidt (ed.), *Mahāparinirvāṇasūtra*, p. 400. For the Pali version, see Dīghanikāya 16 (II, p. 157).

[37] For Śakra, see for instance the *Sakkapañhasutta* (DN 21). For the corresponding Sanskrit text, see E. Waldschmidt, *Bruchstücke buddhistischer Sūtras aus dem zentralasiatischen Sanskritkanon* (²Kleinere Sanskrit-Texte IV, Wiesbaden, 1979), p. 58 ff.

the Buddha, in which case he may be counted as one of the Śuddhāvāsa (or Akaniṣṭha) gods of the Rūpadhātu.[38]

The *Mahāsamaya/Mahāsamāja* Sūtra in both the Pali and Sanskrit versions (as well as in its Chinese and Tibetan translations) is a *locus classicus* for an enumeration of various popular Indian divinities (*devatā*, *devakāya*: such as the gods Viṣṇu, Candra, Sūrya, Śakra; the goddesses Umā [Pali Ummā]; the four Mahārājas; Yakṣas, Nāgas, etc.) who assemble from their celestial abode, approach the Buddha, and take refuge in him.[39] Lists containing several of these figures – sometimes described as *yakṣa*s or *yakṣasenāpati*s – appear in texts as varied as the *Āṭānāṭiya/Āṭānāṭika Sūtra*,[40] the *Suvarṇa(pra)bhāsasūtra*,[41] and the *Mahāmāyūrī*.[42]

In the Mahāyānist system of the Bodhisattva's Ten Stages (*daśabhūmi*), moreover, it is stated that, on the level of the Rūpadhātu, Bodhisattvas of the third *bhūmi* become a Śakra, those of the eighth and ninth

---

[38] See N. Iyanaga, article 'Daijizaiten', *Hōbōgirin*, p. 723 f. (cf. Iyanaga, 'Le Roi Māra du Sixième Ciel et le mythe médiéval de la création du Japon', *CEA* 9 [1996–97], p. 323 ff.). For the name Śaṃkara as an element in the appellations of Buddhist authors, see n. 121 below.

[39] DN 20 (II, p. 253 ff.). For corresponding Sanskrit and Chinese texts, see E. Waldschmidt, *Bruchstücke buddhistischer Sūtras aus dem zentralasiatischen Sanskritkanon* (^{2}Kleinere Sanskrit-Texte IV); and for the Tibetan text see P. Skilling, *Mahāsūtras: Great Discourses of the Buddha*, i (London, 1994), p. 385 ff.

[40] DN 32 (III, p. 204 ff.). For corresponding Sanskrit and Tibetan texts, see H. Hoffmann, *Bruchstücke des Āṭānāṭikasūtra aus dem zentralasiatischen Sanskritkanon der Buddhisten* (^{2}Kleinere Sanskrit-Texte V, Stuttgart, 1987); and P. Skilling, *op. cit.*, p. 460 ff. In many sources, the *yakṣa*s are counted as belonging to the entourage of Vaiśravaṇa/Vaiśramaṇa = Kubera/Kuvera, Great King of the North.

[41] In the *Yakṣāśrayaparivarta*, Chapter xiv in the edition of the Sanskrit text by J. Nobel. Relevant materials are also found elsewhere in the same Sūtra.

[42] See S. Lévi, 'Le catalogue géographique des Yakṣa dans la Mahāmāyūrī', *JA* 1915, p. 19 ff.; and P. C. Bagchi, 'Geographical catalogue of the Yakṣas in the Mahāmāyūrī', *Sino-Indian studies* 3 (1947), p. 21 ff. In the *Mahāmāyūrī* list, Maheśvara and Viṣṇu are for instance included (ed. Bagchi, lines 9 and 13; ed. Takubo, p. 19); see also pp. 24–26, 45 of the same work. For similar material in the *Candragarbhasūtra*, see S. Lévi, 'Notes chinoises sur l'Inde', *BEFEO* 1905, p. 253 ff.

The *Suvarṇa(pra)bhāsa* and the *Mahāmāyūrī* have both been classified as Tantric texts, a class of work to which we shall return below. Concerning non-Tantric sources, see the works already cited above.

*bhūmi*s become a Mahābrahmā, and those of the tenth *bhūmi* become a Maheśvara (or a Śuddhāvāsa celestial).[43]

These divine entities are of course known also from the non-Buddhist – Brāhmanical or Hindu – sources, often under the same designation and with similar if not totally identical functions as in Buddhism. And this circumstance has led scholars to speak of a BORROWING by the Buddhists of Brāhmanical/Hindu deities. It may at the same time be necessary to reckon with a situation of religious compromise or accommodation which permitted the Buddhist – and in particular the Buddhist layman – to worship his ancestral (non/pre-Buddhist) gods while at the same time professing faith, and taking refuge, in the three Jewels of Buddhism: the Buddha, the Dharma and the Community (*saṃgha*).[44]

To account for this situation, a BORROWING PARADIGM/MODEL would no doubt be justified were it clearly the case that Buddhism and Hinduism have been two distinct, and mutually well-demarcated, entities without a partly shared background (previously to any characterized BORROWING or TRANSFER under consideration). But very frequently this view of the matter is historically (and also synchronically) difficult to maintain. It either skirts the question of the complex structure of the levels of the divine in

---

[43] *Daśabhūmikasūtra* iii (ed. Rahder, p. 37), viii (pp. 63, 73), ix (p. 81), x (pp. 92, 94–95), and xi (p. 99); *Bodhisattvabhūmi* (ed. Wogihara, pp. 360–1). For details see N. Iyanaga, article 'Daijizaiten', *Hōbōgirin*, p. 740ff., who has called attention (p. 747a) to the distinction between two kinds of Maheśvara, one of whom is Maheśvara-Śiva, the Lord of the Bhūtas, Vetālas and Piśācas, while the other is the Maheśvara of the Śuddhāvāsa level of the Rūpadhātu, i.e. the Bodhisattva of the tenth *bhūmi*. For Maheśvara identified with (Devaputra) Māra, the ruler of the highest level of the Kāmadhātu (that of the Paranirmitavaśavartin gods), see N. Iyanaga, 'Le Roi Māra du Sixième Ciel et le mythe médiéval de la création du Japon', *CEA* 9 (1996–7), pp. 323–96.

[44] In his article 'Religionssynkretismus in Nepal', in H. Bechert (ed.), *Buddhism in Ceylon and studies on religious syncretism in Buddhist countries* (Göttingen, 1978), p. 151 ff., S. Lienhard has spoken of 'transfer of religious material' (Übertragung religiösen Guts) from one religion to the other together with 'parallelism' and 'identification' as the three main manifestations of religious layering or superimposition (Überlagerung) in the relationship between Hinduism and Buddhism in Nepal. Lienhard evidently uses his term Übertragung as an equivalent of borrowing when he refers (p. 151) to Vajrayāna Buddhism as the recipient (entgegennehmende) religion in relation to Tantric Śaivism as the donor (gebende) religion.

Buddhism; or it more or less tacitly answers this question in a way that is unsatisfactory in so far as it takes no account of the fact that the function of these deities in Buddhism is systemically determined and hence structural, so that they cannot simply be regarded synchronically as extraneous and foreign bodies in Buddhism. The assumption that Buddhism has imported these deities as EXOGENOUS bodies from Hinduism, or that it has entered in the course of its development into some form of SYNCRETISTIC compromise with it, is therefore hardly adequate fully to account for the religious phenomena in question. Moreover, if the BORROWING MODEL is to be accepted on the assumption that Buddhism and Hinduism are indeed two entirely distinct religious entities, it will be necessary to identify the circumstances in which one of these entities borrowed from the other. But writers operating with the BORROWING MODEL have only seldom even posed much less satisfactorily addressed this question. In particular, they have not explained why Buddhism should have felt motivated, or impelled, to borrow from, e.g., Śaivism: that is, why should one religion borrow from another that is, *ex hypothesi*, entirely different from it?

Borrowing is normally something that takes places between two different entities: thus one person borrows from an other person, or from a bank; a government borrows from investors, from its citizens; etc. In this case what is borrowed will be regarded as of worth to borrower and lender, who attach to it an agreed value because they both share common ideas and standards. There of course exist in addition cases where a person is said to borrow from himself, for example when one borrows from one's own capital. Was this perchance the idea which certain writers had in mind when adopting a BORROWING MODEL? And was Buddhism then perhaps being thought of by them as borrowing from its common ('pan-Indian') capital? Most writers who have operated with the borrowing model did not, however, indicate that such was their view of the matter. And when this model was employed in speaking of Buddhists' use of material known to Śaivism, the two traditions have evidently been thought of by these scholars as separate religious and social entities. (The old hypothesis, once frequently mooted, that Buddhism borrowed, and indeed somehow developed, from pre-classical Sāṃkhya is another example of a discussion which did not clearly take into account the difference between, on the one side, two movements or schools sharing, at least in part, a common cultural background and then operating with related categories and methods and, on the other side, a defined and discrete movement or school (Buddhism) making a characterized borrowing from an other movement or school (early Sāṃkhya).)

With respect to the significant, positive and benevolent – or at the very least to the neutral – rôle played in Buddhism by figures of the Indian pantheon, attention may be drawn to an interesting passage from the *Ratnagotravibhāga* (*Mahāyānottaratantraśāstra*).

In the Guṇādhikāra – the third chapter of this quite old and very important Mahāyānist Śāstra dealing with the qualities of the Tathāgata (*buddhaguṇa*) – there are found two verses which – in poetically coloured language recapitulating in elaborate *upajāti* (*indravajrā*) metre the doctrine of the thirty-two Marks (*mahāpuruṣalakṣaṇa*) belonging to the Buddha's Sambhogakāya that had been explained in the preceding *śloka*s of this work – compare the Tathāgata's hair with sapphire-coloured locks (*mahendranīlāmalaratnakeśaḥ*, iii.24c) and the firm body of the Tathāgata with Nārāyaṇa's strength (*nārāyaṇasthāmadṛḍhātmabhāvaḥ*, iii.25a).[45] Here the reference to the mighty god Nārāyaṇa is explicit, whilst the mention of the *mahendranīla* – i.e. the *indranīla* or sapphire – seems in the context only to allude implicitly to Indra (or, perhaps more specifically, to Śiva Gaṅgādhara in whose hair flows the Gaṅgā on her descent earthwards?). It is to be noted that neither of these attributes is mentioned as a *lakṣaṇa* in the passage of Haribhadra's *Abhisamayālaṃkārālokā* commenting on the relevant verse of the *Abhisamayālaṃkāra* (viii.12) or in the *Mahāvyutpatti* (ed. Ishihama and Fukuda, nos. 233–265).

In *Ratnagotravibhāga* iii.22 there is further listed the *brahmasvaratā* 'brahmic voice' of the Svayambhū, i.e. the Tathāgata. This is a standard

---

[45] The standard Tib. equivalent of Nārāyaṇa is Sred med kyi bu. In the *Kāraṇḍavyūha* (i.11) – where a version of the story of Nārāyaṇa is to be found linked with the story of the Asura Bali and the Vāmanāvatāra of Viṣṇu, and where Nārāyaṇa has moreover been assimilated to Daśarathaputra (= Rāma) – the Tib. equivalent of Nārāyaṇa is mThu bo che. (This episode has been studied by C. Regamey, 'Motifs vichnouites et śivaïtes dans le Kāraṇḍavyūha', in: *Études tibétaines dédiées à la mémoire de Marcelle Lalou* [Paris, 1971], pp. 411–32.) In the *Daśabhūmikasūtra* (1A) Nārāyaṇaśrīgarbha is the name of a Bodhisattva. And in the *Survarṇa(pra)bhāsasūtra* (xiv.45), mThu bo che = Nārāyaṇa (rather than Nāgayana as in the MSS used by Nobel for his edition) appears as a *yakṣa*.

lakṣaṇa counted as the twenty-third in Haribhadra's list, and as the thirteenth in the *Mahāvyutpatti* enumeration (no. 245).

In addition, in the fourth chapter of the *Ratnagotravibhāga* treating of the Buddha's immaculate qualities in connexion with his salvific activity, there is found a comparison between the Tathāgata and Brahmā under the commentarial rubric 'likc Great Brahmā' (*mahābrahmavat* = *tshaṅs pa chen po bžin*) (iv.13, 53-56). And under the commentarial rubric 'like a manifestation as Indra' (*śakrapratibhāsavat* = *brgya byin du snaṅ ba bžin*) in the same chapter we find a comparison with Śakra (iv.13, 14–30).

In these passages the *Ratnagotravibhāga* is seemingly reworking old mythic material which Buddhism evidently shared with the common ('pan-Indian') mythology. To speak of 'popular religion' in relation to such a Śāstra would amount to unjustifiably injecting an inappropriate category into the discussion.

It should be recalled in addition that the seventh chapter of the *Varṇārhavarṇastotra*, Mātr̥ceṭa's Hymn in praise of the Praiseworthy (i.e. the Buddha), is entitled Brahmānuvāda (Tib. *tshaṅs pa daṅ mthun par gsuṅ bar bstod pa*).[46] In it notions held in common with Brahmanism have been interpreted in a Buddhist sense, and the Buddha has been represented as the 'true' *brahman*.

Mythological and iconographic notices on divinities such as Brahmā, Maheśvara (Śiva) and Viṣṇu have also found a place in the encyclopaedic **Mahāprajñāpāramitopadeśa* (*Ta-chih-tu-lun*) ascribed to Nāgārjuna.[47]

---

[46] cf. J.-U. Hartmann, *Das Varṇārhavarṇastotra des Mātr̥ceṭa* (Göttingen, 1987), p. 215 ff.

[47] See E. Lamotte, *Le traité de la Grande Vertu de Sagesse*, i (Louvain, 1944), pp. 134, 137 f., 466, f., 561 f. Cf. id., *Histoire du bouddhisme indien*, i, p. 435. For a detailed survey of the place occupied by Maheśvara/Śiva in Buddhist traditions, see N. Iyanaga's monographic article 'Daijizaiten' in *Hōbōgirin*, pp. 713–65; and his '*Honji suijaku* and the logic of combinatory deities', in: M. Teeuwen and F. Rambelli (ed.), *Buddhas and Kami in Japan* (London, 2003), pp. 145–76. For Viṣṇu, see Hōbōgirin, article 'Bichū'; and C. Regamey's article in *Études tibétaines dédiées à la mémoire de Marcelle Lalou* (cited in n. 45 above).

A further divinity held in common – at least if one is to judge by the name – by Hindus and Buddhists is Gaṇeśa/Gaṇapati (Tib. Tshogs [kyi] bdag [po]). He is otherwise known as Vināyaka, and his double nature from the Buddhist's point of view is reflected in two Tibetan renderings of his name: rNam par 'dren pa 'leader, remover (of obstacles)' and Log (par) 'dren (pa) 'mis-leader' (i.e. lord of obstacles; compare the appellations Vighna = bGegs and Vighnāntaka = bGegs mthar byed, bGegs sel ba, etc., as names of Gaṇeśa). Although Gaṇapati's iconography and functions have both developed somewhat differently in the two religions, they evidently share in part a common origin.[48]

*

Among utterances ascribed in the old canon to the Buddha himself can be cited verses that no doubt give us some idea of one older Buddhist attitude towards divinities of the ambient religion who might be

---

[48] Such ambivalence is of course not a development peculiar to Buddhism. The frequent ambivalence of Sanskrit vocabulary has been traced back to the Veda by L. Renou, 'L'ambiguïté du vocabulaire du Ṛgveda', *JA* 1939, pp. 161–235, who notes it for, e.g., *yakṣa* and *gandharva*. Gaṇapati's origins in Rudra/Śiva were pointed out by Renou, 'Les origines védiques de Gaṇeśa', *JA* 1937, pp. 271–4.

Gaṇapati/Gaṇeśa, in Hindu mythology the son of Mahādeva/Śiva, is regarded in Buddhism, in his propitious form, as an emanation of the compassionate Avalokiteśvara. As for Vināyaka/Vighna, he is danced upon for example by Aparājitā (*Sādhanamālā* no. 204). He figures also in the *maṇḍala*s of Dharmadhātuvāgīśvara, Durgatipariśodhana (as Vajravināyaka), Bhūtaḍāmara, and Kālacakra. Three forms have been listed in the *Rin 'byuṅ* and in Paṇ chen Blo bzaṅ dpal ldan's *Rin 'byuṅ lhan thabs* (vol. ṅa, section 17). In Tibet, it is the *phyi sgrub* form of Gaṇapati that is theriomorphic.

On this god, in addition to the standard works on Indian and Tibetan iconography, see A. Getty, *Gaṇeśa* (Oxford, 1936); Haridas Mitra, 'Gaṇapati', *Viśva-Bharati Annals* 8 (1955), pp. 1–120; H. Bechert, 'Mythologie der singhalesischen Volksreligion', in: H. Haussig (ed.), *Wörterbuch der Mythologie*, 1. Abteilung: Die alten Kulturvölker (Stuttgart, n.d.), p. 584; Lokesh Chandra, 'Gaṇeśa in Japan', in: *Indo-Asian studies* 3 (1977), pp. 121–46; R. L. Brown (ed.), *Ganesh, Studies of an Asian god* (Albany, 1991), which includes C. Wilkinson, 'The Tantric Gaṇeśa: Texts preserved in the Tibetan canon', pp. 235–75, and J. Sanford, 'Literary aspects of Japan's Dual-Gaṇeśa cult', pp. 287–335 (discussing the god's connexion with Avalokiteśvara); and G. Bühnemann, 'Two forms of Gaṇapati in the Indo-Tibetan Buddhist tradition', *WZKS* 38 (1994), pp. 201–11.

described as belonging to a common ('pan-Indian') substratum or ground. In both the *Mahāparinibbānasutta* of the Dīghanikāya (II, p. 88) and the *Mahāvagga* (Vinaya I, pp. 229–30) we read:

... yā tattha devatā assu tāsaṃ dakkhiṇām ādise
tā pūjitā pūjayanti mānitā mānayanti naṃ/
tato naṃ anukampanti mātā puttaṃ va orasaṃ
devatānukampito poso sadā bhadrāṇi passatîti//

Whatever divinities may be there, to them the [wise person] shall make an offering; paid respect to they pay respect, being honoured they honour him. They then gratify [him], as a mother would her own son. Gratified by the divinities, the person always sees auspicious things.

Parallel verses are found in the Sanskrit version of the *Mahāparinirvāṇa-sūtra* (ed. E. Waldschmidt, p. 154; compare the Tibetan in the translation of the Vinaya of the Mūlasarvāstivādins, *ibid.*, p. 155):

yo devatāḥ pūjayati śrāddhaḥ puruṣapudgalaḥ/
śāstur vākyakaro bhavati buddhair etat praśaṃsitam//

yasmin pradeśe medhāvī vāsaṃ kalpayati paṇḍitaḥ/
śīlavantaṃ bhojayitvā dakṣiṇām ādiśet tataḥ//[49]

te mānitā mānayanti pūjitāḥ pūjayanti ca/
athâinam anukampanti mātā putram ivâurasam/
devānukampitappoṣaḥ sukhī bhadrāṇi paśyati//

The valiant person who, possessing faith, honours gods executes the command of the Teacher: this is praised by the Buddha. At the place where an intelligent wise man makes his abode, nourishing the virtuous, he should then make an offering. Paid respect to the [gods] pay respect and being honoured they pay honour: they gratify him as a mother would her own son. Gratified by the gods, happy, a person sees auspicious things.

Here, then, the person paying respect to and honouring these divinities is described not only as *śrāddha* 'possessed of faith' (*dad pa can*) but also as executing the word of the Teacher (*saṅs rgyas kyi bka' bžin byed gyur pa*), while the recipient of the *dakṣiṇā* corresponds to the one described as virtuous (*śīlavant*).

In the *Varṣāvastu* of the Mūlasarvāstivādin Vinaya, moreover, there is found an allusion to the participation of local protective divinities in the

---

[49] The expression *dakṣiṇām ādiśet* is translated into Tibetan by *yon bsṅo ba* 'dedicate the good accruing from a salutary deed; assign a ritual gift/honorarium'. (Compare the concept of *puṇyapariṇāmanā* = *bsod nams yoṅs su bsṅo ba* 'dedication of good'.)

official ritual activity of a monastic community, even though they are of course not themselves counted as monks.[50] These divinities appear to be known as *naivāsika*s 'residents (incumbents?)', a class there associated with the *yakṣa*s, *amanuṣya*s, and *vyāḍa*s. In the Tibetan translation of this Vinaya, these divinities are termed either *gñug mar gnas pa* or *gnas (b)sruṅ*; elsewhere *naivāsika* is rendered *gži pa* (which is opposed to *glo bur du 'oṅs pa* = *āgantuka* in the *Mahāvyutpatti*). By commentators on the Vinaya this class of divinity is then glossed by *gtsug lag khaṅ gi sruṅ ma*, those specifically named being Hārītī, Mahādevī, and Pañcika/ Pāñcika.[51]

Recollection, or commemoration, of divinities (*devatānusmr̥ti*) constitutes furthermore one of the six (or ten) *anusmr̥ti*s (Pali *anussati*) known to Buddhist texts from early times, together with that of *buddha*, *dharma*, *saṃgha*, etc.

It is exceedingly difficult to describe Buddhism in terms of the familiar categories monotheism/polytheism/atheism taken from the Abrahamic religions; and the English version of H. von Glasenapp's *Buddhismus, eine atheistische Religion* sought to obviate part of the problem by substituting 'non-theistic' for 'atheistic'(see below, n. 62). Similarly, the Abrahamic dichotomy polytheism/monotheism is of very questionable relevance to forms of Brahmanism/Hinduism, and 'kathenotheism' has sometimes been used instead.

---

[50] In certain later sources at least, some local protective divinities have been described as *upāsaka* = *dge bsñen*. For the Tibetan category of *dge bsñen*, see, e.g., R. de Nebesky-Wojkowitz, *Oracles and demons of Tibet* (The Hague, 1956), p. 304 and *passim*.

[51] See the piece of religio-philological and literary detective work by G. Schopen, 'Counting the Buddha and the local spirits in: A monastic ritual of inclusion for the rain retreat', *JIP* 30 (2002), pp. 359–88. G. Schopen, 'Doing business for the Lord', *JAOS* 114 (1994), p. 553, has moreover argued that '... what *dharmaśāstra* says in regard to a whole host of topics, may now have to be seen in the light of similar discussions in Buddhist *vinaya*, and certainly Buddhist *vinaya* – especially, it seems, the *Mūlasarvāstivāda-vinaya* – may have particularly close ties to brahmanical concerns, and this, in turn, may again suggest that it was redacted by a community deeply embedded in the larger Indian, brahmanical world. It may in fact turn out to be *the* mainstream Indian *vinaya*.' We shall turn to this topic below, p. 37 ff.

*

Turning briefly to epigraphical evidence, we notice that in a Kharoṣṭhī inscription in Gāndhārī Prakrit of Senavarma, king of Oḍi, datable to the first century CE and recording the restoration of a *stūpa*, honour is paid to Brahmā Sahampati, Śakro devānāṃ indraḥ, the four Mahārājas (i.c. the guardians of the quarters), and also to the twenty-eight Yakṣa generals (*yakṣa-senāpati*), and Hārītī (the counterpart in Buddhism of Śītalā and Māriyammai) with her entourage (*saparivarā*). In the inscription, the mention of the *pūjā* offered to them follows on that in honour of the Bhagavant-Arhant-Samyaksambuddha, the Pratyekabuddhas, Arhants, Śrāvakas, Anāgāmins, Sakṛdāgāmins, Srotaāpannas, and all Ārya-pudgalas.[52]

These gods and celestials constitute, then, a fairly representative group of common Indian divinities as recognized in a Buddhist milieu and belonging to what might be called a partly shared Indian substratum or ground.[53]

---

[52] See O. von Hinüber, *Beiträge zur Erklärung der Senavarma-Inschrift* (AWL Mainz, Abhandl. der Geistes- u. sozialwiss. Kl., Nr. 1, Stuttgart, 2003), pp. 34–35, with G. Fussman, 'Documents épigraphiques kouchans (III)', *BEFEO* 71 (1982), p. 1–46. – Compare further the Kharoṣṭhī inscription in Gāndhārī of the Apraca/Avaca king Viṣṇuvarma, dated to the late first century BCE or the very early first century CE and published by R. Salomon, *South Asian Studies* 11 (1995), pp. 27–32. After the Buddhist worthies, this inscriptions mentions Brahmā, Śakra, and the four Mahārājas, as well as *sarvasattva* (!).

[53] On the intricate question of the interrelationship between Brahmanical/Hindu and Buddhist religion and ritual, many scholarly views could be cited. Special reference can be made to the following. C. Regamey, 'Motifs vichnouites et śivaïtes dans le Kāraṇḍavyūha', in: *Études tibétaines à la mémoire de Marcelle Lalou*, p. 411, wrote: 'L'influence réciproque entre le bouddhisme indien et les diverses traditions brahmaniques est un fait généralement reconnu. [...] On peut toutefois se poser la question de savoir jusqu'à quel point ces influences témoignent d'une réelle connaissance réciproque des croyances et des doctrines respectives. [...] Quant à la fameuse fusion tantrique, on pourrait l'attribuer à l'influence d'une tendance générale agissant aussi bien sur les hindouistes que sur les bouddhistes sans que le contact entre les deux courants religieux y fût nécessaire.' In this connexion Regamey pertinently referred to P. Horsch, *Die vedische Śloka- und Gāthā-Dichtung* (Bern, 1966), and 'Buddhismus und Upaniṣaden', in *Pratidānam* (F.B.J. Kuiper Felicitation Volume, The Hague, 1968), pp. 462–77. N. Iyanaga, article 'Daijizaiten (Maheś-

vara)', in: *Hōbōgirin* 6 (Paris-Tokyo, 1983), pp. 732–3, wrote: 'Les rapports réels que le bouddhisme a entretenus dans l'histoire avec les autres religions de l'Inde restent obscurs dans l'état présent des connaissances. [...] [L]es polémiques étaient activement menées sur le plan spéculatif et métaphysique. Mais en ce qui concerne les cultes quotidiens, le conflit peut avoir été beaucoup moins aigu : du moins, du côté du bouddhisme, c'est la tolérance qui semble avoir prévalu le plus souvent. Cependant, le prosélytisme a dû être actif d'un côté et de l'autre, et sur ce plan-là il peut y avoir eu des conflits réels, surtout lorsque des intérêts politiques étaient en jeu.' M. Strickmann, *Mantra et mandarins* (Paris, 1996), p. 24, wrote: 'Je suis convaincu que les āgama du śivaïsme médiéval et les tantra du bouddhisme médiéval représentent simplement différentes versions, différentes rédactions d'une seule et même chose. On peut même aller jusqu'à l'affirmer avec une certaine assurance, puisque l'élément commun n'est ni la doctrine ni la théorie. [...] Si, au contraire, on considère le rituel et les pratiques effectives, on peut voir alors que c'est là ce qu'ils ont en commun.'

A not dissimilar view of the matter was expressed by D. Seyfort Ruegg, 'Sur les rapports entre le bouddhisme et le "substrat religieux" indien et tibétain', *JA* 1964, pp. 77–95. See more recently our 'A note on the relationship between Buddhist and "Hindu" divinities in Buddhist literature and iconology: The *laukika/lokottara* contrast and the notion of an Indian "religious substratum"', in: R. Torella *et al.* (ed.), *Le parole e i marmi* (R. Gnoli Felicitation Volume, Rome, 2001), pp. 735–42.

3. Docetism in Mahāyāna Sūtras

Divine entities of the *laukika* level can appropriately find their place within the form of docetism that characterizes Mahāyāna Buddhism, that is, through the Teacher's (i.e. the Buddha's or Bodhisattva's) use of an expedient device, or salvific means (*upāya*), known as his *vikurvaṇa* (= *rnam par 'phrul ba*) 'transformative manifestation, emanation' and *nirmāṇakāya* (*sprul ba'i sku*) 'projection, phantom body'. Such a *nirmāṇa* is, then, so to say a second-order ectype of its original, first-order, achetype, be the latter a Buddha or high Bodhisattva, who may emanate or project it as a soteriological device with the purpose of assisting a trainee (*vineya, vaineya*; Tib. *gdul bya*).

The Candrādi-utpatti Chapter of the Nepalese version in prose of the *Kāraṇḍavyūhasūtra* (i.4), in a teaching given by the Lord to the Bodhisattva Sarvanīvaraṇaviṣkambhin, describes Avalokiteśvara as a sort of theogonic, *viśvarūpa*-like, figure from whom emanate Candra, Āditya (Sūrya), Maheśvara, Brahmā, Nārāyaṇa, Sarasvatī, Vāyu, Dharaṇī and Varuṇa, that is, the chosen deities honoured by the sentient beings whom this compassionate Great Being assists. Maheśvara is there said to be wrongly perceived by beings during the degenerate Iron Age (*kaliyuga*) as *ādideva*, as emanator (*sraṣṭṛ*) and creator (*kartṛ*) of the world. The *Kāraṇḍavyūha*'s description is stated to correspond to the recital of Avalokiteśvara's Qualities (*guṇodbhāvanā*) earlier communicated to the Lord by the former Tathāgata Vipaśyin.[54] Whilst this passage is not

---

[54] *Kāraṇḍavyūha* i.4 (the Candrādi-utpatti chapter); this passage is not among the Gilgit fragments of this Sūtra published by A. Mette, *Die Gilgitfragmente des Kāraṇḍavyūha* (Swisttal-Odendorf, 1997), but similar material is found in the metrical version (ed. Lokesh Chandra, 1999, Chap. iv). The gloriously resplendent, and fiery, cosmic *viśvarūpa* aspect of Viṣṇu-Kṛṣṇa as perceived by Arjuna is described in *Bhagavadgītā* xi. Cf. C. Regamey, 'Motifs vichnouites et śivaïtes dans le Kāraṇḍavyūha', *Études tibétaines dédiées à la mémoire de Marcelle Lalou*, pp. 411–32. – On Viśvarūpa in Indian art and iconography see T. Maxwell, *Viśvarūpa* (Bombay-Calcutta-Madras, 1988). And for a Nepalese image of Viśvarūpa, see A. Gail, 'Nepalica iconographica', in: B. Kölver (ed.), *Aspects of Nepalese traditions* (Stuttgart, 1992), p. 79.

For the figure of Avalokiteśvara/Lokeśvara and his iconography, beside the studies by M.-T. de Mallmann in her *Introduction à l'étude d'Avalokiteśvara* (Paris, 1948)

found amongst the Gilgit fragments of the *Kāraṇḍavyūha* published by A. Mette, the latter fragments include a section in which is reported a conversation between the *devaputra* Maheśvara and his spouse Umā concerning the *guṇodbhāvanā* of Avalokiteśvara, where the devotion of this divine couple to Avalokiteśvara and his six-syllable formula (*ṣaḍakṣarī vidyā*, i.e. '*oṃ maṇi padme hūṃ*') is described.[55]

In the second part of the Nepalese version in prose of the *Kāraṇḍavyūha*, the Mahāvidyāmaṇḍalavarṇana chapter (ii.6) concerned with Avalokiteśvara's six-syllable formula (*vidyā*), there are listed Brahmā, Viṣṇu, Maheśvara, Candra, Āditya, Vāyu, Varuṇa, Agni, Yama-Dharmarāja, and the four Great Kings (*mahārāja*, i.e. the celestial Guardians of the Quarters). And several lines later in the same section a further enumeration of divinities who seek Avalokiteśvara's *ṣaḍakṣarī mahāvidyārājñī* adds Śakra (Devānām Indraḥ) to the list.[56] The Maheśvaranirvyūha/niryūha (ii.7) provides an additional list of divinities that reads: *deva-nāga-yakṣa-gandharvâsura-garuḍa-kinnara-mahoraga-manuṣyâ-manuṣya-maheśvara-nārāyaṇapūrvagamāni devaputr<asahasr>āṇi* (?).[57]

This EMANATIONAL and DOCETIC concept and model is not confined to the *Kāraṇḍavyūha* alone, and it is well exemplified for instance in the *Saddharmapuṇḍarīkasūtra*, notably in the Avalokiteśvaravikurvaṇanirdeśa in Chapter xxiv (the Samantamukhaparivarta) which lists a number

---

and in her *Introduction à l'iconographie du tântrisme bouddhique* (Paris, 1975), see J. Locke, *Karunamaya: the Cult of Avalokitesvara-Matsyendranatha in the Valley of Nepal* (Kathamandu, 1980); J. Losty, 'An early Indian manuscript of the Kāraṇḍavyūhasūtra', in: D. Mitra and G. Bhattacharya, *Studies in art and archaeology of Bihar and Bengal* (Delhi, 1989), pp. 1–21. Cf. J. Holt, *Buddha in the crown: Avalokiteśvara in the Buddhist tradition of Sri Lanka* (New York, 1991).

[55] See A. Mette, *Die Gilgitfragmente des Kāraṇḍavyūha*, p. 110 ff.; id., 'Beschreibung eines Kultbildes im Gilgit-Manuskript des Kāraṇḍavyūha', *BIS* 9–10 (1996), pp. 217–23. Cf. A. Mette, 'Die Stotras des Kāraṇḍavyūha', *BEI*, 15 (1997), pp. 145–69.

[56] These two passages of the Nepalese version also have no exact correspondence among the Gilgit fragments published by A. Mette. But there is similar material in the metrical version of the Sūtra (ed. Lokesh Chandra, Chap. xvi).

[57] In the corresponding passage of the Gilgit fragments published by Mette (p. 128), the list also includes Maheśvara and Nārāyaṇa amongst many other spirits and *numina*: *deva-nāga-yakṣa-gandharvâsura ... maheśvara-nārāyaṇapūrvaṃgamāni daśa devaputrasaha[sr]<āṇi>*. – On Chap. ii of this Sūtra, see also p. 57 below.

of corporeal manifestations (*rūpa*) by which the Dharma is taught in the Sahālokadhātu to various trainee disciples (*vaineya*). Beside the Buddha himself, the Bodhisattva, and the Śrāvaka, these *rūpa*s include Brahmā, Śakra, Īśvara, Maheśvara, Vaiśravaṇa, and Vajrapāṇi. In its Chapter xxiii, the Gadgadasvaraparivarta, the same Sūtra speaks of the *rūpas* of the Bodhisattva Gadgadasvara when he has entered the *sarvarūpa-saṃdarśana-samādhi* and teaches the Sūtra to his various trainees.[58] For *vikurvaṇa*/*vikurvāṇa* (Tib. *rnam par 'phrul ba*) – as well as for *vikurvaṇā* and *vikurvā* – the meaning 'miracle' has been provided by F. Edgerton in his *Dictionary*; but the rendering 'transformation, (docetic) manifestation' seems closer to the sense intended.

Between the mythologemes of Avalokiteśvara and, in particular, Maheśvara as Lokeśvaras there exists a close link. In the *Dharmadhātu-stava* (57) ascribed to Nāgārjuna,[59] moreover, reference is made to Maheśvara-Amitāyus (Amitāyus/Amitābha being the Jina associated with the Bodhisattva Avalokiteśvara).

To regard divinities included in such Sūtra-lists – or at least the greater ones among them of whom similar lists are found in other Buddhist texts – as being specifically Hindu ones eclectically borrowed by, or syncretistically infiltrated into, Buddhism would be, it seems, to take much too one-sided a view of the matter. They are, rather, deities conceived of as belonging to the mundane level who are worshipped by still immature trainees, but who in fact take their refuge in the infinite compassion of Avalokiteśvara and his six-syllable *vidyā*.

In the Vaineyadharmopadeśa chapter of the Nepalese version in prose of the *Kāraṇḍavyūha* (i.8), such divine figures are described as guarding and teaching the *dharma* to their respective disciples or trainees. Thus, after those persons to be trained (*vaineya*, *vineya* < *vi-nī*; Tib. *gdul bya* < *'dul ba*) by the Tathāgata, Pratyekabuddhas, Arhats and Bodhisattvas, there are mentioned those trained by Maheśvara, Nārāyaṇa, Brahmā, Indra, Āditya, Candra, Agni, Varuṇa, Vāyu, the Nāgas, Vighnapati, the

[58] In Chapter i, the Nidānaparivarta, Īśvara, Maheśvara, Brahmā Sahāmpati and a host of other divinities and *numina* are enumerated among the auditors of this Sūtra.

[59] See D. Seyfort Ruegg, 'Le *Dharmadhātustava* de Nāgārjuna', in: *Études tibétaines dédiées à la mémoire de Marcelle Lalou*, p. 468.

Yakṣas, Vaiśravaṇa, etc. In this context, 'training' refers of course to the procedure by which a disciple is assisted and instructed in a fashion that conforms to his psychological and spiritual nature and predisposition.

Now, if Buddhist thought has recognized the existence of various kinds of trainee disciples (*vaineya*) – not only Buddhists but also non-Buddhist *tīrthika*s – each having his or her own religious concepts and devotion to his or her chosen divinity, the divine entities belonging to the lower levels of the world that are thus accepted by some trainees may accordingly be nothing but contingent manifestations, ones perhaps projected, so to say, by the Compassionate Beings belonging to the higher (supramundane) level in the docetic perspective frequently adopted in Buddhism. The entire world of *saṃsāra* may then be a kind of stage on which the liberating activity of the Buddha and the Bodhisattvas is played out. And the divine entities of India (and Tibet, or of any other Buddhist country) that belong to the mundane level may be regarded as forming part of this whole.

But in so far as they are contingent reflexes, i.e. projections or transformative emanations, of the Great Beings of the supramundane level, these divine entities of the mundane level have no independent and autogenous soteriological or gnoseological function in Buddhism. They are regarded by an informed Buddhist as divine beings, but in a lower degree and, usually, in a derivative mode.

Thus, beside the SUBSTRATUM paradigm considered above, there exists a DOCETIC paradigm based also on the idea that a divinity or hero is considered the transformative, ectypal, EMANATION (*nirmāṇa* = *sprul pa*, *vikurvaṇa*/*vikurvāṇa* = *rnam par 'phrul ba*) of a protective being such as a Buddha or higher Bodhisattva.

4. Kārttikeya-Mañjuśrī in the *Mañjuśrīmūlakalpa*

In Chapter ii of the *Mañjuśrīmūlakalpa* – the Maṇḍalavidhinirdeśaparivarta – there appears the entity named Kārttikeya-Mañjuśrī, a curious divine figure who as it were embodies a *mantra*. In this work, later classified as a Kriyātantra belonging to the *tathāgatakula*, this figure is described (p. 33) as a boy (*kumāra*), and as an attendant (*anucara*) and executor (*sarvakarmika*) of the Bodhisattva Mañjuśrī Kumārabhūta, otherwise referred to in the same text as Mañjughoṣa. This figure is found in a passage alluding *inter alia* to the *Atharvaveda*, and also mentioning Brahmā, Garuḍavāhana Cakrapāṇi, and Mahāmaheśvara together with the latter's son Skanda (= Kārttikeya). Further on, in his iconographical description in a passage (p. 43) which also mentions Brahmā Sahāmpati/Sabhāpati and Īśāna, Lord of the *bhūta*s, and Umā, this Kārttikeya-Mañjuśrī is described as mounted on a peacock. Elsewhere (e.g. at p. 62), in keeping with his appearance also as a boy, the Bodhisattva Ārya-Mañjuśrī is represented as adorned with the ornaments of a prince (*kumārālaṃkārālaṃkṛta*) and as wearing his hair dressed in five locks (*pañcacīrakaśiraska*) as was customary for a boy. In a Maṇḍala of this important Kriyātantra, several great Indian divinities have been associated with their respective *mantra*s. And the Bodhisattva Kumārabhūta Mañjuśrī is connected with an embodiment known as Kārttikeya-Mañjuśrī, who shares divine iconographical features with Śiva's son Kārttikeya/Skanda/Ṣaṇmukha.[60]

Other chapters of the same Tantra contain further references to *mantra*s pronounced by Śiva, Viṣṇu, Brahmā, etc., and which are incorporated in the ritual (*kalpa*) of the *Mañjuśrīmūlakalpa*.

---

[60] Part of chapter ii of the Tantra was studied by Ariane Macdonald(-Spanien), *Le Maṇḍala du Mañjuśrīmūlakalpa* (Paris, 1962). Kārttikeya is discussed there on pp. 118 and 122–3 (an equivalent of the Skt. form Kārttikeya-Mañjuśrī is, however, not reflected exactly in the denominations found in the Tibetan translation of this text, namely gDoṅ drug gi bu žes bya ba'i 'jam dpal gžon nu/gŽon nu smin drug gi bu). – On Mañjuśrī *pañcacīraka* (Tib. *zur phud lṅa*), Pañcaśikha, and Brahmā Sanatkumāra, see M. Lalou, *Iconographie des étoffes peintes* (Paris, 1930), chap. v; and E. Lamotte, 'Mañjuśrī', *T'oung-Pao* 48 (1960), pp. 2–3.

Verse ii.31 of the same text refers in an interesting manner to *kalpa*s set out in Vaiṣṇava Tantra:

ya eva vaiṣṇave tantre kathitāḥ kalpavistarāḥ/
upāyā vaineyasattvānāṃ mañjughoṣeṇa bhāṣitāḥ//

Those numerous rituals described in Vaiṣṇava Tantra are salvific devices for beings to be trained once pronounced by Mañjughoṣa.

Whether (ritual) ECLECTICISM is the most appropriate description of these processes, as suggested by Phyllis Granoff in her valuable study of 'Indian eclectic religious culture', may be a matter of definitions.[61] And whether DOCETISM and EMANATIONISM are in play here is also not quite certain. At all events, the idea conveyed can perhaps be best understood in the light of the Kriyātantra theory that – in a process of 'conversion' and ritual transformation of the Laukikas belonging to the sixth *kula* 'clan' – these divinities of the mundane level offer up their respective *mantra*s to a Buddha (see below, p. 63 f.). Here in the *Mañjuśrīmūlakalpa* it is Mañjughoṣa, a Bodhisattva of the highest stage (*bhūmi*), who is represented as promulgating *kalpa*s belonging to Vaiṣṇava Tantra.

---

[61] Passages from several chapters of the *Mañjuśrīmūlakalpa* have been examined by P. Granoff, 'Other people's ritual: Ritual eclecticism in early mediaeval Indian religions', *JIP* 28 (2000), pp. 399–424 (see also id., 'My rituals and my gods: Ritual exclusiveness in mediaeval India' *JIP* 29 [2001], pp. 109–34).

In discussing ritual eclecticism in the earlier of these two articles, Granoff however states (p. 404 and n. 5) that she considers that the contrast *laukika* : *lokottara* amounts to the opposition Hindu : Buddhist. There no doubt exists a link – perhaps even a sort of isomorphism – between these two sets of oppositions. But that, in Buddhist Tantra, the category *laukika* cannot be exactly coterminous with what is usually called Hindu would seem to follow from the fact that the *laukikakula* of the Buddhist Kriyātantra (see below, pp. 63–67) is not entirely made up of specifically Hindu gods. It would be possible to equate *laukika* with Hindu only were one to define as 'Hindu' all the divinities and numina not included in the Buddhist *lokottara* category – a definition that would, however, probably be both over-wide and somewhat circular.

5. The worldly/mundane (*laukika*), and the matter of the popular and lay

It needs to be made clear from the start that the CONTINUITY of Buddhism with its Indian milieu and matrix which is at issue here – that is, the absence of defined and fixed frontiers that would mark off entirely distinct and separate entities – does not necessarily apply at all levels in Buddhist religion and philosophy. In particular, it concerns the level that Buddhists have tended to call the 'worldly' or 'mundane' (*laukika*), in contradistinction to what they have termed the 'supramundane' or 'transmundane' (*lokottara*). This structured opposition will be discussed in detail below.

It needs also to be made explicit that when referring to Buddhism as a religion it is in no way intended to imply that it is basically theistic.[62] The

---

[62] Still useful older discussions are H. von Glasenapp, *Buddhismus und Gottesidee* (AWL Mainz, Abhandlungen der Geistes- und Sozialwissenscaftlichen Klasse, Wiesbaden, 1954), and *Der Buddhismus, eine atheistische Religion* (Munich, 1966; subsequently translated into English with the revised title *Buddhism, a non-theistic religion*). See also H. Jacobi, *Die Entwicklung der Gottesidee bei den Indern* (Bonn, 1923); G. Chemparathy, 'Two early Buddhist refutations of the existence of Īśvara as the Creator of the universe', *WZKSO* 12–13 (1968–9), pp. 83–100; id., *An Indian rational theology* (Vienna, 1972); N. Iyanaga, article 'Daijizaiten", *Hōbōgirin*, p. 725; J. Bronkhorst, *Karma and teleology* (Tōkyō, 2000), p. 49 ff.; E. Steinkellner, 'Hindu Doctrines of Creation and Their Buddhist Critiques', in: P. Schmidt-Leukel (ed.), *Buddhism, Christianity and the Question of Creation. Karmic or Divine?* (Ashgate, 2006), pp. 15–31; as well as the publications cited in the following note.

In Chap. iv of the metrical version of the *Kāraṇḍavyūhasūtra*, the figure of Avalokiteśvara/Lokeśvara absorbed in *lokasaṃsarjana-samādhi* (Concentration of 'co-emission' of the world) and *lokodbhava-samādhi* – and described, (quasi) theistically, as *ādibuddha*(*ātmasambhūta*), *ādideva*, *viśvasr̥j*, *sraṣtr̥*, etc – is described in the frame of an emanationist theogony (root *nir-mā-*; see above, p. 31 ff.) of which he is the origin; but he has presumably to be distinguished from what is usually understood as a Creator God. (Quasi) theistic and creationist representations are not rare also in parts of Vajrayānist literature, including rDzogs chen in its Tantra entitled (*Byaṅ chub kyi sems*) *Kun byed rgyal po*. Nonetheless, a tract rejecting a creator god – the **Īśvarakartr̥tvanirākr̥tir, Viṣṇor ekakartr̥tvanirākaraṇam* – is attributed to a (no doubt Deutero-)Nāgārjunapāda (for references see D. Seyfort Ruegg, *The literature of the Madhyamaka school of philosophy in India* [Wiesbaden, 1981], p. 30). Candrakīrti,

familiar equation 'religion = theism' is of course largely a Judeo-Christian (pre)judgement which has today become little more than a popular pre-judice. In fact, as is well known, Buddhism neither postulates nor accepts a God who is the creator (*kartṛ*, *sraṣṭṛ*) of the world and its inhabitants, or a God who directly controls and intervenes in the destinies of men. In this respect, then, Buddhism is non-theistic (rather than atheistic in the usual sense of this word). In its later history we do, however, find pronouncedly anti-theistic tracts. But on the just mentioned 'mundane' level Buddhism has accepted, if only provisionally, what people – the 'world' (*loka*) – call gods and divinities (Skt./Pali *deva*, *devatā*, *yakṣa/yakkha*, etc.; Tib. *lha*, *gnod sbyin*, etc.). These entities in fact play a not inconspicuous rôle in both scriptural and post-canonical Buddhist sources.[63] But, in Buddhism, celestials and gods (at least of the *laukika*

Prasannapadā i.1 (p. 39) criticizes the idea of a creator-god. Other works rejecting the idea of a creator-god were composed by Śubhagupta (dGe [b]sruṅ[s], the *Īśvarabhaṅgakārikās*), Jñānaśrīmitra (the *Īśvaravāda*), and Ratnakīrti (the *Īśvarasādhanadūṣaṇa*). See also H. Krasser, *Śaṅkaranandanas Īśvarāpākaraṇasaṅkṣepa mit einem anonymen Kommentar und weiteren Materialien zur buddhistischen Gottespolemik* (Vienna, 2002). (This is not the place to consider the development in the course of the history of Buddhism – in addition to a sort of *bhakti*-movement attested in particular in the *Stotra/Stava* literature – of certain theistic tendencies, including the Amida-cult in Japan and the idea of a creative *buddha* – Kun tu bzaṅ po = Samantabhadra – in Tibet.)

63 See e.g. J. Masson, *La religion populaire dans le canon bouddhique pâli* (Louvain, 1942); E. Lamotte, *Histoire du bouddhisme indien* (Louvain, 1958); M. Marasinghe, *Gods in early Buddhism* (Vidyalankara, 1974); K. R. Norman, 'The Buddha's view of Devas', in: *Beiträge zur Indienforschung* (Festschrift E. Waldschmidt, Berlin, 1977), pp. 329–36 (= *Collected papers*, ii, pp. 1–8) on the Pali classification into *saṃmuti*-, *upapatti*- and *visuddhi-deva*s (see p. 92 below); id., 'Devas and Adhidevas in Buddhism', *JPTS* 9 (1981), pp. 145–55 (= *Collected papers*, ii, pp. 162–71); D. Seyfort Ruegg, 'On the supramundane and the divine in Buddhism', in: N. Katz (ed.), *Buddhist and Western philosophy* (New Delhi, 1981), pp. 421–4; M. Wijayaratna, *Le culte des dieux chez les bouddhistes singhalais* : *La religion populaire du Ceylan face au bouddhisme Theravāda* (Paris, 1987); G. Schopen, 'Counting the Buddha and the local spirits', *JIP* 30 (2002), pp. 359–88 (among other things on *naivāsika*, on which see above, p. 27); id., 'On Buddhist monks and dreadful deities: Some monastic devices for updating the Dharma', in: H. Bodewitz and M. Hara (ed.), *Gedenkschrift J. W. de Jong* (Tōkyō, 2004), pp. 161–84.

An important later Indian source concerning deities and mythology in a (non-Tantric) Buddhist context is Udbhaṭasiddhasvāmin's *Viśeṣastava* (or *Viśiṣṭastava*?) with

variety on which see below) are all subject to the conditioned (*saṃskṛta*) processes of the round of existence (*saṃsāra*) and in fact make up one of the five (or six) states of existence (*gati*).

It must also to be specified that – contrary to a widespread view – the phenomena in question do not necessarily have anything directly to do with a so-called 'popular' or 'lay' Buddhism – concepts that may in fact raise at least as many problems as they are supposed to solve.[64]

Prajñāvarman's *Ṭīkā*, the same author's **Sarvajñamaheśvarastotra*, and Śaṃkarasvāmin's (or Śaṃkarapati's?) **Devatāvimarśastuti* (or *Devatātiśayastotra*) with Prajñāvarman's *Ṭīkā*. On these works see below, pp. 73, 93, 163.

For Sri Lanka in particular, see H. Bechert (ed.), *Buddhism in Ceylon and Studies on religious syncretism in Buddhist countries* (Symposien zur Buddhismusforschung, i, Göttingen, 1978); id. 'Mythologie der singhalesischen Volksreligion', in: H. Haussig (ed.), *Wörterbuch der Mythologie*, 1. Abteilung: Die alten Kulturvölker, 15. Lieferung (Stuttgart, n.d.); and M. Wijayaratna, *op. cit.*. The god of Kataragama (and Skanda/Kumāra) is a famous case. For Nepal and the Newars, see e.g. D. Gellner, *Monk, householder and Tantric priest* (Cambridge, 1992), p. 98 ff. On the place of Indian mythology and deities in Tibet, see R.-A. Stein, 'La mythologie hindouiste au Tibet', in: G. Gnoli and L. Lanciotti (ed.), *Orientalia Iosephi Tucci memoriae dicata*, iii (Rome, 1988), pp. 1407–26. And for gods and *kami* in Japan, see B. Frank, 'Les Deva de la tradition bouddhique et la société japonaise: L'exemple d'Indra/Taishakuten', in: A. Forest *et al.* (ed.), *Bouddhisme et sociétés asiatiques* (Paris, 1990), pp. 61–74; id., *Le panthéon bouddhique au Japon – Collections d'Émile Guimet* (Paris, 1991), p. 68 (*honji suijaku* and *gongen* 'apparition circonstantielle'); id., *Dieux et bouddhas au Japon* (Paris, 2000); M. Teeuwen and F. Rambelli (ed.), *Buddhas and Kami in Japan* (London, 2003); D. N. Bakshi, *Hindu divinities in Japanese Buddhist pantheon* (Calcutta, 1979). See also the studies in F. Fukui and G. Fussman (ed.), *Bouddhisme et cultures locales* (Paris, 1994).

[64] For a critique of the idea of lay Buddhism, in addition to the brief observations in D. Seyfort Ruegg, 'A recent work on the religions of Tibet and Mongolia', *TP* 61 (1976), pp. 313–14, see G. Schopen, 'Filial piety and the monk in the practice of Buddhism', *TP* 70 (1984), p. 110 ff.; id., 'Two problems in the history of Indian thought: The layman/monk distinction and the doctrines of the transference of merit', *StII* 10 (1985), p. 26; and id., 'Monks and the relic-cult in the *Mahāparinibbānasutta*: An old misunderstanding in regard to monastic Buddhism', in: K. Shinohara and G. Schopen (ed.), *From Benares to Beijing* (Oakville, 1991), p. 187. On the attitude of a layperson, or Buddhist *upāsaka*, towards the cult of Maheśvara, see N. Iyanaga, article 'Daijizaiten', *Hōbōgirin*, pp. 719, 732–3. Devotion to divinities such as Brahmā, Śakra, Īśvara, Nārāyaṇa, Vaiśravaṇa, etc., is represented as characteristic of the worldling (*pṛthagjana*) – who may of course be a religious as well as a layperson – in the *Mahāvairocanasūtra* (Chap. i; Tajima, pp. 68–70).

No single theory or explanatory hypothesis can of course be expected to resolve without residue all the questions and problems that may arise in connexion with the topics at issue here: no single key, no open-sesame, will unlock all cases. The following remarks are offered, then, simply with a view to clarifying some relevant points. For the structured – i.e. contrastive and complementary – opposition *laukika* : *lokottara* has often served as an organizing principle for ordering a complex world of religious and cultural representations.

The idea of a specifically lay Buddhism has been advanced, e.g, by E. Lamotte, 'Le bouddhisme des laïcs', in: *Studies in Indology and Buddhology* (S. Yamaguchi Felicitation Volume, Kyōto, 1955), pp. 73–89, and *Histoire du bouddhisme indien*, pp. 686–705; and by A. Hirakawa, *A history of Indian Buddhism from Śākyamuni to early Mahāyāna* (translated and edited by P. Groner, Honolulu, 1990), p. 105 f. (For a critique of Hirakawa's views, see S. Sasaki, 'A study of the origins of Mahāyāna Buddhism', *Eastern Buddhist* 30 [1997], pp. 79–113, especially p. 81.) For Tibet, a parallel distinction has been made between *mi chos* and *saṅs rgyas kyi chos* (*buddha-dharma*). An attempt, perhaps not altogether successful, to identify lay and 'pop(ular)' elements from Tibetan sources was made by D. Martin, 'The Star King and the Four Children of Pehar: Popular religious movements of 11th–12th century Tibet', *AOH* 49 (1996), pp. 171–95; cf. id., 'Lay religious movements in 11th and 12th century Tibet', *Kailash* 18 (1996), pp. 23–55. – What has been said above is not, of course, meant to detract from the established fact that, in Mahāyāna, there have existed the figure and ideal of a layman-Bodhisattva (such as Vimalakīrti); cf. D. Seyfort Ruegg, 'Aspects of the study of the (earlier) Indian Mahāyāna', *JIABS* 27 (2004), p. 27.

6. The common Indian religious ground or substratum and the opposition worldly/mundane (*laukika*) : supramundane/transmundane (*lokottara*)

What accounts for the fact that gods, divinities and celestials bearing the same (or very closely related) names are to be found in Buddhism as well as in other religions of India? As far as Indian Buddhism is concerned, the answer, briefly stated, may well be that these entities are Indian, that Buddhists were Indians, and therefore that Buddhism was in the first place an Indian religion that made use of widely spread Indian ideas. To suppose that Buddhism arose and developed in some sort of water-tight compartment separate from its Indian milieu and matrix will then be historically without foundation. Indeed, this supposition would make almost impossible any treatment of Buddhism as a religion and as a system of thinking of India. Variants of the above-mentioned supposition are, nevertheless, not infrequently met with in discussions of Indian religious art and iconography and of Buddhism in general. It will therefore be useful to take a closer and more detailed look at several of the problems involved.[65]

---

[65] The idea of a pan-Indian religious ground/substratum common to both Buddhism and Brahmanism/Hinduism (and of course to other Indian religions) was already broached by the present writer in his article of 1964 'Sur les rapports entre le bouddhisme et le "substrat religieux" indien et tibétain' cited in n. 53 above. The term 'substratum' was then adopted by N. Iyanaga in his important article 'Daijizaiten', *Hōbōgirin* vi (1983), p. 715a. This concept of a common substratum, a pan-Indian ground, has been criticized as both too 'Platonic' and too 'structuralist' and comparable to Saussure's 'langue' (as opposed to his 'parole') by R. Davidson, *Indian esoteric Buddhism* (New York, 2002), pp. 171–2. For A. Sanderson's view, see further below.

It should be made clear that the term 'substratum' is being used here roughly in the sense of (religious or cultural) (back)ground, or patrimony/heritage, and also that the 'Substratum Model' being envisaged does not itself presuppose (or exclude) the possibility of the presence in Buddhism (and Hinduism) of so-called 'pre-Aryan' or 'non-Aryan' components, towards which matter it is theoretically and historically neutral. Concerning the expression 'religious substratum', its appropriateness here is perhaps open to discussion. In the first place, in the present context, the question may arise of distinguishing between a religious substratum, adstratum, superstratum, and even archistratum. In the cases to be considered, it does not appear that the pan-

Of fundamental importance is the fact that most of the divinities and celestials in question were to be classified in Buddhist thought as belonging in the first place to the level termed 'worldly' or 'mundane' (*laukika*), as opposed to the supramundane/transmundane (*lokottara*) level to which belong only those entities having a true soteriological and gnoseological function on the Buddhist Path of liberation and Gnosis.

We are thus presented with a basic, and structurally constituted, contrastive and complementary opposition the two terms of which are not as it were horizontally related like the opposition Hindu : Buddhist in India (and Bon po : Buddhist in Tibet[66]) – or indeed like other oppositions such as lay : monastic (or monachal),[67] affective : cognitive, or, *a fortiori*, actual doing (e.g. ritual behaviour) : idealizing saying (and writing in, e.g., didactic and normative texts) – but, rather, vertically related in the hierarchical, structured, opposition *laukika* : *lokottara*.

Indian components in Buddhism are either a superstratum or an adstratum. Whether they might be regarded as some sort of archistratum is perhaps to be investigated. But it would seem that the archistratum relation, and also the superstratum and adstratum relations, would pertain most closely to some kind of BORROWING MODEL (on which see below). In any event, where the idea of 'religious substratum' will differ importantly from that of a linguistic substratum is in the fact that there exists a historical-genetic continuity between a given religion and its substratum – e.g. between Buddhism on the one side and on the other side its Indian matrix, a pan-Indian pantheon, etc. – whereas between a given language and its linguistic substratum – e.g. between Sanskrit as an Old Indo-Aryan language and Dravidian or Munda as non-Indo-Aryan languages – there is no genetic continuiy, the link being instead areal (and typological). In our 'A note on the relationship ...' (as in n. 53), p. 738, it was pointed out that 'the "religious substratum" is not directly comparable with, e.g., a linguistic substratum where an exogenous element may actually be observed in a language-system linguistically different from the foreign one regarded as constituting the substratum. Let it be explicitly stated that, in the matter under discussion, the postulated "religious substratum" is not *exogenous* to the system in which it is observed, but (more or less) closely related genetically to the latter (so much so, indeed, that on occasion it might be described as *endogenous* in relation to the latter).' Concerning the qualification 'pan-Indian' in the expression common ('pan-Indian') substratum, see p. 89 below.

66 Concerning the relationship between Tibetan Buddhism and Bon, see Appendix I and specially n. 232.

67 See above, n. 64. For the opposition monastic : lay, see D. Seyfort Ruegg, 'Aspects of the study of (earlier) Mahāyāna', *JIABS* 27 (2004), p. 24 ff.

What then are the gods, godlings, celestials, and *numina* classified as *laukika*? A section of the *Mahāvyutpatti* (nos. 3111–3172) lists the names of some sixty-one *laukikadevatā* (Tib. *'jig rten pa'i lha*), beginning with Brahmā Hiraṇyagarbha (Tshaṅs pa dbyig gi sñiṅ po) and ending with Vighna (bGegs). Separate lists are also given of Nāgarājas (no. 3224 ff.), ordinary Nāgas (no. 3307 ff.), Yakṣas (no. 3364 ff., including Vaiśravaṇa), Gandharvas (no. 3378 ff., including Dhṛtarāṣṭra), Asuras (no. 3389 ff.), Garuḍas (no. 3401 ff.), Kinnaras (no. 3411 ff.), and Kumbhāṇḍas (no. 3434 ff., including Virūḍhaka). Ten different classes of celestials, terrestrials and subterrestrials have been enumerated in the same source (nos. 3214–3223), namely *deva*, *nāga*, *yakṣa*, *gandharva*, *asura*, *daitya*, *garuḍa*, *kinnara*, *mahoraga*, and *kumbhāṇḍa*.

From the Buddhist standpoint, all these entities, inclusive of the *deva*s, are subject to the world process characterized by the relation of cause and effect – the law of the connexion between actions (*karman*) and their maturation (*vipāka*) – which governs the entire round of existence (*saṃsāra*) to the various levels of which they all belong. Laukika divinities therefore belong to a different category from the one to which belong fully Awakened (*buddha*) beings – the *lokottara* Tathāgatas who have attained Nirvāṇa (*parinirvṛta*) – and also from Ārya-Bodhisattvas of the highest stage (*bhūmi*), all of whom are representative of, and as it were symbolize, the soteriological and gnoseological principles of Buddhism. (Whilst the Buddhas/Tathāgatas are beyond the world of *saṃsāra* – they are described as *lokātīta*, etc. – even as their benevolent salvific action (*kāritra*, etc.) proceeding from their compassionate resolve (*praṇidhi*, etc.) continues to have an effect on beings in the world, by virtue of their resolve the higher Bodhisattvas are in the world though not of it. Beginning with his *darśanamārga*, the Bodhisattva proceeds on the *lokottaramārga*.)

There appears to exist no reason to suppose that, in India, gods such as Brahmā and Śakra found already in Buddhist canonical sources, as well as other godlings and *numina* recognized by Buddhists, were exogenous and alien intrusions or imports from Hinduism that, for some reason, had to be incorporated, somehow or other, into Buddhism in the course of its historical development. The two religious traditions in question have their roots for the most part in the same common GROUND or SUBSTRATUM of religious representations, a fact which would seem adequately to account for ther presence in Buddhism also.

7. Symbiosis, confrontation, the subordination of the *laukika* through subjugation, and the issue of 'Buddhism *vs.* Hinduism': evidence from some Yogatantras

It has sometimes been assumed that common Indian divinities assigned in Buddhist thought to the *laukika* level stood in a relation of antagonism and hostility to the specifically Buddhist tutelaries of the *lokottara* level, and in particular to the Great Wrathful Ones (*mahākrodha-rāja, khro bo chen po*) of the Vajrayāna who may be depicted iconographically as dancing or treading upon the prostrate bodies of these divinities.

The question of the extent to which there existed hostile CONFRONTATION between Hinduism and Buddhism, and between 'Hindu' divinities and celestials (in the narrow sense of the word 'Hindu' exclusive of Buddhism) – or those belonging to a common Indian religious GROUND/SUBSTRATUM – and specifically Buddhist deities is clearly of fundamental importance for the general history of religion in India, for the analysis of the system of *kula*s and *maṇḍala*s of the Vajrayāna, and for the understanding of Buddhism and its iconology and iconography as a whole.[68] It is no doubt true that the rivalry and antagonisms which, from

---

[68] The view that there existed a hostile confrontation, even an inveterate antagonism, between Buddhism and Hinduism that was depicted in certain icons has been quite widely held. It was advanced by, e.g., Benoytosh Bhattacharyya, *Sādhanamālā*, ii (Baroda, 1928), pp. cxxx ff.; and id., *Indian Buddhist iconography* ([2]Calcutta, 1958), pp. 158, 187, 388–9. On p. 344 ff. of the latter book Bhattacharyya has described as 'Hindu gods in Vajrayāna' a number of figures that might better be described as 'pan-Indian' (cf. p. 89 below), or as belonging to a religious GROUND/SUBSTRATUM common to Buddhism and Brahmanism/Hinduism. For the interpretation of icons in terms of secular confrontation and sectarian antagonism (on the Śarabha/Śarabheśamūrti model), see *inter alia* J. Banerjea, *The development of Hindu iconography* (Calcutta, 1956), pp. 5, 231, 275

Already on the appearance of the first edition of Bhattacharyya's *Indian Buddhist iconography* (London, 1924) his confrontational interpretation was rejected in a review by A. K. Coomaraswamy, *JAOS* 46 (1926), pp. 187–9. Since that time interpretations fairly close to Bhattacharyya's, according to which the divinities in question were 'Hindu', have been fairly widely maintained, for example by M.-T. de Mallmann, 'Divinités hindoues dans le tântrisme bouddhique', *Arts asiatiques* 10 (1964), pp. 67–86, and 'Hindu deities in Tantric Buddhism', *ZAS* 2 (1968), pp. 41–53.

time to time, must have arisen between the followers of Buddhism and the old cults did produce conflict in addition to SYMBIOSIS, and to the cases of compromise and syncretism, that their co-existence side by side could have generated.[69] Close contacts can indeed be expected to have on

---

This kind of interpretation was questioned by the present writer in his 'Sur les rapports entre le bouddhisme et le "substrat religieux" indien et tibétain', *JA* 1964, p. 77 ff., and elsewhere since (for example in a review of Mallman's *Introduction à l'iconographie du tântrisme bouddhique* in *JAOS* 98 (1978), pp. 544–5).

[69] On the problem of 'syncretism' in relation to Buddhism, beside the observations in D. Seyfort Ruegg, 'Sur les rapports entre le bouddhisme et le "substrat religieux" indien et tibétain', *JA* 1964, pp. 77–95, and 'A note on the relationship between Buddhist and Hindu divinities in Buddhist literature and iconology: The *laukika/lolottara* contrast and the notion of an Indian "religious substratum"', in: R. Torella *et al.* (ed.), *Le parole e i marmi* (R. Gnoli Festschrift), pp. 735–42, see, concerning South and Inner Asia, H. Bechert (ed.), *Buddhism in Ceylon and Studies on religious syncretism in Buddhist countries* (as in n. 44) which includes Bechert's s own important survey of the question in his introduction (p. 19 ff.: 'A comparative view of religious syncretism in Buddhist countries'), and, on pp. 146–77; S. Lienhard, 'Religionssynkretismus in Nepal' (cited above in n. 44; also published as 'Problèmes du syncrétisme religieux au Népal', *BEFEO* 65 [1978], pp. 239–50), and *Diamantmeister und Hausväter: Buddhistisches Gemeindeleben in Nepal* (Vienna, 1999); J. Locke, *Karunamaya, the cult of Avalokiteśvara-Matsyendranath in the Valley of Nepal* (Kathmandu, 1980); H. Brinkhaus, 'References to Buddhism in the Nepālamāhātmya', *JNRC* 4 (1980), pp. 274–86; W. Heissig and H.-J. Klimkeit (ed.), *Synkretismus in den Religionen Zentralasiens* (Wiesbaden, 1987); W. Heissig, *Götter im Wandel: gesammelte Aufsätze zum Synkretismus der mongolischen Volksreligion* (Wiesbaden, 1996); B. Kölver, 'Some examples of syncretism in Nepal', in: B. Kölver (ed.), *Aspects of Nepalese traditions* (Proceedings of the Seminar held under the auspices of Tribhuvan University Research Division and the German Research Council, March 1990; Stuttgart, 1992), pp. 209–22; D. Gellner, *Monk, householder and Tantric priest*, esp. pp. 100–04; id., 'Sketch of the history of Lalitpur (Patan)', *Contributions to Nepal Studies* 23 (1996), pp. 125–57 (on the identification of Karuṇāmaya with Kṛṣṇa and Viṣṇu and with Matsyendranātha, a form of Śiva, pp. 140–41, and, more generally, on 'competing interpretations', 'contextual syncretism' and the 'stategy of inclusivism' with Hindu accretions being regarded as unnecesary); and F. Sferra, 'Some considerations on the relationship between Hindu and Buddhist Tantras', in: G. Verardi and S. Vita (ed.), *Buddhist Asia 1* (Università degli Studi di Napoli "L'Orientale", Centro di Studi sul Buddhismo, Kyōto, 2003), pp. 57–84. – For Sri Lanka, in addition to Bechert (ed.), *Buddhism in Ceylon ...* (as in n. 44), see R. Gombrich, *Precept and practice. Traditional Buddhism in the rural highlands of Ceylon* (Oxford, 1971). For Burma see N. R. Ray, *Brahmanical gods in Burma* (Calcutta, 1932). For Thailand see Gauri Devi, *Hindu deities in Thai art* (Śatapiṭaka

occasion led to tension and hostility, and perhaps then to confrontational

---

Series no. 387, New Delhi, 1996). For Cambodia see, e.g., J. Filliozat, 'Sur le çivaïsme et le bouddhisme du Cambodge, à propos de deux livres récents', *BEFEO* 70 (1981), pp. 59–99; K. Bhattacharya, 'Religious syncretism in Ancient Cambodia', in: T. Dhammaratana *et al.*, (ed.), *Mélanges offerts au Vénérable Thích Huyên-Vi* (Paris, 1997), pp. 1–12; A Sanderson, 'The Śaiva religion among the Khmers (I)', *BEFEO* 90-91 (2003–4), pp. 349–462. On Buddhist 'syncretism' in Indonesia, in particular Bali, see C. Hoykaas, *Balinese Bauddha Brahmans* (Amsterdam, 1973); T. Goudriaan and C. Hoykaas, *Stuti and Stava* (*Bauddha, Śaiva and Vaiṣṇava*) *of Balinese Brahman priests* (Amsterdam, 1971); and J. Ensink, 'Śiva-Buddhism in Java and Bali', in: H. Bechert (ed.), *op. cit.*, pp. 178–98. See further J. F. Staal, *Mantras between fire and water: Reflections on a Balinese rite* (Amsterdam, 1995), p. 47.

In Japan, the very significant Buddhist concept of *honji suijaku* – a compound translatable as 'original or fundamental nature' (i.e. *dharmakāya*: Mahāvairocana) and 'manifestation, imprint, trace' (for instance a *kami* or a Shintō god) – and the complex problem of syncretism with Shintō divinities have been studied by, amongst others, J. Kitagawa, ' Buddhist transformation in Japan', *HR* 4 (1965), pp. 319–36; A. Matsunaga, *The Buddhist philosophy of assimilation* (Tokyo, 1969); M. Kiyota, *Shingon Buddhism* (Los Angeles-Tokyo, 1978), p. 74 ff.; R. Heinemann, 'Buddhistisch-schintoistischer Synkretismus in Struktur und Praxis des Tempels Rinnōji in Nikkō, Japan', in: H. Bechert (ed.), *op. cit.*, pp. 199–213; T. Yamaori, '*Buddha*-s and *Kami*-s: about the syncretic relationship between Shintō and Buddhism', in: *Bouddhisme et cultures locales* (as in n. 63), pp. 179–98; U. Mammitzsch, 'Maṇḍala and landscape in Japan', in: A. Macdonald (ed.), *Maṇḍala and landscape* (New Delhi, 1997), pp. 1–39; the work by B. Frank cited above in n. 63; and, on *shinbutsu shūgō* 'amalgamation of Kami-deities and Buddhas', see M. Teeuwen and F. Rambelli (ed.), *Buddhas and Kami in Japan*: *Honji suijaku as a combinatory paradigm* (London, 2003), who in their joint introduction seem to make no use of the Indian mundane : transmundane paradigm (used already in *Hōbōgirin* vi (1983), p. 751 f., in Iyanaga's article 'Daijizaiten'). See also N. Iyanaga, article 'Daikokuten' (Mahākāla) in *Hōbōgirin* vii (1994), pp. 839–920, as well as his other articles cited in the present study.

On syncretism, cf. e.g. C. Colpe's article 'Syncretism' in the *Encyclopaedia of Religion* 14, col. 218b–227b, and the brief overview by L. H. Martin, 'Historicism, syncretism, comparativism', in: Iva Doležalová *et al.* (ed.), *Religions in contact* (Brno, 1996), pp. 31–38. – The problem under discussion here in addition touches on, and partly overlaps with, the anthropological notion of 'Sanskritization' as presented some decades ago by M. N. Srinivas, 'Notes on Sanskritization and Westernization', *FEQ* 15 (1956), pp. 481–96; see more recently his *The cohesive role of Sanskritization* (Madras, 1989), p. 56 ff. See further V. Raghavan, 'Variety and integration in the pattern of Indian culture', *FEQ* 15 (1956), pp. 497–505; and F. Staal, 'Sanskrit and Sanskritization', *JAS* 22 (1963), pp. 261–75. Cf. also J. Houben (ed.), *Ideology and status of Sanskrit* (Leiden, 1996).

'INCLUSIVISM' of the kind postulated by Paul Hacker (see below, pp. 80, 97 f.).[70]

But in this case too, it seems that the application of the twin contrastive categories of the worldly/mundane and the supramundane/transmundane may allow us to achieve a better understanding of this crucial matter. For in Buddhist thought the structured opposition *laukika* : *lokottara* does not of itself normally correspond to a secular antagonism, on the historical and sociological levels, between Hinduism and Buddhism. It is, rather, a conceptual, and structural, religious opposition. And to interpret such an opposition, which is synchronic rather than diachronic, in terms of historical and secular antagonism – i.e. as Buddhism *vs.* Hinduism – would amount to reductionism, and to unwarranted euhemerism (cf. n. 2 above). In our classical sources, of course, the expressions Hindu/Hinduism do not yet appear at all, for these terms belong to a later stage in the history of Indian religious thought and civilization. The words *tīrthika*/*tīrthaṃkara* (Tib. *mu stegs can*, *mu stegs pa*/*mu stegs byed pa*), which in Buddhist usage may refer to the Brahmanical/Hinduistic, do however appear very often; and the relations between Buddhists and these *tīrthika*s were complex, often involving confrontation (both historical and conceptual) and rivalry.

What now of the many icons representing a figure – often described as 'Hindu' – being danced or trodden on (*ākrānta*, also *[praty]ālīḍha*) by a Buddhist tutelary deity, especially of the Great Wrathful (*mahākrodharāja*, Tib. *khro bo chen po*) category?[71] Since such icons have in fact not

---

70 In his article 'Zur Geschichte und Beurteilung des Hinduismus', *OLZ* 1964, col. 241, Hacker described the victory of Śarabha-Vīrabhadra-Śiva over Nṛsiṃha-Viṣṇu (see below, p. 60) as 'das gültige mythische Bild für den Inklusivismus'.

That confrontation and antagonism between Buddhism and Hinduism may be reflected in the position in Buddhist thought of Maheśvara as the great god of the Tīrthikas has been shown by N. Iyanaga in his article 'Daijizaiten', *Hōbōgirin*, p. 725 f. In this article Iyanaga has collected instances of anatagonism, not to speak of perhaps politically inspired secular hostility, between Buddhism and Hinduism (p. 732 f.). Compare n. 2 above.

71 The word *ākrānta* has for instance been employed with reference to Pinākin = Śiva in the introductory verse of Vajrapāṇi's *Laghutantraṭīkā* (ed. C. Cicuzza, Rome, 2001, p. 43). The words *(sam)ākrānta* and *ālīḍha* are both found in the *abhisamaya*s (*mṅon*

infrequently been interpreted by writers on Buddhist art and iconography as being intended to depict, in a pronouncedly dramatic and drastic fashion, the triumph of Buddhism over Hinduism, do we not have here an expression of historical – and secular – antagonism between these two religions? Or are we here in the presence of icons that are comparable with what are called in the parlance of Hindu iconology *saṃhāramūrtis* as opposed to *anugrahamūrtis*?

An observer who looks merely at the *materiality* of the icon and proceeds from the assumption that Buddhism and Hinduism are two antagonistic creeds – and also indeed the advocate of the 'inclusivist' interpretation of their relationship – sees the relevant icons as depicting the victory of Buddhism over Hinduism in secular CONFRONTATION and conflict. But in so doing the observer risks overlooking the ideology – and *iconology* – informing the images and their iconography. In this way the icons in question have become little other than 'monstrosities', joining the number of what in another context have been called 'much maligned monsters'.[72]

The Buddhist literature that may accompany the rituals and meditative practices to which these icons relate indeed very frequently make no mention of *this* kind of opposition between Buddhism and an other religion. And what we find instead is the concept of the *transcending* of the worldly (*laukika*) level and, eventually, of its *transformation/transmutation/trans-valuation* to the transmundane (*lokottara*) plane. We also find the idea that the *lokottara* symbol protects (*rakṣ-* = *sruṅ ba*) – rather than merely subjugates – the figures symbolizing the mundane level.

It has to be noted that certain deities classified not as supramundane tutelaries but as mundane (*laukika*) protectors have also been represented

---

rtogs), and in the corresponding iconographic descriptions, of protective deities as provided in the *Sādhanamālā* and in similar texts.

Concerning the motif of subjugation in East Asian Buddhism, see F. Rambelli, 'Buddha's wrath: Esoteric Buddhism and the discourse of divine punishment', *Japanese Religions* 27/1 (2002), pp. 41–68. And on the theme of wrath in Indian and Tibetan Buddhist iconography, see R. Linrothe, *Ruthless compassion*: *Wrathful deities in early Indo-Tibetan art* (London, 1999).

72 The allusion here is to other Indian icons which were not understood either culturally or aesthetically and iconologically, and which formed the subject of a study by Partha Mitter, *Much maligned monsters* (Oxford, 1977).

as treading upon figures described as inferior daimons. Examples are the four Great Kings (*mahārāja* = *rgyal po chen po*) – i.e. the Caturmahārājakāyikas Vaiśravaṇa, Dhṛtarāṣṭra, Virūḍhaka, and Virūpākṣa – who are the guardians of the world (*lokapāla* = *'jig rten skyoṅ ba*) and of the four quarters of space (*dikpāla* = *phyogs skyoṅ*) of the Kāmadhātu and are accordingly classified as *laukika* divinitics in the *Mahāvyutpatti* and elsewhere (see pp. 19, 69). (This classification of the four Great Kings, and of Vaiśravaṇa in particular, is, however, not definitively fixed forever inasmuch as *laukika* protectors are liable to be 'promoted' and then counted as *lokottara* protective deities.[73]) In other words, in certain cases, the mere fact that a deity is represented iconographically as treading on an inferior being does not indicate that it is automatically to be classified as a supramundane (*lokottara*) tutelary. It is thus possible for a protective divinity on the *laukika* level, such as a *lokapāla*, to be represented as overcoming inferior powers.

The historicizing and secularizing interpretation referred to above is hardly supported by the body of texts relating to these icons; and it appears to represent a quite unilateral understanding suggested by an interpretation of the materiality of the icon, and of the opposition expressed through it. For there is little doubt that the symbolism of the icon may in fact pertain to another sort of opposition, namely that between the *laukika* and *lokottara* levels in Buddhist thought. This kind of contrast or opposition will be of a structural (and synchronic) sort rather than one within the historical or secular dimension. As such, it takes on a quite distinct significance in Buddhist thought, and for the study of religion in general.

Consider now a concrete example of such an image and the relevant textual sources. To support the contention that an icon representing a wrathful tutelary deity (*[mahā]krodha*) dancing or treading upon a prostrate being, one iconographically homologous with a Hindu divinity,

---

[73] See, e.g., Kloṅ rdol Ṅag dbaṅ blo bzaṅ, *bsTan sruṅ dam can rgya mtsho'i miṅ gi rnam graṅs* (section ya of the gSuṅ 'bum); Paṇ chen Blo bzaṅ dpal ldan, *Rin 'byuṅ lhan thabs*, ṅa, f. 463a; and below, p. 160 and Appendix II. On the matter of transformation/transmutatiom/trans-valuation from the *laukika* to the *lokottara* level see below, pp. 57, 93, 177 f., and 183 ff.

represents a clash between Buddhism and Hinduism, reference has been made to a text from the *Tattvasaṃgrahatantra* (ii.6: 'Trilokavijayamahāmaṇḍalavidhivistara') which was published in fragmentary form already in 1932 by G. Tucci, who at that time also discussed the meaning of this Vajrayānist narrative.[74] It recounts the subjugation of Maheśvara/Mahādeva – the chief creator and destroyer god for all beings who stands above all other gods (*īśvaraḥ kartā vikartā sarvabhūteśvaro devatādhidevaḥ*), the master of the the three worlds (*trailoyādhipati*) – by Vajrapāṇi, who is described both as a *yakṣa* and as a *bodhisattva* identifiable with Samantabhadra and who acts as the agent of the great Lord (*bhagavant*) Vairocana.[75] It is to be noticed that in this Tantra Mahādeva, quali-

---

[74] *Indo-Tibetica*, i (Rome, 1932), pp. 135–40 and p. 93; see also *Indo-Tibetica* iii/1 (Rome, 1935), pp. 165–6; iii/2 (Rome, 1936), p. 82 ff. Later, in his *Tibetan painted scrolls* (Rome, 1949), p. 217, Tucci summed up his view of the matter in the following words: '[T]he Tantric schools, Shivaite and Buddhist, strove as rivals to conquer the soul of the masses [...]. Buddhism mostly accepts the gods of Hinduism [...] inserting them as acolytes among its own gods; it places them outside and around the maṇḍalas as *laukikas* [...]. But in other cases, confronted by the hostile attitude of Hindu circles, Buddhism decided to declare its superiority over those gods in a striking manner, by having its own gods trample upon them [...]. In these cases the attitude of Buddhism is changed: in the first case a difference of planes has been made, by virtue of which the nirvanic plane transcended the samsaric *ipso facto*. In the latter plane gods share the fate of all that is subject to change and are overthrown not as hostile forces but because they partake of an illusive existence, which must be entirely surpassed. But in other Tantras (almost all belonging to the Anuttarayoga class) the relation between the two religions is stated to be one of strife and antithesis [...]. They fight to conquer the world, as for instance in the account of the rivalry between Kālabhairava and bDe mc'og [Śaṃvara/Samvara].' One will agree with Tucci's distinction between what is, in the present study, termed horizontal subordination (as in a *maṇḍala*) and vertical subordination (as in the case of icons where the main divinity tramples on a representative of a lower plane) (see below). But it is not clear precisely how Tucci wished to demarcate and distinguish the categories he identified; and his observations on strife and antagonism call for further reflection.

[75] The entire Sanskrit text is now available in the editions of the *Tattvasaṃgrahatantra* by I. Yamada (New Delhi, 1981), pp. 160–210, and by Lokesh Chandra (New Delhi, 1987), pp. 55–71.

For this and similar passages see D. Seyfort Ruegg, 'Sur les rapports ...', *JA* 1964, p. 85 with notes 10–12; R.-A. Stein, *Annuaire du Collège de France* (Résumé des Cours) 72 (1972), pp. 499–510, 73 (1973), pp. 463–70, and 74 (1974), pp. 508–17; id., 'La mythlogie hindouiste au Tibet' (cited above, n. 63), p. 1409 (with the refer-

fied as *duṣṭa(sattva)*, figures not so much as the great god bearing this name in the Hindu tradition – i.e. Śiva/Śaṃkara/Maheśvara/Mahādeva – but rather as the regent of the three worlds (*triloka*) who, subdued and humbled by Vajrapāṇi, is compelled to accept the latter's 'convention' (*samaya*) and 'vow' (*saṃvara*). At the beginning of the narrative Mahādeva shows himself to be full of 'pride' (cf. below, pp. 61, 71–72, 84, 169), recalcitrant and, for the time being, unamenable to 'training' (*avineya*). In the ensuing struggle Vajrapāṇi treads on Mahādeva with his left leg while he presses down Umā, Mahādeva's spouse, with his right one. But in the event, in virtue of the great compassion (*mahākāruṇā*) of Vajrapāṇi and indeed of the Bhagavant Vairocana, and following on the Lord's uttering the formula of friendliness (*maitrīhṛdaya*), Maheśvara takes refuge in the Buddha, Dharma and Saṃgha. The purpose of this process is, then, not merely to conquer Maheśvara/Mahādeva and his kind and forcibly to make them subservient to Vajrapāṇi's command

---

ences to further discussions given in his n. 7); D. Snellgrove, *Indo-Tibetan Buddhism* (London, 1987), pp. 134–41; R. Davidson, *Indian esoteric Buddhism*, p. 148 ff. See also N. Iyanaga's important article 'Daijizaiten', *Hōbōgirin*, p. 747 ff. (cf. Iyanaga, 'Le Roi Māra du Sixième Ciel et le mythe médiéval de la création du Japon', *CEA* 9 [1996–97], p. 323 ff.; and id., '*Honji suijaku* and the logic of combinatory deities' in: M. Teeuwen and F. Rambelli (ed.), *Buddhas and Kami in Japan*, pp. 145–76). Forms assumed in Tibet by this myth have been discussed by M. Kapstein, 'Samantabhadra and Rudra', in: F. Reynolds and D. Tracy (ed.), *Discourse and practice* (Albany, 1992), pp. 65–72. Kapstein (p. 59) points out with reference to Karma Pakshi that 'some sources do suggest that it is in principle possible to calculate the date of Rudra's subjugation'; but he adds (p. 75 n 16) that Karma Pakshi like (b)sNubs chen Saṅs rgyas ye šes and mKhan po Nus ldan rdo rje 'is primarily interested in the symbolic dimension of Rudra's tale. In other words, some sources may indeed take the myth of Rudra's subjugation literally as an event in historical time; but more often it is understood ahistorically and symbolically. For R. Mayer's work on the subject see below, n. 202.

This idea and its reflection in iconography are of course not confined to the Indian and Tibetan traditions of Buddhism. For the Sino-Japanese tradition going back to Amoghavajra, see R. Tajima, *Les deux Grands Maṇḍala et la doctrine de l'Ésotérisme shingon* (Tōkyō-Paris, 1959), pp. 147–9, 212–3; N. Iyanaga, 'Récits de la soumission de Maheśvara par Trailokyavijaya d'après les sources chinoises et japonaises', in : M. Strickmann (ed.), *Tantric and Taoist studies in honour of R.-A. Stein* iii (*MCB* 22 [1985]), pp. 635–745. For an illustration on a Japanese painting of the Heian period of the subjection of Daijizaiten (Maheśvara) by Gōzanze (Trailokyavijaya), see *Hōbōgirin* 6, Plate xlv.

(*ājñā*), but – once they have humbly accepted the *samaya* and *saṃvara*, so to speak 'converting' them to the Teaching (*śāsana*), and have taken refuge (*śaraṇagamana*) in the Three Jewels – finally to purify and bring them to liberation by a process of 'training' (*vi-nī-* = *'dul ba* 'subdue, tame, discipline'). Thus Maheśvara, his consort Umā and all the other divinities belonging to his level – Nārāyaṇa and the rest – are finally as it were transmuted in the *vajra*-class, where they are assigned new names and are consecrated (*abhiṣikta*) in their new religious and soteriological functions.[76]

Thus, in the Trilokavijayamahāmaṇḍalavidhivistara chapter of the *Tattvasaṃgraha* (ii.6, pp. 172–173), the modalities and 'mechanics' of this transformation, implemented by Vajrapāṇi, is supplied by a 'Vajra-jewel Consecration' (*vajraratnābhiṣeka*) and a 'Vajra-name Consecration' (*vajranāmābhiṣeka*). And the Tantra specifies that there is thus effected a transformative translation of the *vidyārājyaka*s Maheśvara to Krodharāja, Nārāyaṇa to Māyāvajra, Brahman to Maunavajra, and Indra to Vajrāyudha, etc.; of the *vajrakrodha*s Amṛtakuṇḍali to Vajrakuṇḍali, Piṅgala to Vajrapiṅgala, etc.; of the *gaṇapati*s Madhumatta to Vajraśauṇḍa, Madhukara to Vajramālā, etc.; of the *dūta*s Vāyu to Vajrānila, Agni to Vajrānala, Kubera to Vajrabhairava, etc.; of the *gaṇikā*s Māraṇī to Vajravilayā, Rati to Vajravaśā; and so forth.

The opposition between religiously significant levels together with the transformation/transvaluation – of Vajrapāṇi from *yakṣa* to *bodhisattva*,

---

[76] The expression *vi-nī-*/*vinaya* and its Tibetan equivalent *'dul ba* have often been translated by 'convert/conversion', but the appropriateness of this translation is problematic. On the semantics of *vi-nī-* and *vinaya*, see M. Hara, *J. of the International College of Advanced Buddhist Studies* 7 (2004), pp. 1–54. A study of the late classical and early Christian concept is A. D. Nock, *Conversion* (Oxford, 1933), who has distinguished between conversion from one constituted religious grouping, or creed, to another and adhesion as a movement towards a new understanding without the crossing of a new (creedal) frontier. The term conversion/convert may correspond to either Gk. *epistrophé* or Gk. *metanoia* (usually translated 'repentance') (and also to Gk. (*dia*)*sōzesthai*). – Concerning the question of conversion in the Kathmandu Valley, a sort of test-bed for the study of such processes as operating between Buddhism and Hinduism, see D. Gellner, 'Emergence of conversion in a Hindu-Buddhist polytropy', *Comparative Studies in Society and History* 47 (2005), pp. 755–80, using for 'spiritual cosmopolitanism' the neologism 'polytropy' taken from M. Carrithers, 'On polytropy', *Modern Asian Studies* 34 (2000), pp. 831–61.

and of Mahādeva and other divinities to the *vajra*-level – narrated here appear in effect to correspond to the processes we have been considering. Its centre-piece is the religiously significant opposition between the *laukika* and *lokottara* levels, rather than any historical (and more or less secular) one such as would be involved in the opposition 'Buddhism *vs.* Hinduism'. And the 'apotheosis' of Vajrapāṇi evoked here is, surely, not the product of a 'compromise' between a decaying Buddhism and a triumphant Hinduism as was once suggested by Lamotte.[77]

The subjugator of Maheśvara is known also as Trilokavijaya/Trailokyavijaya, i.e. Vajrahūṃkāra or Vajrasattva. And the subduer of Rudra Vajrapāṇi is known as Nīlāmbaradhara.

In sum, the narrative of *Tattvasaṃgrahatantra* ii.6 would seem to recount the submission of the Lord of the Three Worlds (*trailokyādhipati*) – a symbol of the mundane (*laukika*) level – to the supramundane/transmundane (*lokottara*) level through the agency of Vajrapāṇi acting at the behest of the Lord Vairocana. In the corresponding icon the discursive, sequential and hence diachronic character of the narrative appears condensed and annulled in the visually synchronic, presentational and extra-discursive (albeit still representable and verbalizable) structure of the image.[78]

Further instances of such subjugation of a *laukika* – such as Rudra or Brahmā are in the Buddhist view – by a divinity belonging to the *lokottara* level are too numerous to enumerate here. But as another case in point reference can be made to Vajrakīla (rDo rje phur pa) whose iconography and symbolism have been briefly studied by G. Tucci (*Tibetan painted scrolls*, ii, pp. 588–9 with Plate 199). In Buddhism, the figure of the terrible Rudra – one of the many names of Śiva/Maheś-

---

[77] E. Lamotte, 'Vajrapāṇi en Inde', in: *Mélanges de sinologie offerts à Monsieur Paul Demiéville* (Paris, 1966), p. 149.

[78] Unless one were, on the contrary, to suppose that this type of Vajrayānist icon abandons its presentational aspect and assimilates itself to what has been called 'discursive practice', and that it thus assumes a truly narrative (i.e. diachronic) function. Although of considerable theoretical interest, this question cannot be pursued here.

vara/Mahādeva known since Vedic times – symbolizes a force that is to be mastered by the Vajrayānist practiser-realizer (*sādhaka*).[79]

The subjugation of Maheśvara/Rudra has been been given prominence in sLe luṅ rje druṅ bŽad pa'i rdo rje's (b. 1697) *Dam can bstan sruṅ rgya mtsho'i rnam par thar pa cha šas tsam brjod pa sṅon med legs bšad* (Leh, 1979, vol. i, pp. 4–30). In the relevant section, this work quotes in particular the *Kāraṇḍavyūha* among Sūtras, the *Vairocana*, *Vajraśekhara* and *Guhyagarbha* among Tantras, and Bu ston's *bDe mchog chos 'byuṅ*. The story of the subjugation of Rudra has found a place also in a *gter ma* text such as the *Padma bka' thaṅ* (chap. v-vi).

Of a somewhat different type are icons that depict an iconographically 'Hindu' divinity who has above his head, or in his head-dress, the miniature figure of one of the Jinas of Buddhism. Such a representation evidently indicates that the divinity has been fully adopted into the Jina's *kula* or clan. In the case of a *maṇḍala*, this incorporation is expressed in terms of his horizontal location in space, the divinity being assigned to the spatial direction of which the particular Jina represented over his head is the regent. Rather than a *laukika* divinity trampled underfoot and subjugated by a *lokottara* deity (as in several of the cases considered above), the icon evidently expresses the divinity's complete integration into the spiritual family of the supramundane Jina or Tathāgata by showing over his head the figure of the latter. It is in virtue of such integration that the divinity becomes part and parcel, ritually and doctrinally as well as iconographically, of the Buddhist universe.[80]

---

[79] (Cakra)Saṃvara/Śaṃvara for example dances on the prostrate form of Rudra and his consort. This motif has been touched on by A. W. Macdonald, 'Hindu-isation, Buddha-isation and Lama-isation, or: What happened at La-phyi?", in T. Skorupski (ed.), *Indo-Tibetan studies* (D. Snellgrove Felicitation Volume, Tring, 1990), p. 200 f. On Rudra in Tibet, see R. A. Stein, 'La mythologie hindouiste au Tibet' in: G. Gnoli and L. Lanciotti (ed.), *Orientalia Iosephi Tucci memoriae dicata*, iii (Rome, 1988), p. 1408 f., who refers (in his n. 7) to his earlier studies published in the *Annuaire du Collège de France* beginning in 1971.

[80] Such cases have been considered by M.-T. de Mallmann, *Étude iconographique sur Mañjuśrī* (Paris, 1964), pp. 15, 179 ff. (where the interpretations of R. D. Banerji and J. N. Banerjea have been criticized). On p. 15 M.-T. de Mallmann has written: 'Nous pensons avoir résolu l'énigme posée par les représentations de dieux hindous surmontés de Buddha', thus keeping to her idea that these integrated divinities remain

Hindu – which they may well have been historically, but which they no longer are ritually and soteriologically – i.e. synchronically – once they have been integrated in the *kula* of a Tathāgata, and eventually in the *maṇḍala* of a Buddhist *lokottara* deity. For the rôle of the *kula* and *maṇḍala*, compare above, pp. 36, 45, and below, pp. 63 f., 77 f., 135.

8. Further remarks on the structured *laukika* : *lokottara* opposition

It will of course be impossible here to review exhaustively the materials of all kinds and ages that are relevant to this question of the presence of Hindu(ist)-type figures in Buddhist representations, for they are much too numerous. It may nevertheless be recalled that, in a temple at Nālandā for instance, 'Hindu(istic)' deities such as Śiva and Pārvatī have been placed on its plinth, that is, on that part of a three-dimensional edifice which would correspond structurally to the lower, 'mundane', level.[81] And in two-dimensional diagrams such as a ritual *maṇḍala* these deities, when depicted individually, normally occupy an outer field (rather than being placed immediately under the feet of the principal deity at the centre of the structure).

Moreover, since the *laukika* : *lokottara* contrast runs parallel to the distinction on the Buddhist Path of liberation between the levels of the 'profane worldling' (*pr̥thagjana*) and the saintly 'Noble' of the spirit (*ārya*), it may clearly, and specifically, serve as an opposition having soteriological significance. In both cases it has been employed to express a transcending of the mundane level and/or its transmutation into the supramundane one.

Hierarchical, 'vertical', superordination of a Bodhisattva to Maheśvara is not confined exclusively to Vajrayānist texts. In the Maheśvaranirvyūha/niryūha chapter of the *Kāraṇḍavyūha* (Chap. ii.7, referred to above, p. 32), Maheśvara, who is there described as *devaputra*, falls at the feet of Avalokiteśvara as a sign of respectful submission. He and his consort Umā receive from Avalokiteśvara the solemn predictive declaration (*vyākaraṇa*) that in the future they will be respectively the Tathāgatas Bhasmeśvara and Umeśvara.[82] Here we find neither docetic

---

[81] See S. Huntington, *The "Pāla-Sena" schools of sculpture* (Leiden, 1984), p. 24 (with references to earlier discussions of this temple). Huntington has tentatively dated this particular temple to the seventh century.

[82] For the Gilgit parallel to this passage, see Mette's edition, p. 128 f. On the dialogue between Maheśvara and Umā in the Gilgit version, see above, p. 32.

emanation nor forcible subjugation. Justice is hardly done to the representation being conveyed here by the Sūtra if it is regarded simply as an example of 'Buddhist-Hinduist syncretism'.[83]

From this conception of structured levels, and from corresponding narrative scenes, there appears to derive the figure of Triloka/Trailokyavijaya (Vajrahūṃkāra, Vajrasattva) represented in Vajrayānist thought and iconography as dancing on Maheśvara/Bhairava's head and Gaurī/Kālarātrī's breasts (see *Sādhanamālā [SM]*, ed. Bhattacharyya, nos. 262 and 257; and Abhayākaragupta's *Niṣpannayogāvalī [NY]* no. 11). Further examples are provided by the ritual visualizations (*abhisamaya* = *mṅon rtogs*) and iconography of (Cakra)Saṃvara/Śaṃvara (*SM* nos. 251, 255; *NY* 12),[84] Kālacakra (on Kāmadeva and Rudra: *NY* 26, p. 84), Caṇḍamahāroṣaṇa (Acala) (on Iśāna: *NY* 11), and Vajrayoginī/Vajravārāhī (*SM* nos. 226, 227) (on Bhairava and Kālarātrī).

The fact that Kālacakra tramples Kāmadeva underfoot (*NY* 26) may, moreover, be regarded as indicative of the fact that it is the lower level of the world that is being depicted as subordinate, and not an abstract 'Hinduism' in some form of secular antagonism. (This iconographic type may be compared with the images of Śiva Naṭarāja/Naṭeśvara depicting him dancing on the *apasmarapuruṣa*.) In the *SM* (no. 88, p. 174), Caṇḍamahāroṣaṇa is described more specifically as suppressing the mass of hostile passions (*kleśārivṛndabandhana*) attaching to Hari, Hara, Hiraṇyagarbha, *et al.*

Such icons which represent a vertically, and hierarchically, tiered structure of SUPERORDINATION and SUBORDINATION may be contrasted with the morphologically different composite icons that represent instead the

---

[83] As has been done by A. Mette, 'Beschreibung eines Kultbildes im Gilgit-Manuskript des Kāraṇḍavyūha', *BIS* 9–10 (1996), p. 220. The term 'syncretism' has also been employed by C. Regamey, 'Motifs vichnouites et śivaïtes dans le Kāraṇḍavyūha', in: *Études tibétaines dédiées à la mémoire de Marcelle Lalou*, p. 411 ff.; elsewhere in the same article Regamey spoke of the 'infiltration' of Hindu elements. The significance of the *Kāraṇḍavyūha* in the context of the discussion of so-called 'syncretism' was noted by the present writer in 'Sur les rapports entre le bouddhisme et le "substrat religieux" indien et tibétain', *JA* 1964, p. 84.

[84] Śaṃvara is related to the divinity known as Hevajra/Heruka, also depicted as dancing on the four Māras (identified as Hari [Viṣṇu], Hara [Śiva], Hiraṇyagarbha [Brahmā] and Purandara [Indra] in Abhayākaragupta's *Niṣpannayogāvalī* no. 8, p. 20).

'horizontal' co-ordination of two divine entities such as Harihara (i.e. Viṣṇu and Śiva) and Ardhanārīśvara (i.e. Śiva and his Śakti). In the latter cases, we may have before us expressions of eclecticism and/or eirenicism.

It may finally be recalled here that not only epithets such as *lokanātha* 'protector of the world/people', *lokanāyaka* 'guide of the world' and *lokajyeṣṭha* 'eldest of/in the world' but also *lokajit* 'vanquisher of the world' (*Amarakośa*) have all been applied to the Buddha, the latter epithet being parallel to *jina* 'victor' which is a regular designation of the Buddha or Tathāgata.

In support of the view that Buddhism was being opposed to 'Hinduism' in a more or less agonistic and secular opposition – i.e. 'Buddhism *vs.* Hinduism' – the circumstance might be cited that certain tutelary deities of Buddhism are represented as carrying the severed head of Brahmā (*brahmaśiras*),[85] and that Brahmā has been represented as being trampled underfoot by a Buddhist tutelary.[86]

In classical Hinduism the great god Brahmā was, however, hardly worshipped widely as one of its supreme and most important deities. Moreover, the Hindu god Śiva-Bhairava has himself been represented holding Brahmā's severed head.[87] But, above all, it is necessary to enquire who, from the point of view of Buddhist thought and iconography, the Brahmā in question actually is. The answer appears to be that, very often, he is the divinity known as Brahmā Sahāṃpati/ Sabhāpati (Tib. Mi mjed kyi bdag po tshaṅs pa), that is, the divinity regarded as presiding over the *sahālokadhātu* (Tib. *mi mjed 'jig rten gyi khams*) which was the

---

[85] See B. Bhattacharyya, *Sādhanamālā*, ii, pp. cxxx-cxxxi; id., *Indian Buddhist iconography*, p. 162.

[86] See M.-T. de Mallmann, *Introduction à l'iconographie ...*, p. 127.

[87] On Bhairava's *brahmahatyā* as depicted in his form of Brahmaśiraśchedakamūrti, see E. C. Visuvalingam, 'Bhairava's royal brahmanicide: the problem of the Mahābrāhmaṇa', in: A. Hiltebeitel (ed.), *Criminal gods and demon devotees* (Albany, 1989), pp. 157, 211 n. 3. For the link with the Kāpalikas, see D. Lorenzen, *The Kāpālikas and Kālamukhas* (Berkeley, 1972), pp. 74–81; A. Roşu, 'A propos de rapports entre rasaśāstra et tantra', in: *India and beyond: Essays in honour of Frits Staal* (Leiden, 1997), p. 410.

Buddha-field of the Buddha Śākyamuni.[88] In the *Mahāvyutpatti*, Brahmā Sahāmpati (no. 3113) is in fact listed among the *laukika-devatāḥ*, as is Brahmā Hiraṇyagarbha (no. 3112).[89] As for the divinities known as the Brahmakāyikas, Brahmapāriṣadyas, Brahmapurohitas and Mahā-brahmās, according to the *Mahāvyutpatti* (nos. 3082–5) they belong to the level of the first Dhyāna in the Rūpadhātu. Brahmā is moreover frequently portrayed as a deity who proudly fancies himself to be the creator (*sraṣṭṛ*) of creatures in the worlds.[90]

Once again it thus appears that what is being represented is not the expression of (sectarian and secular) antagonism between two great religions of India but, rather, a structured opposition between two levels, namely the worldly/mundane (*laukika*) and the supramundane/trans-mundane (*lokottara*).[91] The contrary hypothesis, put forward by Benoy-tosh Bhattacharyya and since his time by a number of other writers, in particular by specialists in art history and iconography, has seemingly been maintained without due regard being paid to the relevant sources of the Śrāvakayāna, Mahāyāna and Vajrayāna traditions of Buddhism. The kind of interpretation adopted by these writers would then assimilate Buddhist icons that serve to express the subordination of the *laukika* to the *lokottara* level to, e.g., the Śarabha icon representing Narasiṃha being torn apart by a figure representing Śiva (Śarabheśvaramūrti; see notes 68, 70, 138).

---

[88] On the *sahāloka(dhātu)*, see F. Edgerton, *BHSD*, s.u. *sahā* (= *saha*). For references to Brahmā and Brahmā Sahāṃpati/Sabhāpati, see G. P. Malalasekera, *DPPN* pp. 331 ff., 1081–2; and *BHSD* s.uu. *sahāpati* and *sahāṃpati*. Cf. W. Kirfel, *Die Kosmographie der Inder* (Bonn-Leipzig, 1920), p. 190 f.; J. Przyluski, 'Brahmā sahāṃpati', *JA* 1924, pp. 155–63.

[89] Other forms of (Mahā-)Brahmā known from the Pali tradition are Baka and Sanaṅkumāra. See Malalasekera, *DPPN* s.uu., and p. 337.

[90] For Brahmā in Buddhist thought see the article 'Bon' in the *Hōbōgirin*.

[91] Elsewhere in the Buddhist traditions, the lexemes *brahma-* and *brāhma-* refer to the pure and exalted, as in *brahmacarya* (Tib. *tshaṅs pa'i spyod pa*) and the *brahma-vihāras* (= *apramāṇas*). On further uses of the term or name *brahmá/brahman* in Buddhism as equivalent to *buddha*, see K. Bhattacharya, *L'ātman-brahman dans le bouddhisme ancien* (Paris, 1973); and 'Some thoughts on *ātman-brahman* in early Buddhism', *Dr. B. M. Barua birth centenary commemoration volume* (Calcutta, 1989), p. 66 ff.

Subjugation of *laukika*-level deities, daimons and *numina* is not an action attributed solely and exclusively to the salvific action of great meditation divinities of the tutelary kind. In Tibetan tradition, rDo rje gro lod – one of the eight forms (*gu ru mtshan brgyad*) of the quasi-historical Padmasambhava – is represented as mounted on a tiger, wielding *rdo rje* and *phur bu*, and dominating various deities of the Rūpa and Kāma levels (in which category may be included certain so-called 'Hindu(istic)' deities). Much the same holds also for Padmasambhava's form known as Seṅ ge sgra sgrogs.[92] In the bio-hagiographical literature relating to him, Padmasambhava of course figures regularly as a thaumaturge and the subduer and trainer of local daimons of Tibet and the converter of their cults.

Among the 'Eight Precepts (cum Divinities)' (*bka' brgyad*) of the rÑiṅ ma school of Tibet connected with Padmasambhava, one category is comprised of the 'Jig rten, or 'Mundane', class; it includes the Thirty Great Generals (*sde dpon chen po sum cu*) who are at the head of 'prideful' (*dregs can*) mundane godlings.[93] Another category among the *bka' brgyad* are the Ma mo (Skt. Mātr̥kā), who are mundane female deities.[94] This octadic system appears to have its ultimate origins in India.

---

[92] A classic source is the *bKa' thaṅ sde lṅa*, where he is also considered a projection (*sprul pa* = *nirmāṇa*) of the Buddha Amitābha and the subjugator of Rudra. Cf. G.-W. Essen and Tsering Tashi Thingo, *Padmasambhava* (Cologne, 1991), pp. 106–08.

[93] See, e.g., the *bDe gšegs 'dus pa*, in the Ma mo rgyud skor of the Mahāyoga division of the rÑiṅ ma rgyud 'bum (Kaneko no. 375); and 'Ju Mi pham, *dPal sgrub pa chen po bka' brgyad kyi spyi don rnam par bšad pa dṅos grub sñiṅ po* (*bKa' brgyad rnam bšad*) (Chengdu, 2000), p. 140 ff. On the thirty 'generals' (*sde dpon chen po*), see R. Kaschewsky and Padma Tsering, *sDe-dpon sum-cu*: *Ritual und Ikonographie der "Dreissig Schutzgottheiten der Welt"* (Wiesbaden, 1998), based on the *'Jig rten mchod bstod sgrub pa rtsa ba'i rgyud* in the rGyud section of the bKa' 'gyur and in the Mahāyoga section of the rÑiṅ ma rgyud 'bum (Kaneko no. 387). 'Jig rten mchod bstod is the last member of the *bka' brgyad*, the two preceding members being Ma mo bod gtoṅ and dMod pa drag sṅags, a triad that makes up the *'jig rten pa'i sde*. – For the idea of pride and the *dregs can*, see pp. 52, 71–72, 84, 169.

[94] cf. A.-M. Blondeau, 'Les *Ma mo* : Mythes cosmogoniques et théogoniques dans le *rÑiṅ ma'i rgyud 'bum*', in: H. Eimer and D. Germano, *The many canons of Tibetan Buddhism* (PIATS 2000, 2/10, Leiden, 2002), pp. 293–311.

9. The place and function of the mundane clan (*laukikakula*) in Kriyātantra

What has been said in the last two sections relates particularly to Yoga-tantras and Yogānuttara/Yoganiruttara-tantras (Tib. *[rnal 'byor] bla med kyi rgyud*) – themselves subdivided into Father Tantras (*pha rgyud*, also known as *rnal 'byor bla ma* i.e. Yogottara-tantras) and Mother Tantras (*ma rgyud*, or Yoginī-tantras, also known as Yogānuttara/Yoganiruttara-tantras in the narrower sense of this term) –, that is, to the two highest divisions in a classical Tibetan fourfold classification of Vajrayāna literature.

In the Kriyātantra section of Vajrayāna literature – the first and lowest in this fourfold classification of Tantras which is concerned with ritual actions – the *laukika* category of divinities constitutes a designated subdivision, the Laukikakula (*'jig rten pa'i rigs*). Following a number of authorities, this subdivision is comprised of *deva*s, *asura*s, the *yakṣa*s Pūrṇabhadra and Maṇibhadra, the four *lokapāla*s, and other gods, godlings, and *numina*. To be noted is the fact that to the Padmakula, the second *kula* of Kriyātantra, is assigned the Praise in twenty-one verses of Ārya-Tārā (P, no. 77), where (in verse 6) the *laukika*s Indra, Agni, Brahmā *et al.* are mentioned as being subjugated by her in the peaceful form of her *nirmāṇakāya*.[95]

The Kriyātantras appear to suggest diverse classifications of these gods, divinities and *numina*, which they distribute in 'clans' (*kula* = *rigs*) whose number and exact composition vary in the sources. Tibetan commentators have noticed the classificatory and taxonomic problems that may thus arise, and it was this that caused the Tibetan master Bu ston Rin chen grub (1290–1364) to undertake a systematic classification of the Tantras and their *kula*s, this being necessary both for the analysis of

---

[95] Elsewhere it is her wrathful form that has this function. Cf. P. Arènes, *La déesse sGrol-ma (Tārā)* (Leuven, 1996), who has also studied the commentaries by dGe 'dun grub pa and Tāranātha. This praise of Tārā when included as Chapter iii of P no. 390 is, however, counted as a *bla med kyi rgyud*; cf. mKhas grub dGe legs dpal bzaṅ, *rGyud sde spyi rnam* (ed. Lessing and Wayman), p. 126.

the texts constituting the Tantra-corpus (*rgyud 'bum*) and for their ritual employment.[96]

Bu ston's classification of the Kriyātantras – one of the better known – recognizes the existence in them of six *kula*s 'clans', namely those of the Tathāgata (De bžin gšegs pa), Padma, Vajra (rDo rje), Maṇi (Nor can or Nor bu), *Pauṣṭika (? rGyas pa, viz. lṄa[s] rtsen [Pañcika/Pāñcika], Glaṅ po che, Ba laṅ), and the Laukika (*'jig rten pa*).[97] In his *rGyud 'bum*

---

[96] See Bu ston's *rGyud 'bum gyi dkar chag* and his three *rGyud sde spyi'i rnam par bžag pa* referred to below. Attention was drawn to this topic by the present writer in 'Sur les rapports entre le bouddhisme et le "substrat religieux" indien et tibétain', *JA* 1964, pp. 79–83, and in *Life of Bu ston Rin po che* (Rome, 1966), pp. 25–27, 36, 118.

For Bu ston's *dKar chag*, see H. Eimer, *Der Tantra-Katalog des Bu ston im Vergleich mit der Abteilung Tantra des tibetischen Kanjur* (Bonn, 1989), pp. 28, 34 (with the further discussion in D. Seyfort Ruegg, 'The Tantric Corpus (*rGyud 'bum*) of the Tibetan bKa' 'gyur according to a recent publication', *Buddhist Studies Review* 11 [1994], pp. 180–1). Bu ston's classification is available also in the short (*bsdus pa*), middling (*'briṅ po*) and extended (*rgyas pa*) versions of his *rGyud sde spyi'i rnam par bžag pa* (contained in volumes pha and ba of his bKa' 'bum). For an outline of the extended version, subtitled *rGyud sde rin po che'i mdzes rgyan*, of Bu ston's classification of the four classes of Tantra with their respective texts, see G. Tucci, *Tibetan painted scrolls*, pp. 261–3. Cf. A. Macdonald, *Le maṇḍala du Mañjuśrīmūlakalpa* (Paris, 1962), p. 55 f.

Concerning the terminology used for sacred formulae, among variant explanations cited by him Bu ston has stated that a *gsaṅ sṅags* (*mantra*) relates chiefly to *upāya* and a god (*thabs pho*) and a *rig sṅags* (*vidyā*) to *prajñā* and a goddess (*šes rab lha mo*), whilst a *gzuṅs* (*dhāraṇī*), i.e. a mnemonic making it possible to rememorate and retain what has been comprehended through *prajñā*, relates to a *gzuṅs sṅags* that is linked to both of the preceding. See his *rGyud sde spyi rnam rgyas pa*, f. 260a–b.

Surveys of the Tantras were composed earlier by the Sa skya hierarchs bSod nams rtse mo (1142–1182) and his brother Grags pa rgyal mtshan (1147–1216), their *rGyud sde spyi'i rnam gžag* treatises being of a somewhat different kind from Bu ston's. For some *'jig rten pa'i rgyud* in Grags pa rgyal mtshan's *Kye'i rdo rje'i rgyud 'bum gyi dkar chag* (contained in the text entitled *He ru ka'i chas drug*) and in 'Phags pa Blo gros rgyal mtshan's *rGyud sde'i dkar chag*, see H. Eimer, 'A source for the first Narthang Kanjur: Two early Sa skya pa catalogues of the Tantras', in: H. Eimer (ed.), *Transmission of the Tibetan canon* (PIATS 1995, Vienna, 1997), pp. 50–51.

[97] According to the analysis offered by mKhas grub dGe legs dpal bzaṅ (1385–1438) of the Kriyātantras and Caryātantras, however, the last *three* Kulas are all *laukika*; see his *rGyud sde spyi rnam* (ed. Lessing and Wayman), pp. 102, 132. To the *'jig rten pa'i rigs* of the Kriyātantras and Caryātantras the same source accordingly opposes

gyi dkar chag, Bu ston has explained that the Laukika divinities offer up their formulae (*vidyā*) and, being sustained by the force (*adhiṣṭhita*) of the Teacher, they are all then declared to be of the clan relying on the Teacher (i.e. the Tathāgata).[98]

Let us consider more closely the identity and nature of these Laukikas. Bu ston has stated that they are the *deva*s, *asura*s, *yakṣa*s and the like who do not belong to the first five *kula*s of Kriyātantra. He explains that the Buddha has 'trained' (*'dul ba* = *vi-nī-* 'subdue/tame/discipline'), and caused to enter into a 'convention' (*dam tshig* = *samaya*), the mundane divinities – Rudra, Brahmā, Sūrya, Garuḍa, etc. – who then offer up to him their *mantra*s, and that it is in this manner that these 'pledgers' come to be the beneficiaries of *adhiṣṭhāna* and submit themselves to his command (*bka'*). Still, it is also stated by Bu ston that Laukikas may be found even at times when no Buddha appears in the world.[99] According to Bu ston's further explanation, since certain *mantra*s offered up by the Laukikas are not settled (*gnas pa*) in the four *kula*s (apparently nos. 2–5), they wander (*'khyams pa*) and make up a separate (sixth) Kula. Regarding the question whether they are not included in the first *kula*,

---

the *'jig rten las 'das pa'i rigs* = *lokottarakula*, namely the Kulas of the Tathāgata, Padma and Vajra; see *op. cit.*, p. 102.

In the *Mahāvyutpatti* (nos. 3365, 3375, 3377), lṄa(s) rtsen = Pañcika/Pāñcika is listed as a *yakṣa* together with Vaiśravaṇa/Vaiśramaṇa, Āṭavaka, *et al.*; his consort is Hārītī ('Phrog ma), who is accompanied by her many children, or Mekhalā ('og pag can). He is connected with the border of Kāśmīra in the *Mahāmāyūrī* (ed. Bagchi, line 78; S. Takubo's ed., p. 22, reads *cīnabhūmi* instead). (In Pāli there are attested the forms Pañcaka/Paṇḍaka and Hāritā. These *yakkha*s are both said to have become *sotāpanna*s at the time when the missionary Majjhantika Thera preached to the *nāga* Aravāḷa in the Kāśmīra-Gandhāra region; see *Mahāvaṃsa* xxi.21.) As a god of prosperity and wealth, Pañcika corresponds to Vaiśravaṇa/Kubera/Jambhala. – As for the *gandharva* Pañcaśikha (cf. Pañcacīra) in the Maṇḍala of Dharmadhātu-Vāgīśvara, he is yellow (the colour of prosperity) and plays the *vīṇā*. This name is not listed in the *Mahāvyutpatti*.

98 Bu ston, *rGyud 'bum gyi dkar chag*, f. 17 b: *'jig rten pa'i lha la sogs pas rig pa phul žiṅ/ ston pas byin gyis brlabs pa rnams thams cad kyaṅ ston pa la brten pa'i rigs su gsuṅs so.*

99 See Bu ston's *rGyud sde spyi rnam rgyas pa*, f. 259a; *bsDus pa*, ff. 59b–60a. – When no Buddha has appeared in the world, the divinities in question would of course have no opportunity of offering up to him their *mantra*s and of being adopted into the Kula of the Tathāgata.

that of the Tathāgata, the reply is that one belonging to the Laukikakula proceeds from the Gnosis (*ye šes = jñāna*) of Uṣṇīṣa, etc. And being born from karmic maturation (*rnam par smin pa = vipāka*), they are not members of the Tathāgatakula proper. But since their *mantras* and *vidhis* are offered up with faith (*dad pa = śraddhā*) to the Buddha, they are nonetheless stated to settle (*gnas pa*) in the Tathāgatakula, even though they wander without being really included in this first *kula*. This is, then, the so-called wandering clan (*yoṅs su 'khyams pa'i rigs*). This situation is stated by Bu ston to correspond to the doctrine of the *Subāhuparipṛcchātantra* – one of the 'General Tantras' (*spyi'i rgyud*) of the Kriyātantra class – and to its *Piṇḍārthavṛtti*.[100]

To the first *kulas* referred to as the five *āryakulas* (*'phags pa'i rigs lṅa*),[101] then, the *laukikakula* is opposed. The *mantras* of this last *kula* are said to be undetermined (*mtha' gcig tu ma ṅes pa*) because in it each member pays homage to his respective lord (*bdag po*).[102] In this *kula* the textual matter (*gžuṅ*) is endless (*mtha' yas pa*).[103]

Regarding the fourth and fifth *kulas* of Kriyātantra – the Nor can gyi rigs and the rGyas pa'i rigs – Bu ston quotes the *Subāhuparipṛcchā*, where these two clans (to which is added the sixth or Laukikakula) are included respectively in the Padma-Kula and the Vajra-Kula. Bu ston adds that they both appear intergrated in the Vajra-kula in consideration of their characteristics (*mtshan ñid*) and *mantras*.[104]

---

[100] Bu ston, *rGyud sde spyi rnam rgyas pa*, f. 259b–260a; *'Briṅ po*, f. 105b; *bsDus pa*, f. 60b. Cf. *rGyas pa*, f. 249b: *'jig rten pa'i rigs ni/ saṅs rgyas la dad pa'i lha daṅ lha ma yin la sogs pa rnams kyis raṅ raṅ so sos bšad ciṅ/ ston pas gnaṅ žiṅ rjes su yi raṅ bar mdzad do*. – In Kriyātantra, the Uṣṇīṣa-deities belong to the Tathāgatakula.

[101] *rGyud sde spyi rnam rgyas pa*, f. 260a1; *bsDus pa*, f. 61a1.

[102] Bu ston, *rGyud sde spyi rnam rgyas pa*, f. 254a4;*'Briṅ po*, f. 100a3; *bsDus pa*, f. 59b6.

[103] Bu ston, *rGyud sde spyi rnam rgyas pa* f. 253b4; 'Briṅ po, ff. 95a–b, 99b3; *bsDus pa*, ff. 55a3, 59a6.

[104] Bu ston, *rGyas pa*, f. 259b; *'Briṅ po*, f. 105a–b; *bsDus pa*, f. 60a–b. – The assignment of the Kula headed by Pañcika to the Vajra-, Padma- or Ratna-kula is found in the *Subāhuparipṛcchātantra*; see M. Lalou, 'A la recherche du Vidyādharapiṭaka: Le cycle du *Subāhuparipṛcchā-tantra*', in: *Studies in Indology and Buddhology* (S. Yamaguchi Felicitation Volume, Kyōto, 1955), p. 71.

In short, properly speaking the Laukika divinities do not take birth in the *kula* of the Tathāgata. And their *mantras* 'wander' and merely 'settle' in his clan. Their link with the Tathāgata, which is therefore contingent, is not due to an inherent connexion with his *kula*, but results from the 'faith' they place in him; for it is through this *śraddhā* that they offer up (i.e. surrender) to him their respective formulae (*mantra*) and rites (*vidhi*). In the relevant texts, the Buddha is regularly represented as having converted – or, more precisely, 'trained' (*'dul ba*) – these entities and thus made them submit to what is termed a *samaya* 'convention'.

Hence, according to this analysis, the members of the last 'clan', the sixth or 'mundane' (*laukika*) one with which we are concerned here, are entities of a particular kind who, evidently, found a place from early times in the Buddhists' world-view. Indeed, as a universal and totalizing cosmos, the Buddhist world-order would, very naturally, include the entirety of forces and *numina* recognized in its time in India (and in Tibet and other countries that were later to adopt Buddhism), in other words the Indian (or Tibetan) pantheon inclusive of the 'religious substratum' of gods and godlings. Tantras assigned to the Laukika division of Kriyātantra are concerned with all sorts of 'worldly' concerns including the relief of illness, the pacification of hostile forces and the acquiring of favourable conditions.

Now, as observed above (pp. 22 and 43), there appears to exist no reason to suppose that, in India, gods such as Brahmā and Śakra (Indra) who figure in the Buddhist canon, as well as other *numina* known to Buddhists, were alien, exogenous intrusions or foreign imports from Hinduism that had to be incorporated, somehow or other, into Buddhism in the course of its Indian history. The religions in question have their roots in a common ground of religious representations, a fact that would appear adequately to account for the presence of these divine entities within the Buddhist world-order.

It appears, nonetheless, that the division in Kriyātantra constituted by the Laukikakula and its gods is somewhat narrower, and more specific, than the wider and more universal category of the 'worldly' or 'mundane' (*laukika*) discussed in this study.

10. The *laukika* : *lokottara* contrast in Mahāyāna Sūtras and Śāstras

The motif of the mundane level of *saṃsāra* being overcome by the supramundane/transmundane level of the Ārya, or of the Buddha himself, is not confined to the Vajrayāna alone. Reference has been made above to emanationist and docetist motifs in the Candrādi-utpatti chapter of the *Kāraṇḍavyūha* (*supra*, p. 31) and to the *topos* of subordination and submission in the same Sūtra (*supra*, p. 57). Although these schemas are distinguishable as paradigms and models, it appears that they may converge in so far as a Laukika who has submitted to the supramundane may come to be seen as a sort of emanation of the latter in a docetic perspective. Furthermore, the docetic emanation or projection (*nirmāṇa*) and the divinity of the religious substratum who enters into a convention (*samaya*) and offers his vow (*saṃvara*) as well as his formula (*mantra*) to the representative of the *lokottara* level both operate on the *laukika* level which in either case stands in structured opposition to the *lokottara* level.

A further interesting instance of the idea of the mundane level being overwhelmed by the supramundane in the canonical and commentarial literature of the Prajñāpāramitā may be cited here. On the two Paths of the accumulation of the wholesome salutary factors – the *sambhāra-mārga* – and of practice – the *prayogamārga* – the exercitant is classified as a *pṛthagjana* 'worldling', and is accordingly situated on the *laukika* Path. But on reaching the Path of Vision – the *darśanamārga* – and when continuing onwards on the Path of meditative Realization – the *bhāvanā-mārga* – the exercitant, although still some way removed from the ultimate level of one beyond training (*aśaikṣa*, i.e. the *buddha*), is considered a 'Noble' (*ārya*) on the *lokottara* level. Thus, in the frame of the traditional description of the Buddhist Path, the contrast mundane : supramundane noticed above takes on a primordial significance that is both soteriological and gnoseological.

Buddhism has, in addition, distinguished between the supramundane Path of meditative realization (*bhāvanāmārga*) just mentioned, which is specific to the Buddhist Ārya, and a way of meditative realization (*bhāvanā*) that is on the contrary regarded as mundane (*laukika*), and which is common to all practisers and Yogins. In this case, then, the contrast *laukika* : *lokottara* is employed in order to differentiate between what is specific to Buddhism at its higher levels and what is not specifically Buddhist, in other words what is held in common between the Buddhist and non-Buddhist traditions of India.[105]

A highly significant reference to the subordination of the mundane to the supramundane is to be found in the *Aṣṭasāhasrikā Prajñāpāramitā* (ii, p. 33). In this important canonical text of the Mahāyāna, Śakra, the lord of the gods, together with the fourty thousand Trāyastriṃśatkāyika Devaputras, the four Lokapālas (i.e. the Cāturmahārājakāyikas) with the twenty thousand other Mahārājakāyikas, Brahmā Sabhāpati with the ten thousand other Brahmakāyikas, and the ten thousand Śuddhāvāsa Devaputras[106] all take their places in the great assembly (*parṣad*) of the Buddha's auditors where their lustre (*avabhāsa*, resulting from the maturing of their previous good deeds) is overwhelmed (*abhibhūta*) by the might (*anubhāva*), glory (*tejas*) and sustaining force (*adhiṣṭhāna*) of the Buddha. The divinities thus outshone are specifically those – such as the Thirty-three and the Mahārājakāyikas – situated on the level of the Kāmadhātu – and those – the Brahmakāyikas – connected with the four Dhyānas on the intermediate level of the Rūpadhātu, and the Śuddhāvāsa gods on the high (but still far from supreme) level between the fourth Dhyāna and the Ārūpya level.[107]

In the relevant passage of the *Abhisamayālaṃkāra*, this outshining by the Buddha of the limited lustre of the gods, which comes to an end when their stock of good works is exhausted, has been referred to as an obscuration (*dhyāmīkaraṇatā*) of the gods and godlings by the overwhelming effulgent rays (*bhāḥ*) emitted by the Buddha (ii.1ab):

> *dhyāmīkaraṇatā bhābhir devānāṃ yogyatāṃ prati/*
>
> With respect to aptitude (*yogyatā*), there is obscuration of divinities by rays [emitted by the Tathāgata].[108]

---

[105] For some references see D. Seyfort Ruegg, *Buddha-nature, Mind and the problem of Gradualism*, p. 195 f.

[106] On this last category in the Pali tradition, see Malasekera, *DPPN*, p. 1190. And on the other categories listed here see above, pp. 49 f., 59.

[107] For the taxonomy, see, e.g., *Mahāvyutpatti* nos. 3072 ff.; the Lokanirdeśa chapter (chap. iv) of the *Abhidharmakośa*; and E. Lamotte, *Histoire du bouddhisme indien*, i, p. 759 ff.

[108] The Tibetan translation of *Abhisamayālaṃkāra* ii.1ab reads:

That is, the level of continuing karmically conditioned bondage in the round of existences (*saṃsāra*) is symbolized by the gods and godlings, who are themselves fettered to *saṃsāra* and whose relative lustre is therefore outshone, and thus overwhelmed, by the Buddha's transmundane and supernal radiance.

This passage from the *Abhisamayālaṃkāra*, the basic Śāstra of the Prajñāparamitā, stands at the beginning of its second chapter which treats of knowledge of the Path (*mārgajñatā* = *lam šes pa ñid*) leading ultimately to Omniscience in Buddhahood and, accessorily, of the soteriological and gnoseological concept of the Single Vehicle (*ekayāna*) whereby all Paths are shown finally to converge by being integrated in the supreme and perfect Awakening of Buddhahood surpassing all other spiritual attainments to be achieved by other, lesser paths. The aptitude (*yogyatā*) to which reference is made in *Abhisamayālaṃkāra* ii.1b is the aptitude cultivated by exercitants to generate this knowledge of the Path.[109]

According to Haribhadra's comment, the reference in this verse to the elimination of god-like pride (*māna*) serves to suggest, by an allusive hint (*vakroktyā* = *tshig zur gyis*), the possession by the fit recepient (*ādhāra* = *rten*) of the aptitude necessary for generating the Path.

In Haribhadra's commentary, this section of the *Abhisamayālaṃkāra* has been placed in correlation with the above-mentioned Śakraparivarta – that is, the Indra-Chapter – of the *Aṣṭasāhasrikā*.

The theme of a 'twilight of the gods' – which in various extended contexts is a familiar *topos* in large sections of Buddhist literature – was again taken up centuries later by the Tibetan master Tsoṅ kha pa. In the introductory verse of salutation in his *Legs bšad sñiṅ po* we read: 'To the deity-of-deities, the Lord of Sages (*munīndra*), I pay homage, attending

---

lha rnams ruṅ bar bya ba'i phyir/ /'od kyis mog mog por mdzad daṅ//

This rendering suggests the translation: 'For effecting the aptitude of the divinities there is an obscuration [of their brightness] by [the superior brilliance of the] rays [emitted by the Tathāgata]'. The variant *śyāmīkaraṇatā* is an inferior reading.

[109] On this passage see D. Seyfort Ruegg, *La théorie du tathāgatagarbha et du gotra* (Paris, 1969), p. 189 ff. Cf. E. Obermiller, *Analysis of the Abhisamayālaṃkāra*, Fasc. ii (Calcutta Oriental Series, No. 27, London, 1936), pp. 197–8.

with respect (*gus pa* = *bhāva*, *bhakti*) before the lotus-feet of him who treats – just as the sun would the fire-fly – those [turning round] in the world of rebirths: Śambhu, Meghavāhana [Indra], Hiraṇyagarbha [Brahmā], the lord Anaṅga [Kāmadeva], Dāmodara [Viṣṇu-Kṛṣṇa] and the like who are all puffed up with swollen egoism (*abhimāna*) loudly uttering roars of overweening pride (*dregs pa*), [but] who then, once they have perceived his bodily form, [on their part bow down in homage before him] with their lovely diadems'.[110] That is to say, just as the sun by its very radiance, and without any additional effort, will totally outshine the fire-fly, so the Buddha, solely through his radiant nature, and without any additional effort, overwhelms even great gods still karmically fettered to the world.

Chronologically located between, on the one side, the narrative of the *Aṣṭasāhasrikā* passage or the distinctly soteriological-gnoseological purport of the *Abhisamayālaṃkāra* verse cited above and, on the other side,

---

[110] Tsoṅ kha pa Blo bzaṅ grags pa (1357–1419), *Draṅ ṅes legs bšad sñiṅ po*, f. 1b:

bde 'byuṅ sprin la žon daṅ gser gyi mṅal/ /lus med bdag po tha gu'i lto la sogs//

srid na dregs pa'i ṅa ro cher sgrogs pa'i/ /rlom pas 'gyiṅ rnams kyis kyaṅ gaṅ gi sku//

mthoṅ ba'i mod la ñi mas me khyer bžin/ /mdzad par gyur tshe mdzes pa'i cod pan gyis//

gaṅ gi žabs pad gus pas bsten byed pa/ /thub dbaṅ lha yi lha la phyag 'tshal lo//

In his *Draṅ ba daṅ ṅes pa'i don rnam par 'byed pa'i mtha' dpyod 'khrul bral luṅ rigs bai ḍūr dkar po'i gan mdzod, sKal bzaṅ re ba kun skoṅ*, f. 1b, dPal 'byor lhun grub has paraphrased Tsoṅ kha pa's salutation in the following metrically elaborate verse:

gaṅ žig srid 'dir rlom pas rab bsñems mes po dpal bdag spyan stoṅ ldan pa sogs//

gaṅ gi mdun na me khyer bcom bžin žum pa lhur len gtsug rgyan nor bus kyaṅ//

gaṅ gi žabs rdul ñer mchod thub dbaṅ thub pa'i chu skyes kun gyi gñen gcig pu//

gaṅ žig zas gtsaṅ sras su grags pa'i gdugs dkar srid rtser 'god de'i žabs kyi pad mar 'dud//

Concerning this important concept of 'pride' (*[abhi]māna*, *rlom pa*, *dregs pa*) consisting in a celestial's holding himself to be a great and powerful god superior to all, it may be noted that the *dregs pa/dregs ldan/dregs pa can* form a category of worldly (*'jig rten pa*) deities, for example in the context of the *'jig rten mchod bstod*. Cf. R. de Nebesky-Wojkowitz, *Oracles and demons of Tibet*, chap. 16 (pointing out, however, another use of the term *dregs pa* to designate a higher category of protector).

the more conventionally literary, and quasi mythic, context met with in Tsoṅ kha pa's text, 'Hindu(ist)' materials have been exploited by Udbhaṭasiddhasvāmin in his **Viśeṣa/Viśiṣṭa*(?)*-stava* and **Sarvajñamaheśvarastotra*, by his brother Śaṃkarasvāmin (Śaṃkarapati?) in his **Devatāvimarśastuti/Devātiśayastotra*, and then by Prajñāvarman in his extensive commentaries on the first and last of these hymns. The latter two works are especially rich documents attesting to the special use that has been made of such materials by Buddhists in India. In the colophon of the Tibetan translation of the **Sarvajñamaheśvarastotra*, Udbhaṭasiddhasvāmin is described both as a Brahman (*bram ze*) and as a (Buddhist) *upāsaka* (*dge bsñen*). And in Tāranātha's *rGya gar chos 'byuṅ* (ed. Schiefner, pp. 51–52) he and Śaṃkarasvāmin figure as having originally been Śaivas; but after a pilgrimage to Kailāsa – the mountain in western Tibet sacred to both Hindus as the abode of Śiva and to Buddhists as a holy place (*gnas*) – where Mahādeva/ Maheśvara/Śiva manifested himself as really a Bauddha, he followed his brother Śaṃkarasvāmin in becoming a professed Buddhist, the Buddha being then represented in his **Sarvajñamaheśvarastotra* as the true and authentic possessor of the qualities commonly attributed to Śiva.[111] As for Udbhaṭasiddhasvāmin's **Viśeṣa/Viśiṣṭa-stava*, now unavailable in Sanskrit, it is interesting to note that it is no mere literary relic or fossil preserved in the bsTan 'gyur; for its Tibetan translation has been reprinted in recent times, and it has attracted modern Tibetan commentaries, one (by 'Bras mi ñag mkhan sprul Blo bzaṅ skal ldan) written in the nineteenth century and another (by Khu nu bsTan 'dzin rgyal mtshan) written in the twentieth century.

What Buddhist tradition has done here is as it were to TRANSMYTHOLOGIZE, and thus to transmute, the (so-called) 'Hindu(ist)' deities

---

[111] On Udbhaṭasiddhasvāmin's **Viśeṣa/Viśiṣṭastava* and Prajñāvarman's *Ṭīkā*, see J. Schneider, *Der Lobpreis der Vorzüglichkeit des Buddha* (Bonn, 1993); and on Udbhaṭasiddhasvāmin's **Sarvajñamaheśvarastotra*, see J. Schneider, 'Der Buddha als der wahre Śiva', *BIS* 8 (1995), pp. 153–87. On the **Devatāvimarśastuti/Devātiśayastotra*, see Lobsang Norbu Shastri, *Supra-divine praise* (Sarnath, 1990); M. Hahn, 'Śaṅkarasvāmin's *Devatāvimarśastuti*', in *Vividharatnakaraṇḍaka* (Fest. A. Mette, Swisttal-Odendorf, 2000), pp. 313–29. – On the Kailāsa region as a place of contact between religions, see below, pp. 80, 123, 165 f.

in question, including even some supreme gods of Brahmanical mythology, making of them simple *laukika* or 'mundane' divinities, in a procedure that, *mutatis mutandis*, might perhaps be described as euhemerism in reverse.

The motif of the Buddha's overwhelming radiance considered above echoes a *topos* found already in the Buddha-hagiography. According to the Kr̥ṣigrāmaparivarta of the *Lalitavistara* (xi, pp. 129–130), at the time of the future Buddha's first meditation when seated in the shade of a Jambu tree, five R̥ṣis, strangely hindered in their flight overhead, considered whether this radiant boy was perchance Vaiśravaṇa, Māra, Brahmā-Sahā(ṃ)pati, Indra the *vajra*-bearer, Rudra, Kr̥ṣṇa, Sūrya, Candra, or perhaps a Cakravartin-King. Yet, even as the young Bodhisattva, he outshone them all in his glory (*lakṣmī*) or majesty (*śrī*), and in his flaming brightness (*tejas*), in addition to checking the magical power (*r̥ddhi*) of the poor astounded and abashed R̥ṣis, as was indeed perceived by a *vanadevatā* present at this marvellous event. This *topos* is followed in the same episode by the 'miracle' of the shade of the Jambu tree, whose shadow remained stationary round the meditating Bodhisattva even when the sun had passed the zenith and was declining, so that its scorching rays were unable to affect or vie with him.[112]

---

[112] On this passage, and on parallels in the *Saṃghabhedavastu* of the Vinaya of the Mūlasarvāstivādins, the *Divyāvadāna* and the *Mahāvastu*, see J. W. de Jong, 'Buddha's first meditation in the Lalitavistara', in R. Torella (ed.), *Le parole et i marmi* (R. Gnoli Felicitation Volume), pp. 229–36.

11. An iconic depiction of the victory of Śākyamuni Buddha over a heterodox teacher mentioned in a Tibetan source

In a Tibetan Buddhist source we find a trace of an iconic representation of the Buddha overcoming a heterodox (*tīrthika* = *mu stegs pa*, etc.) teacher. It is located in the important *sDom gsum rab dbye* by the great hierarch Sa skya paṇḍita Kun dga' rgyal mtshan (1182–1251),[113] where we find the following description of a mural depiction of the Buddha Śākyamuni's victory over Īśvara (*dbaṅ phyug*), teacher of the heterodox Tīrthikas (f. 40a–b):

'khrul pa'i grub mtha' sun 'byin pa'i/ /rnam gžag cuṅ zad bšad kyi[s] ñon//
mu stegs ston pa dbaṅ phyug sogs/ /mnan pa'i saṅs rgyas mthoṅ nas ni//
de bzlog pa yi bris sku žig/ /mu stegs dbyaṅs can dga' bas byas//
mkhas pa chen po dzñāna šris/ /de daṅ rtsod pa'i rtsod grva ru//
raṅ gžan gñis ka'i sde pa daṅ/ /rgyal po sogs kyi dpaṅ po'i grvar//
saṅs rgyas mnan pa raṅ bzo yin/ /des na 'khrul pa yin par bsgrags//
des kyaṅ dbaṅ phyug mnan pa yi//saṅs rgyas raṅ bzo yin žes bsgres//
de la mkhas pas 'di skad brtsad/ /saṅs rgyas mnan pa khyed kyi gžuṅ//
khuṅs ma rnams nas bšad pa med/ /mu stegs mnan pa ṅed kyi rgyud//
gdod ma ñid nas yod pa yin/ /des na ṅes kyi raṅ bzo min//
de nas spobs pa med gyur tshe/ /rgyal po khyod kyi yul 'di ru//
'di 'dra'i raṅ bzo 'phel na ni/ /da duṅ raṅ bzo gžan 'byuṅ bas//
bstan pa spyi la gnod pa 'di/ /kho raṅ la yaṅ cis mi gnod//
'di dra'i raṅ bzo'i chos lugs ni/ /saṅs rgyas pa la byuṅ na yaṅ//
rgyal po khyod kyis dgag dgos so/ /de skad bsgo nas gyeṅ ris bsubs//

I shall succinctly explain a systematic method for refuting a mistaken doctrinal system (*siddhānta*). Listen! Having observed the Buddha [depicted as] overcoming (*mnan pa*) [in his teaching] heterodox teachers such as Īśvara, the Tīrthika *Sarasvatīnanda made a painted image [depicting] the opposite. [Then,] in a debating hall where he was debating with him, in a school where members of both his own and opposed schools and [persons] such as the king were acting as arbiter-witnesses (*sākṣin*), the great scholar Jñānaśrī proclaimed that [such a representation of] the Buddha's defeat was an arbitrary invention and that it was therefore mistaken. The [heterodox teacher

---

[113] For calling my attention to this passage I am indebted to David Jackson, who compares the beginning of Sa paṇ's reply to Chag Lo tsā ba's question (vol. na, f. 229b) where Śākyamuni's superiority to Śaṃkara, Viṣṇu, Brahmā, etc., has been affirmed. This representation thus recalls the passage just cited from Tsoṅ kha pa (pp. 71–72 above).

> *Sarasvatīnanda] matched this claim [asserting] that [the representation of] the Buddha defeating Īśvara was [itself] an arbitrary invention. Against this the same scholar [Jñānaśrī] then argued: 'In your basic texts the defeat of the Buddha has not been set out. [But] from the start there is found in our Tantra the defeating of Tīrthikas.'[114] Then, [*Sarasvatīnanda] having been reduced to silence, [Jñānaśrī bade the King]: 'Sire, if such arbitrary inventions become widespread in this land of yours, further arbitrary inventions will henceforth spring up, so that this will damage the [Buddha's] Teaching in general. How then will this not be damaging to oneself [i.e. to yourself in particular]? Also, if for Buddhists [too] there were to arise a doctrinal system which is such an arbitrary invention, you must, Sire, put an end to it.' Having thus bidden [the King, Jñānaśrī] erased the mural depiction (*gyeṅ ris* = *gyaṅ ris*) [made by the Tīrthika *Sarasvatīnanda].

What is in question in this passage is, firstly, not an icon representing a protective deity trampling on a 'Hindu(istic) divinity' but, rather, a depiction of the Buddha defeating a Tīrthika in the course of his teaching activity. That is, the reference is to a refutation of a heterodox teacher's erroneous *siddhānta*, as is made clear at the beginning of the passage. Secondly, it is to be noted that Sa skya paṇḍi ta has here made no reference to the contrastive pair or complementary opposition *laukika* : *lokottara* with which we are concerned in this study. Thirdly, this document dating from the thirteenth century provides some sort of precedent for Benoytosh Bhattacharyya's modern secular, and historicizing, interpretation of certain Buddhist images, however iconographically disparate they in fact are.

For Sa skya paṇḍi ta's understanding of the subordination to the Aikṣvāka (Bu ram šiṅ pa, i.e. Śākyamuni) of Śaṃkara, Jalaśayana, Brahmā, *et al.* – which is comparable to Tsoṅ kha pa's in the passage from the *Legs bšad sñiṅ po* cited above (pp. 71–72), – reference can be made to his 'Reply to Chag Lo tsā ba' (*Chag lo tsā ba'i žus lan*, f. 229b).

---

[114] Whereas Brahmanical *śruti* texts take no account of the Buddha Śākyamuni, Buddhist canonical texts beginning with the Āgamas/Nikāyas do mention the Buddha discussing with Tīrthikas, and defeating them in discussion.

12. Subordination of the *laukika* level by peripheralization within a concentric *maṇḍala* structure

Examples have been given in the preceding sections where a prostrate divinity of the *laukika* category is represented being danced or trodden upon by a great tutelary deity of Buddhism belonging to the *lokottara* level. This has been understood as SUBJUGATION of the subordinate 'mundane' level by the SUPERORDINATE 'transmundane' level, and as a vertically depicted hierarchic stratification. This holds for both two-dimensional and three-dimensional images and cosmograms (*maṇḍala*) used for either ritual or meditative purposes. And as has also been seen, this understanding is applicable in addition to cases where no trampling is depicted or referred to.

This is the case in particular in certain concentrically structured *maṇḍala*s, which may of course be either two-dimansional or three-dimensional (Tib. *blos blaṅs*). Noteworthy in this respect are the *maṇḍala*s of Dharmadhātuvāgīśvara, Bhūtaḍāmara, and Kālacakra, each of which includes a number of such subordinate divinities assembled peripherally round the main deity – the Lord of the *maṇḍala* – who is placed in the centre of the cosmogram.[115] Included among these lesser divinities are Brahmā, Viṣṇu, Maheśvara and their consorts or Śaktis; Gaṇapati (Vināyaka);[116] and so forth. In these last cases it is, then, possible to speak of horizontal inclusion, and of SUBORDINATION through DECENTRING and PERIPHERALIZATION, as opposed to SUPERORDINATION through CENTRALITY in a *maṇḍala* structure.

As is frequently the case in these matters, however, the relationship between the two levels of the *laukika* and the *lokottara* is not always entirely straight-forward and frozen. Thus Maheśvara – both a personifica-

---

[115] See Abhayākaragupta, *Niṣpannayogāvalī* nos. 21, 23 and 26, *maṇḍala*s which have been analysed by B. Bhattacharyya, *Niṣpannayogāvalī* (Baroda, 1949), by M.-T. de Mallmann, *Introduction à l'iconographie du tântrisme bouddhique*, and by Yong-hyun Lee, *The Niṣpannayogāvalī by Abhayākaragupta* (Seoul, 2004). Concerning Kalki(n) accompanied (and assisted) in his battle with the Mlecchas by Hari-Hara, etc., see *Kālacakratantra* i.162 f., and below, p. 123.

[116] On Gaṇapati see above, n. 48.

tion of primordial nescience (*avidyā*) and a manifestation of the Buddha Vairocana – may be placed in the outer field of certain *maṇḍala*s; but elsewhere he is shown occupying the central position in a *maṇḍala* of his own.[117] This has evidently to do with the transformative power of the Tathāgata and his Teaching, a once subjugated force that has submitted to its 'trainer' then becoming an emanation (*nirmāṇa*) of this tutelary by virtue of entering into a convention (*samaya*) and accepting by a vow (*saṃvara*) to protect the Teaching.

Philosophically speaking, the structured opposition *laukika* : *lokottara* is in fact not immutably stabilized and forever frozen into a hypostatized opposition, for the two opposed terms of the contrast are open to neutralization, to a sort of 'zeroing', in the frame of the classical theory of Emptiness of self-existence (*svabhāvaśūnyata*) and non-substantiality (*nairātmya*).

[117] See N. Iyanaga's article 'Daijizaiten' in the *Hōbōgirin*, p. 721 and pp. 751–2.

13. Ritual, geographical, iconological and architectural collocation (juxtaposition), hierarchic stratification, and centrality as against peripheralization

It might be suggested that – instead either of a diffuse or undifferentiated syncretism uniting two different religious traditions (a relation roughly describable as 'Buddhism-*cum*-Hinduism') or of a virtually secular antagonism opposing the two (a relation describable as 'Buddhism *versus* Hinduism' or *vice versa*) – we very often meet with what might be called the COLLOCATION or JUXTAPOSITION of the two traditions. This collocation of the two traditions would then be in some respects analogous to the geographical PROPINQUITY that has existed in Northeastern India between the nearby religious centres of Vārāṇasī and Sārnāth or Gayā and Bodh-Gayā, the first place in each pair being an essentially Brahmanical/Hindu site whilst the second is a predominantly Buddhist one.

In the Kathmandu valley of Nepal, a comparable pattern is to be found in the relation between the towns of Bhatgaon (Bhaktapur) and Pāṭan (Lalitpur) which, respectively, have been predominantly Hindu and Buddhist; whilst Kāthmāṇḍu, which religiously speaking stands between these two towns in so far as it has many sites belonging to both religious traditions, is flanked by the major mainly Buddhist sites of Svayambhūnāth and Bodhnāth.[118] In addition, the relationship in question may be marked, for example in the Kathmandu Valley, by the existence of shrines that are common to both traditions, so that collocation or juxtaposition of the two traditions may on occasion even assume the form of their geographical unilocality in a single holy site.[119]

---

[118] See J. Locke, *Buddhist monasteries of Nepal* (Kathmandu, 1985).

[119] On Paśupatināth and Būṛā Nīlakaṇṭh as, respectively, Śaiva-cum-Buddhist and Vaiṣṇava-cum-Buddhist shrines, see, e.g., S. Lienhard, 'Religionssyncretismus in Nepal' (as in n. 44 above), p. 153 ff., who has adopted the term 'PARALLELISM' to denote the phenomenon in question. – Concerning stylistically closely related icons from the same site (and possibly even from the same workshop) belonging to both Hinduism and Buddhism see below, n. 155.

In Tibet mention may be made of the area of Mount Kailāsa/(Gaṅs) Ti se and Lake Mānasa (Mānassarovar)/Ma pham (g-yu) mtsho which is sacred not only to Buddhists (as an abode of Cakrasaṃvara/Śaṃvara), and also to Bon pos, but equally to Hindus (as the abode of Śiva and the mythical source of the sacred Gaṅgā), and where we thus find a noteworthy collocation of these religious traditions.[120]

This particular collocation of the two traditions of Buddhism and Brahmanism/Hinduism often presents itself synchronically as a horizontal JUXTAPOSITION in space of two distinct entities, despite the partly common roots of each and hence their diachronic CONTINUITY. And in this case there will, generally speaking, be neither total SYNCRETISTIC convergence and conflation of the two traditions nor open hostile CONFRONTATION between them. Only in certain circumstances (that require specification) will such collocation/juxtaposition develop, horizontally as it were, into either true SYNCRETISTIC CONVERGENCE or, in certain cases, mutual HOSTILITY. Just as frequently, if not even more often, the collocation manifests itself, so to say vertically, in a kind of structured STRATIFICATION, and vertical hierarchic ordering, wherein one tradition is represented as superordinate and the other as subordinate, in the manner already alluded to above. This relationship might, *prima facie*, appear to be close to what Paul Hacker has termed 'INCLUSIVISM', but it does not in fact appear identical with Hacker's own definition of this concept (see below). And it will of course be necessary to consider whether subordination of the *laukika* to the *lokottara* is nothing but a more polite way of giving expression to epistemic subjugation and hostility.

---

[120] Concerning the Buddhist and Bon traditions relating to the Kailāsa area, see Appendix I, n. 236 below. This area was the locale of the contest between Mi la ras pa and the Bon po master Na ro bon chuṅ recounted in Mi la's *rNam thar* (version published in Chinghai [1981], p. 376 f.) and in his *mGur 'bum* (chap. 22 and 24; cf. H. Hoffmann, *Quellen zur Geschichte der tibetischen Bon-Religion* [Mainz, 1950], pp. 230 f., 266 ff.).

For the neighbouring region of La phyi, another area linked with Mi la ras pa, A. W. Macdonald has discussed the juxtaposition and stratification of religious traditions in his article 'Hindu-isation, Buddha-isation, then Lama-isation, or: What happened at La-phyi?', in: T. Skorupski (ed.), *Indo-Tibetan studies* (D. Snellgrove Felicitation Volume, Tring, 1990), pp. 199–208. Macdonald there touches on the *motif* of the subjugation of Maheśvara/Mahādeva/Bhairava/Rudra by Vajrapāṇi under the aegis of Cakrasaṃvara.

Attention was already called above to the parallel procedure of HORIZONTAL INCLUSION by SUPERORDINATION through CENTRALITY, as opposed to SUBORDINATION through PERIPHERALIZATION.

It would seem, then, that for this complex situation SYMBIOSIS may be a more appropriate general description than either SYNCRETISM or INCLUSIVISM, or out-and-out hostile CONFRONTATION, even though tendencies towards one (or more) of the latter are no doubt detectable in certain cases.

Such interreligious collocations, seemingly more SYMBIOSIS than syncretism, have of course been observed at numberless sites. An example is furnished by an early petroglyph dating to about the beginning of the common era from Chilas (Gilgit area) where, beside the drawing of a *stūpa* on a rock, an inscription reads *śivadasasya* 'of Śivadāsa', and where the dedicator bearing this Śivaite name is apparently to be associated with Buddhism. In the dedication on a Buddha-image from the North West and belonging to a much later time is found the name of a certain donor named Saṃkarasenạ (sic) described as a *paramopāsaka*.[121]

---

[121] See G. Fussmann, 'Les inscriptions kharoṣṭhī de la plaine de Chilas', in: K. Jettmar, *Antiquities of Northern Pakistan: Reports and studies*, i (Mainz, 1989), pp. 12–13. Fussman has aptly observed (pp. 12–13): 'Il semble bien que dès cette époque [i.e. lst century AC–lst century PC], dans le Nord-Ouest de l'Inde, śivaïsme et bouddhisme aient fait bon ménage... Les inscriptions kharoṣṭhī que j'ai mentionnées à la page précédente prouvent que ces relations privilégiées entre le śivaïsme et le bouddhisme (car on ne saurait parler de syncrétisme, tout au plus s'agit-il de symbiose) remontent loin dans le temps: les premiers témoignages certains datent des alentours de notre ère'. And on a certain Śivarakṣita as the donor of a Buddhist relief, see G. Fussman, 'Documents épigraphiques kouchans II', *BEFEO* 67 (1980), p. 55. Concerning the donor Śaṃkarasenạ, the *paramopāsaka* whose name figures on the base of a Buddha-image, see further G. Fussman, 'Chilas, Hatun et les bronzes bouddhiques du Cachemire', in: K. Jettmar, *Antiquities of Northern Pakistan: Reports and studies*, ii (Mainz, 1993), pp. 43–44, dating this image to the early eighth century.

Several other names beginning with Śaṃkara are known from Buddhist literary history. Thus, as noted above (n. 111), the author of the **Devatāvimarśastuti/Devatātiśayastotra* was Śaṃkarasvāmin (bDe byed bdag po, *Śaṃkarapati?), a brother of Udbhaṭasiddhasvāmin (mTho btsun grub rje), the author of the **Viśeṣa/Viśiṣṭastava*, who – according to Prajñāvarman's commentaries – both made a pilgrimage to Śiva/Śaṃkara's abode on Kailāsa where they found their deity paying homage to Arhats and where they converted to Buddhism at the command of Śiva himself. Udbhaṭasiddhasvāmin composed a **Sarvajñamaheśvara-nāma-stotra* where Maheś-

---

vara is identified with the Omniscient, i.e. the Buddha. As for Śaṃkaranandana, an important master in the tradition of Buddhist Pramāṇa studies dated *c.* 940/50–1020/30, he was by birth a Brahman and is indeed known in Tibetan as Bram ze chen po; on him and his relation to Hinduism see H. Krasser, 'On the date and works of Śaṃkaranandana', in R. Torella *et al.* (ed.), *Le parole e i marmi* (R. Gnoli Felicitation Volume), pp. 489–507, an article which contains important materials concerning the relationship between Buddhism and Śaivism and their symbiosis in the late tenth and early eleventh centuries. Earlier, in the tradition of Buddhist Pramāṇa studies, the name Śaṃkarasvāmin is already attested for a pupil of Dignāga; he was the author of the *Nyāyapraveśa*. An identical formation is Śivasvāmin, the name of the ninth-century author of the *Kapphiṇābhyudaya*, a poem based on a Buddhist *avadāna*. And a comparable name is Umāpatidatta/°deva, the author of two texts relating to Vajrayoginī (one in the *Guhyasamayasādhanamālā*, and both in the bsTan 'gyur). Another comparable name in the Buddhist Pramāṇa tradition is Īśvarasena, a teacher of Dharmakīrti. (It is interesting to note that so many of the great names in the area of Indian logic and epistemology were linked with Śaivism.)

14. Further issues in the *laukika* : *lokottara* contrastive and complementary opposition

The remarks offered above on the subject of the significance and valency of the *lokottara* level in Buddhist thought bring us to another point that needs to be considered in connexion with the structured contrastive pair *laukika* : *lokottara*. Given that Buddhist soteriological theory allows for the transcending of the *laukika* level and the passage to the *lokottara* level, as seen above on the evidence of several sources, this pair is dynamic rather than STATICALLY DUALISTIC; for it does not posit two fixed, frozen and reified levels sealed off from each other.[122]

This contrastive and complementary opposition has so far been invoked here as a means for describing systemically certain Buddhist representations concerning the divine and sacral as it is distributed over two levels the first of which, the *laukika*, embraces what has been termed the common Indian religious SUBSTRATUM OF GROUND. But the full significance of the opposition worldly/mundane : supramundane/transmundane has not thereby been fully brought out, for only on the gnoseological, meditative and ritual levels does it reveal its full, and central, significance for Buddhist thought. However useful a heuristic device this opposition may then be for the historian of Indian religions, its ultimate *raison d'être* and finality in Buddhism lie in the dimensions of soteriology and gnoseology, about which a few words may now be in order.

Here and now, the practiser or exercitant – the Sādhaka or Yogin – as a human individual is of course located, soteriologically speaking, within

---

[122] To say that a relationship is not dualistic is, of course, not to suggest that it is monistic, the point here being that the relation is a dynamic rather than a static one between two levels, and that one may be transcended thus allowing a passage to the other. It must, moreover, be kept in mind that principles of Madhyamaka thought are in the background of much in Buddhist thought, in particular the dynamic relationship between the levels of pragmatic usage (*vyavahāra*) and ultimate reality (*paramārtha*). This is so even if it is not possible to equate the *lokottara* and the *paramārtha*. The ascription of the *laukika* to the *vyāvahārika* is, however, straightforward. The contrast *laukika* : *lokottara* will be annulled in the final perspective of ultimate non-duality (*advaya*, i.e. on the level of the *paramārtha*); see for instance the *Vimalakīrtinirdeśa*, Chap. viii. (Lamotte's translation, pp. 306–07)

the round of existences (*saṃsāra*); and gnoseologically he is located on the level of pragmatic usage (*vyavahāra*), that is, philosophically speaking, on the surface level (*saṃvṛti*, as opposed to the ultimate level of *paramārtha*) (cf. p. 91 below) The aim of practice in Mahāyāna and Vajrayāna thought is to realize the ultimate non-duality (*advaya*) of *saṃsāra* (along with the level of *[tathya]saṃvṛti*) and *nirvāṇa* (together with ultimate reality, the *paramārtha*). And this realization is represented as being achieved through meditative-philosophical understanding of Emptiness (*śūnyatā*), to which end Buddhist thought has proposed several ways of approach.

In Vajrayāna, the Sādhaka's practice has been largely structured round a complex process of what might be called self-identification with the supramundane divinity through *abhimāna* = *ṅa rgyal* 'pride, selfhood' (or *ahaṃkāra* 'self-affirmation'). The practiser is to regard himself as identical with – i.e. undifferentiated from – his tutelary divinity (*iṣṭadevatā, adhideva; yi dam*), for no ordinary person can be regarded as fit to approach the divine and sacral. And there consequently takes place an entry or descent (*'jug pa, 'bab pa*) of the noetic (or noumenal) hierophany (*ye šes pa*) in the sacralised subject (*dam tshig pa*), that is, in the Sādhaka identified with the divinity and his characteristic, defining symbols and cognizances. In this process of the Sādhaka's self-identification with the supramundane divine, the opposition *laukika* : *lokottara* appears as crucial; for while the practiser finds himself, in his existential condition here and now, on the mundane level, the tutelary which is the focus of ritual-meditative practice stands for the supramundane level with which the practiser is to infuse himself through the ritual-meditative process of (self-)identification.

In the Vajrayāna and its art, ritual and meditation accordingly have a MEDIATING – and so to say MESOCOSMIC – function, for they serve as a means of establishing communication between the microcosmic Sādhaka in *saṃsāra* and the macrocosmic transmundane, the 'locus' of the tutelary divinity. In short, a fundamental principle in Vajrayāna is that the Sādhaka should visualize, and realize, himself as not different from the supramundane level of his tutelary, this self-identification being indeed the necessary condition for effecting the required COMMUNICATION, TRANSFORMATION and TRANS-VALUATION between the mundane and supramundane levels. (See also Appendix II below.)

Now it is essential to note that were this self-identification nothing but gratuitous self-deification – that is, an identification in relative space and time of the practiser qua objective individual being with the divine conceived of as an objective supramundane entity – this would be an egregious, and altogether absurd, example of overweening selfhood and hubris. But in the last analysis there can be no room here for such hubristic excess of self-affirmation, and the Sādhaka's self-identification with the transmundane divinity is rather to be understood as a process whereby the noetic hierophany of the *lokottara* level is as it were precipitated into, and realized on, the Sādhaka's level in a trans-temporal and trans-spatial refiguration, once the Sādhaka has undergone the requisite preparation making this precipitation and realization of the transmundane possible in a specific mediating and communicative situation. This process is, then, a special form of *theōsis* characteristic of Buddhism, a tradition that is not, however, theistic in any customary sense but one in which the divine is most certainly sensed and recognized, and where even a particular form of devotion (*bhakti*, *bhāva*; Tib. *gus pa*) is well attested (see pp. 72, 93). This process will appear paradoxical (if not contradictory) only to a casual observer caught in the customary theistic categories of, e.g., the Abrahamic religions who engages in 'etic' comparison without having first completed the necessary 'emic' analyses.

In this mediating and communicative practice of Vajrayāna ritual and meditation, then, we have to do with an abolishing or annulment of the gap between the *laukika* and the *lokottara* as it is conventionally concretized in a dichotomously conceptualized polarity of mundane and supramundane 'loci'. Such neutralization, or 'zeroing', of the duality of the two levels, effected as it is in a situation where the practiser is penetrated by the *lokottara*, is to be understood in terms of the Vajrayānist – and Mahāyānist – non-substantiality of the individual (*pudgalanairātmya*) and of all factors of existence (*dharmanairātmya*), that is, of Emptiness of self-existence (*svabhāvaśūnyatā*).

Hence, although it might have at first seemed that the logically complementary concepts of the mundane and supramundane were symmetrically opposed and mutually exclusive, and that they therefore refer to totally heterogeneous entities and ontological levels, this is not really the case for either the Vajrayānist or Mahāyānist.

In the Buddhist view of things, as opposed concepts with a discursively constructed (*prapañcita*) conceptual structure, there exists between the two terms, and between the soteriological and gnoseological levels designated by them, a certain solidarity inasmuch as the supramundane is conceptualizable and expressible as opposed, in a binary relation, to the mundane (and vice versa). Consequently, so long as it is opposed in dichotomizing conceptual construction (*vikalpa*) to the mundane, the supramundane cannot truly correspond to the supreme reality of Buddhism, which by definition transcends such conceptual development and dichotomization. And the same applies to *nirvāṇa* when conceived of as the dichotomously posited opposite and complementary of *saṃsāra*. Hence, *nirvāṇa* corresponds to ultimate reality – the *paramārtha* – only when the discursively constructed conceptual, and linguistic, opposition between it and *saṃsāra* has been neutralized or 'zeroed' in Emptiness (*śūnyatā*, i.e. *niḥsvabhāvatā* or *nairātmya*).

This would suggest that, in the final analysis, the supramundane will take on its true significance and valency only outside any binary conceptual opposition, that is to say once the opposition between it and the mundane has been either provisionally suspended or finally abolished through ritual, meditative and philosophical means. Thus, the Indian and Tibetan *kusu lu pa* and the East Asian practiser of Ch'an/Zen may realize reality in every-day life, and they then have an intimation of the non-duality of *saṃsāra* and *nirvāṇa* (or *satori*); but preliminary and temporally delimited realization is then to be followed by the final realization of *nirvāṇa*, or the supreme and perfect Awakening (*anuttarasamyaksambodhi*) of the *buddha*. In Mahāyāna and Vajrayāna Buddhism, the religious as well as the philosophical has to do with realizing this abolishment of duality.

In summary, in Buddhist thought, this non-duality is realized in Emptiness. And in religious practice the Bodhisattva's and the Vajrayānist Yogin's actions are as it were grounded in *śūnyatā* and infused with non-objectifying Great Compassion (*mahākaruṇā*) in which the differentiation between the Bodhisattva, his compassionate action and the object of compassion – i.e. the *trimaṇḍala* – is abolished, and where there no longer is to be found any phenomenal sign (*nimitta*) to objectify and cling to, no reification and no substantial self-existence (*svabhāva*).

15. Continuity, the substratum model in relation to the borrowing model, and the *laukika* : *lokottara* opposition as an 'emic' classification

Mention has been repeatedly made above of cultural continuity between Indian Buddhism and Indian civilization.

In India, the lines of demarcation between the Buddhist and the Brahmanical/Hindu, and also between the *śramaṇa* and the *brāhmaṇa*, sometimes appear to have at least as much to do with practice, and orthopraxy, as they do with theory and doctrine, and with orthodoxy. A *śramaṇa* may be defined as much by his practice as by his doctrines, views or beliefs. Whilst a *brāhmaṇa* retains a tuft of hair (*śikhā*), the *śramaṇa* shaves his head completely. The latter gives up the sacred thread (*sūtra*, *yajñopavīta*) of the Hindu twice-born (*dvija*) and wears the ochre robe (*kaṣāya*); he does not follow the Vedas or the *varṇāśrama-dharma* of the Hindu; and so on.

Of course, between these traditions there also exist points of doctrinal difference, e.g. the Buddhist's non-acceptance of an *ātman* and of a creator god (*īśvara*) or one who controls men's destinies. Still, not only in Buddhism but also in large sectors of earlier Brahmanical thought, God either as a creator or as the arbiter of men's destinies plays no rôle. And the Pūrva- or Karma-Mīmāṃsā is non-theistic, as is the Sāṃkhya. Even in the Uttara-Mīmāṃsā, or Advaita-Vedānta, *īśvara* hardly occupies a central place. In a certain sense, moreover, even the Buddhist theory of no-self (*anātmavāda*), as opposed to Brahmanical *ātmavāda*, is not always strictly speaking criterial in demarcating Buddhism from Brahmanism. Certainly, the schools of Buddhism refuse to postulate an *ātman* as a permanent and indestructible soul, as an entelechy or spiritual substance inhabiting beings in *saṃsāra* and still to be found in *nirvāṇa*. Yet some schools of Buddhism have not hesitated to make use of the word *ātman*, or *paramātman* 'trans-*ātman*', when speaking of ultimate unconditioned reality, the *asaṃskr̥ta*. This usage represents a means of definition and description – a kind of 'showing' – of ultimate reality by a process of differentiation and reversal (perhaps also by antiphrasis).[123]

[123] This applies to the *tathāgatragarbha* theory in Buddhist Sūtras and Śāstras, on which see D. Seyfort Ruegg, *La théorie du tathāgatagarbha et du gotra* (Paris, 1969). On the matter of description by differentiation and reversal, see *Théorie*, pp. 362–92.

Contrary to what has often been supposed, the earlier Buddhist textual sources do not seem to know the Upaniṣads. As for the Vedānta, it appears clearly, perhaps for the first time in a major Buddhist text, in Bhāviveka's *Madhyamakahṛdayakārikā*s, chap. viii (cf. iii.288 f.), and in the *Tarkajvālā*-commentary on it. P. Horsch, 'Buddhismus und Upaniṣaden', in: *Pratidānam* (F.B.J. Kuijper Felicitation Volume, The Hague, 1968), pp. 462–77, concluded that there are no clear references in the earlier Buddhist literature to the Upaniṣadic *ātman/brahman*. Several more recent works on the subject of the relation between Buddhism and the Upaniṣadic *ātman*-theory (e.g. K. R. Norman, 'A note on *attā* in the *Alagaddūpama-sutta*', *Collected papers*, ii, p. 200 ff., and R. Gombrich, *How Buddhism began* [London, 1996]) have not addressed the objections raised by Horsch (who examined on p. 467 the passage studied by Norman in his article just cited). An article that appeared in the same year as Horsch's, H. Nakamura, 'The Vedānta philosophy as was revealed in Buddhist scriptures', in *Pañcāmṛtam* (Śāradīya Jñāna Mahotsava 3, Śrī Lāl Bahādur Śāstrī Rāṣṭrīya Saṃskṛta Vidyā Pīṭha, Delhi 2024 [= 1968], pp. 6, 8–12), was somewhat less categorical than Horsch. And in his *History of early Vedānta philosophy*, i (Delhi, 1983), Nakamura expressed the opinion that the concept of Brahmā and Upaniṣadic ideas are to be found scattered throughout the early Buddhist scriptures (pp. 135–9). See also K. Bhattacharya, *L'ātman-brahman dans le bouddhisme ancien* (Paris, 1973); id., 'Some thoughts on ātman-brahman in early Buddhism', in: *Dr. B. M. Barua birth centenary volume* (Calcutta, 1989), pp. 63–83; id., *Some thoughts on early Buddhism with special reference to its relation to the Upaniṣads* (Post-graduate and Research Department Series No. 41, Pune, 1998). – This is of course not the place to go into the matter of the *pudgalavāda* of the Vātsīputrīyas/Sammatīyas.

In the Mahāyānist *Mahāparinirvāṇasūtra* in particular, there is found a positive view of the *ātman* properly understood – that is, as interpreted in the frame of Buddhist thought rather than as maintained by many Brahmans – and the relationship between the Buddhist and the Brāhman is there presented in a particularly interesting, and nuanced, form. Cf. D. Seyfort Ruegg, *Le traité du tathāgatagarbha de Bu ston Rin chen grub* (Paris, 1973), Index s. v. *Mahāparinirvāṇasūtra*; id., *Buddha-nature, Mind and the problem of Gradualism in a comparative perspective* (London, 1989), p. 19 ff. In passages of this Sūtra (quoted in *Buddha-nature* ..., pp. 22–23), Hindu ascetics – having heard the Buddha explain how it was that he taught non-self (*nairātmya*) and how it is that the Buddha-nature, or *tathāgatagarbha*, is nonetheless 'self' (*ātman*) – are shown taking refuge in the Buddha's teaching and producing the *bodhicitta*.

To affirm a certain continuity between Indian Buddhism and Indian civilization, and to propose a ('pan-Indian') SUBSTRATUM MODEL to help describe and understand the relationship between the two, is of course by itself less a final and definitive interpretation or judgement than it is a means of elucidating the issues at hand. But CONTINUITY seems to be somewhat overlooked when, for example, we hear of the BORROWING of Brahmanical/Hindu divinities in Buddhism, a procedure which evidently implies that the Indian religious ground or substratum is foreign and exogenous to Buddhism. To put it pointedly, Indian Buddhists could hardly have borrowed what was already in their religious and cultural heritage. The question is, then, just how this shared heritage has been regarded and used by Buddhists. (If a 'pan-Indian' substratum, or divinity, is spoken of here, the refererence is not necessarily to one found everywhere in India but to one common to Buddhism and another Indian religion, e.g. Brahmanism/Hinduism.)

Now it needs to be stated explicitly that a SUBSTRATUM MODEL is not being envisaged here in a spirit of reductionism. That is, to state the obvious fact that Buddhists in India were Indians, and that Buddhism was contiguous and in large part continuous with Indian civilization, is not reductionistically to assert that Indian Buddhism was nothing distinctive and specific, that it was but a 'sect' of Brahmanism/Hinduism, and that Indian Buddhists (who, as is known, were not infrequently Brahmans) were nothing but Hindus (in the narrow sense of this word). The cultural (if not creedal) continuity in question, of which Buddhists have often shown themselves to be aware, does not imply total religio-philosophical identity, to which the Buddhists certainly did not assent, any more than it *per se* necessarily demonstrates careless INDIFFERENTISM, or SYNCRETISM (or INCLUSIVISM, on which see below). One or the other of these factors may on occasion have played a part, but it does not seem possible to reduce the phenomena under discussion exclusively to any one of them (or to some combination of them).

The SUBSTRATUM MODEL does imply a SYMBIOSIS (or an OSMOSIS) between Buddhism and Hinduism that is both a historically conditioned diachronic one and a culturally determined synchronic one. The question then is just how this symbiosis or osmosis actually functioned, and how a substratum model might serve to clarify their workings.

On the face of it, the concept of a substratum is (like syncretism, symbiosis, etc.) a more or less 'etic' one, that is, one that belongs to a metatheoretical discourse on Indian data that operates interculturally with comparative ideas and analyses rather than, initially, with 'emic' ones, i.e. with indigenous and intracultural Indian concepts. To be useful and heuristically fruitful, the applicability of an 'etic' concept to the study of Buddhism can be worked out in detail only once the 'emic' categories have been carefully identified and analysed.[124] Otherwise the indigenous concepts of our sources run the risk of being stretched on the Procrustean bed of exogenous presuppositions and prejudgements. A question that arises immediately is, then, how the substratum model may be related to concepts and categories known from the Buddhist sources themselves, in other words to 'emic' categories embedded in the structures and dynamics characterizing the traditions of Buddhism.

To avoid misunderstanding, it has to be emphasized that the idea of a partly shared religious and cultural SUBSTRATUM, (back)ground or patrimony/heritage being envisaged here does not, of course, automatically and totally exclude any possibility of instances of BORROWING by Buddhists from Brahmanism/Hinduism in certain characterized cases specifiable through historical and philological analysis. Far from being entirely incompatible, the SUBSTRATUM and BORROWING MODELS may in fact be complementary. Indeed, it is the existence of such a shared ground or substratum that will yield the conditions required for borrowing to take place within a given civilization.[125] Moreover, a substratum model neither presupposes nor excludes the presence of so-called pre-Aryan or non-Aryan components, towards which hypotheses it is theoretically neutral. Nor of course does the concept of a substratum necessarily rule out the presence in it of 'higher' theoretical thought and religio-philosophical doctrine. Finally, the kind of substratum envisaged here is not of the same kind as a linguistic substratum which, by definition, is allogenic to the language in which it is identified; for the purposes of the present enquiry, the substratum, precisely because it is largely shared by both, is thought of as endogenous to Buddhism as well as to Brahmanism/Hinduism.[126]

---

[124] On the subject of the 'emic' and 'etic' see below, p. 135 ff.

[125] However, 'beachcomber' and 'cargo-cult' versions of the borrowing model would be incompatible with the substratum model; see below, p. 108 f.

[126] For the difference between the above-mentioned concept of a shared religious and

One very significant 'emic' concept embedded in the very structure and dynamics of Buddhist tradition which is pertinent to the issues under discussion is, precisely, the *laukika* : *lokottara* opposition, the structured – contrastive and complementary – opposition between the worldly/mundane and the supramundane/transmundane levels in Buddhist religious and philosophical thought with which this study is concerned. The further structured opposition *samvr̥ti* (or *vyavahāra*) : *paramārtha* – i.e. the surface-level of pragmatic usage as opposed to the level of ultimate reality – might perhaps also suggest itself here because the SUBSTRATUM – the *laukika* – will, in the frame of Buddhist thought, belong to the *vyavahāra* level (cf. p. 84 above). But, on the one hand, the *lokottara* level is not simply coterminous with the (*niṣparyāya-*)*paramārtha* level, which is a more restricted and philosophically defined category. (Whether the *lokottara* level can be said to correspond to the *saparyāya-paramārtha*, or *paramārthānukūla*, of philosophical analysis – and thus to 'point to' or 'show' the ultimate level of the *niṣparyāya-paramārtha* – is a matter for reflection; compare below, p. 186.) On the other hand, the *saṃvr̥ti* or *vyavahāra* level appears to embrace not only the *laukika* but also at least a part of what is regarded as *lokottara*.

As already observed above (pp. 57, 69 f.), the contrastive pair *laukika* : *lokottara* has been employed in Buddhist descriptions of the progressive Path of the spiritual exercitant. It has also been seen (pp. 69 f.) how Buddhism has, in addition, distinguished between the supramundane Path of meditative realizaton, which is specific to the Ārya, and a way of meditative realization (*bhāvanā*) which is termed mundane (*laukika*) and is common to practisers and Yogins independently of their being Āryas. In this particular case, the contast *laukika* : *lokottara* has been employed in Buddhist thought to differentiate between what is specific to it, at least on its higher levels, and what is not specifically Buddhist, in other words what is held in common by the Buddhist and Brāhmanical (etc.) traditions.

---

cultural substratum or ground and that of Hindutva, see p. 2 above and pp. 112 and 152 below. On the concepts of substratum, adstratum and archistratum, see n. 65 above.

The soteriological and gnoseological concept of the Single Vehicle (*ekayāna*) has been mentioned above (p. 71). In connexion with this *ekayāna*, the *Laṅkāvatārasūtra* has referred to the transformation of the ways of the gods (*devayāna*) and of Brahmā (*brahmayāna*) – and indeed, of the differentiated three Vehicles (*yāna*) of the Śrāvaka, Pratyekabuddha and Tathāgata to the extent that they are conceived of as independent paths leading to ultimately distinct goals – into, and through, the gnoseologically and soteriologically unitary principle of the One Vehicle.[127]

In the *Lalitavistara*, moreover, the infant Siddhārtha is shown to observe that, at his birth, the trischiliocosmos (*trisahasra*) was shaken and that the gods – Śakra, Brahmā, Candra, Sūrya, Vaiśravaṇa, Kumāra *et al.* – all bowed their heads at his feet, for he was indeed the 'god above gods' (*devātideva*).[128]

In the Pali canon, a distinction is made between a god by convention (*saṃmutideva*) – such as a king or prince – and those who are called gods in virtue of divine rebirth due to their meritorious deeds (*upapattideva*) on the one side and on the other those counted as gods because of their purity (*visuddhideva*).[129] The last of these three categories corresponds to the *buddha* or *tathāgata*, to the *arhat* whose impurities are removed (*khīṇāsava*) and to the *paccekabuddha* (*Cullanidessa* ii 307, Nālandā ed. p. 238).

The Buddha has often received the epithet of *lokātīta* 'transmundane', for example in Nāgārjuna's *Lokātītastava*. The theme of the subordinating integration of the Indian gods and godlings in the Buddhist cosmos has been treated in later commentaries on the Stava/Stotra

---

[127] *Laṅkāvatārasūtra*, ii.203–05; see also the Sagāthaka chapter, 457–8 and 445. Cf. our *Théorie du tathāgatagarbha et du gotra*, Part II.
In connexion with the concept of annulment, neutralization and 'zeroing' referred to in the present study, it is useful to recall this Sūtra's concept of non-Vehicle (*ayāna*, pp. 65, 243, 297 and 306) whereby the idea of *yāna*s is abolished.

[128] *Lalitavistara*, viii, p. 119.

[129] The term *atideva* is used of the Buddha in *Theragāthā* 489, and of the Arhat in Saṃyuttanikāya i.141.18. See also the *Kaṇṇakatthalasutta* (Majjhimanikāyya ii, 125) and the *Saṅgāravasutta* (ibid. ii 209–13). Cf. K. R. Norman, 'The Buddha's view of Devas', *Beiträge zur Indienforschung* (E. Waldschmidt Festschrift, Berlin, 1977), pp. 329–36; id., 'Devas and Adhidevas in Buddhism', *JPTS* 9 (1981), pp. 145–55 (n. 62).

literature, such as Prajñāvarman's *Ṭīkā*s on Udbhaṭasiddhasvāmin's **Viśeṣa/Viśiṣṭa(?)-stava* and Śaṃkarasvāmin's **Devatāvimarśastuti/Devātiśayastotra*. It is also above all in hymnic literature that there comes clearly to the fore in Buddhism a *bhakti* current which, judging by the probable dates of the texts, is no more recent than all but the very oldest references to *bhakti* in Hindu literature.

In terms of the *laukika* : *lokottara* opposition, then, the *laukika* level corresponds in large part to a common Indian substratum or ground that is structurally and systemically subordinate to the higher, and specifically Buddhist, level of the *lokottara*. As already remarked (p. 83), however, the relationship of the worldly/mundane to the supramundane/transmundane is not a totally frozen and static one of permanent subordination and subjection. For the *laukika* level may be raised to and transmuted into the *lokottara* plane through a process of TRANSFORMATIVE MEDIATION whereby a *laukika* divinity, undertaking as he does an engagement or vow (*saṃvara*) to maintain the Buddha's teaching and adhering to a convention (*samaya*), may become a 'Noble' Stream-Winner (*ārya srotaāpanna*). As also observed above (pp. 83–86), the means of this TRANSFORMATION and TRANS-VALUATION are ritual, meditative and philosophical.

In the spread of Buddhism first within India and then abroad – in Central, East and Southeast Asia – the *laukika* level has provided as it were the religious space in which local divinities and *numina*, along with so-called 'Little Traditions', could be conceptually accommodated. In Tibet, local and mountain divinities (*yul lha*, *gži bdag*, also *sa bdag*, *gter bdag*, etc.) were integrated as protectors, etc., into the Buddhist cosmos and pantheon (see below). The *laukika* level has accordingly provided a kind of slot on the basis of which TRANSFORMATION and TRANS-VALUATION could then be effected. In this way the relation non-Buddhist : Buddhist was no more a STATIC one than is the relation *laukika* : *lokottara* as described above in relation to the Buddhist Path and to Vajrayāna. The terms in these contrastive reltionships are in fact DYNAMIC ones.

16. Some 'etic' categories previously invoked by scholars

Beside SYNCRETISM, various categories and models, descriptive and analytical, have previously been employed in studying Buddhism in relation to the ambient religions and culture of India, and then of the lands where it later became established, as well as with respect to its distinct traditions and registers.

The antithetical categories *popular* : *learned*, *lay* : *monastic*, and *ordinary believer* : *religious specialist* (or *virtuoso*) have been variously invoked by scholars. A further antithesis invoked has been the Weberian one of *this-worldly* : *other-worldly*. Durkheim's antithetical pairs *belief* : *rite* and *sacred* : *profane* have also been employed. For his part M. Spiro proposed a threefold division into *apotropaic*, *kammatic* and *nibbanic* Buddhisms. An analysis contrasting the *affective* and the *cognitive* has in addition been advanced jointly with the antithesis between *behaviour* or *practice* and *precept*. Still other writers have made use of the anthropologists' antithesis 'Little Tradition : 'Great Tradition' as developed by Redfield and Marriott.

Few would probably wish to deny that tensions, antitheses and oppositions expressible by these concepts and terms have been operative within the wide domain of the historical development and geographical expansion of Buddhist thought.[130] In the matter of the inclusion within Buddhism of divinities belonging to a common Indian religious substratum, and in the context of the contrast *laukika* : *lokottara*, the antitheses lay : monastic, ordinary believer : religious specialist, and this-worldly : other-worldly could no doubt be invoked with some justification. Still, it has remained anything but clear how most appropriately to apply these 'etic' concepts in the complex and multi-faceted religio-philosophical traditions of Buddhism. Moreover, any dualistic opposition that is reified, and basically static and frozen, can do little, it seems, adequately to convey the eminently dynamic relationships so often existing between levels in Buddhism, where a lower level is not just affectively retained (either more or less unconsciously, or in some cognitively debased or

---

[130] Compare below, p. 131.

filtered form), but transfigured and trans-valued to a higher level. These are some of the many things that the *laukika* : *lokottara* opposition has been used to convey.

17. Paul Hacker's concept of 'inclusivism'

A further notion requiring attention in the present context is Paul Hacker's concept of INCLUSIVISM. Hacker developed his theory of inclusivism because of his dissatisfaction with the idea, often entertained by writers on India, of the essentially tolerant nature of Hinduism.[131] Hacker's last published definition runs as follows:

> Inclusivism is a concept I use to describe data from the area which we term Indian religion and, in particular, Indian religious philosophy. Inclusivism means declaring that a central conception of an alien religious or weltanschaulich group is identical with this or that central conception of the group to which one belongs oneself. To inclusivism there mostly belongs, explicitly or implicitly, the assertion that the alien declared to be identical with one's own is in some way subordinate or inferior to the latter. In addition, no proof is generally furnished for the identity of the alien with one's own.
>
> (P. Hacker in: G. Oberhammer [ed.], *Inklusivismus, eine indische Denkform*, p. 12: Inklusivismus ist ein Begriff, den ich zur Beschreibung von Daten aus demjenigen Bereich benutze, den wir indische Religion und speziell indische Religionsphilosophie nennen. Inklusivismus bedeutet, daß man erklärt, eine zentrale Vorstellung einer fremden religiösen oder weltanschaulichen Gruppe sei identisch mit dieser oder jener zentralen Vorstellung der Gruppe, zu der man selber gehört. Meistens gehört zum Inklusivismus ausgesprochen oder unausgesprochen die Behauptung, daß das Fremde, das mit dem Eigenen als identisch erklärt wird, in irgendeiner Weise ihm unterordnet oder unterlegen sei. Ferner wird ein Beweis dafür, daß das Fremde mit dem Eigenem identisch sei, meist nicht unternommen).[132]

---

[131] See P. Hacker, 'Religiöse Toleranz und Intoleranz im Hinduismus', *Saeculum* 8 (1957), pp. 167–79. Cf. A. Wezler, 'Zur Proklamation religiös-weltanschaulicher Toleranz bei dem indischen Philosophen Jayantabhaṭṭa', *Saeculum* 27 (1976), pp. 329–47; W. Halbfass, *India and Europe*, chapter 22; id., Introduction to *Philology and confrontation* (Albany, 1995), pp. 10, 12 (between these two publications the themes of inclusivism, tolerance and concordance were studied by Halbfass in his *Studies in Kumārila and Śaṅkara* [Reinbek, 1983] and *Tradition and reflection* [Albany, 1991]); P. Granoff, 'Tolerance in the Tantras: its form and function', *JOR* 56–62 (1986–92), pp. 283–302; id., 'The Yogavāsiṣṭha: The continuing search for a context', in: *New horizons of research in Indology* (Silver Jubilee Volume, Poona University, ed. V. N. Jha, Poona 1989), pp. 181–205; and W. Slaje, 'Sarvasiddhānta-siddhānta: On "Tolerance" and "Syncretism" in the Yogavāsiṣṭha', *WZKS* 36 (1992, Supplementband), pp. 307–22.

[132] P. Hacker, 'Inklusivismus', in: G. Oberhammer (ed.), *Inklusivismus, eine indische*

Two forms of inclusivism have been distinguished by Hacker:

(i) One (*op. cit.*, p. 17 ff.), the commonest form according to him, is the inclusivism of weakness and inferiority, where a group or tendency seeks to assert itself and to prevail over another more powerful group or tendency. In this case, what is included remains basically unchanged.

(ii) The second form (*op. cit.*, p. 23 ff.) Hacker has termed the inclusivism of strength and a sense of superiority, where a rising and dynamic group reinterprets the ideas and values of an older and (at least temporarily) inferior group. As an instance of this form in early Buddhism Hacker has cited from the Pali canon – the Theravāda as he called it – the borrowing, adaptation and reinterpretation (Umdeutung) from 'Aryanism' (sic!) of the god Brahmā (p. 23). Hacker finds that in later Buddhism such integration of elements from 'Aryanism' was no longer required. In this second form of inclusivism, what is borrowed is also reinterpreted, purified and ethicized, as in the case of Brahmā (*op. cit.*, pp. 27–28).

In both these main forms as defined by Hacker, inclusivism is restricted to India alone (*op. cit.*, p. 28). He has thus differentiated what he termed inclusivism from religious (and philosophical) tolerance. His definition of it is also different from that usually given of syncretism.

Characteristically, Hacker has contrasted his concept of inclusivism with the Christian reception of ideas from the ancient world, or from paganism, known as just use (*usus iustus*) – in other words the Greek *chrêsis* – which presupposed a careful sifting, transformation and restriction of non-Christian ideas. According to Hacker, what distinguishes Indian inclusivism from Christian *usus iustus* is the fact that the early Chistians resorted to it neither under the overwhelming influence of paganism nor with a desire to deceive the heathen. Rather, they had specific theological grounds for the employment of non-Christian ideas.[133]

Hacker's analyses have been discussed and evaluated by W. Halbfass, G. Oberhammer and A. Wezler in the volume published in 1983 containing his article quoted above entitled 'Inklusivismus'.[134] There, alongside inclusivism, A. Wezler has suggestively called attention to the relevance of the Indian idea of substitution (*ādeśa*), underscoring the

---

Denkform (Vienna, 1983), p. 12.

133 cf. also P. Hacker, '"Topos" und chrêsis', in: *Kleine Schriften*, p. 348.

134 In: G. Oberhammer (ed.), *Inklusivismus, eine indische Denkform*. For further critical discussions of Hacker's concept see the works cited above in n. 131.

importance of this procedure in grammar as well as elsewhere in Indian thought (p. 77 ff.).

Hacker's concept of inclusivism is certainly of great interest for the Indologist, and it may possibly reward further investigation in connexion with the study of the relationship between Buddhism and the ambient religions of India. But Hacker's postulation of 'Aryanization' as the explanation for the presence of Indian divinities (Brahmā, etc.) in the Buddhist cosmos seems not only strangely historicist, but quite simply irrelevant to the matter at hand. And his use here of the notion of the foreign or alien (fremd) is question-begging in so far as it takes as an established premiss the unproved proposition that the largely shared Indian religious substratum is somehow 'alien' to Buddhism.[135] The applicability of Hacker's notion of inclusivism to Buddhism in India and elsewhere is, accordingly, not unproblematic in the form in which he presented it. And it will require further clarification and, no doubt, refinement by scholars accepting his basic conception of it before it could be effectively employed in analysing and describing the basic issue addressed in the present study.

---

[135] For further remarks on Hacker's use of the notion of the foreign and alien, see D. Seyfort Ruegg, 'La traduction de la terminologie technique de la pensée indienne et bouddhique depuis Sylvain Lévi', in: L. Bansat-Boudon and R. Lardinois (ed.), *Sylvain Lévi (1863–1935), Études indiennes* (Bibliothèque de l'École des Hautes Études, Sciences religieuses, vol. CXXX, Turnhout, 2007), Appendix 3.

18. Harihariharivāhanodbhava-Lokeśvara: An example of Hacker's 'inclusivism'?

The composite icon known as Harihariharivāhanodbhava-Lokeśvara provides an interesting test for the application of Hacker's concept of INCLUSIVISM as distinct from tolerance and syncretism. This particular form of Avalokiteśvara is represented iconographically as mounted on Viṣṇu, who rides on his vehicle Garuḍa, which is in turn seated on a lion, all three 'mounts' (*vāhana*) of this form of Lokeśvara being referred to by the same polysemic word *hari*. The name of this divinity accordingly designates Lokeśvara (i.e. Avalokiteśvara) springing up over three *hari*s, namely Hari = Viṣṇu, Hari = Garuḍa and Hari = lion (as a vehicle for Viṣṇu, and for Lokeśvara himself).[136]

This complex image thus appears to differ structurally in a significant way from those icons considered above in which the tutelary divinity is represented dancing, or treading, on one or more prostrate subordinate figures drawn from the Indian pantheon and representing the *laukika* level. A different analysis is therefore in order, as is perhaps suggested additionally by the fact that the word *udbhava* – rather than, e.g., *ākrānta* or *ālīḍha* used in other cases (see above, p. 48) – has been employed to denote the relationship of the main figure (Lokeśvara) to the three *hari*s beneath him.

Horst Brinkhaus has sought to explain this polymorphic figure in terms of Hacker's concept of inclusivism,[137] namely in terms of subordination in the frame of a dualistic (p. 423), and agonistic, confrontation

---

[136] The version of the *Svayambhūpurāṇa* edited by Haraprasad Sastri (Calcutta, 1894), p. 495 (quoted by H. Brinkhaus on p. 425 of his article cited at the beginning of the following note), gives the name as Harihariharivāhanodbhūta (instead of °udbhava). This form of Avalokiteśvara/Lokeśvara is illustrated in the British Library manuscript of the *Kāraṇḍavyūha* reproduced, and dated to c. 1100–1125, by J. Losty, 'An early Indian manuscript of the Kāraṇḍavyūhasūtra', in: D. Mitra and G. Bhattacharya (ed.), *Studies in art and archaeology of Bihar and Bengal* (Delhi, 1989), figure 46 and p. 14.

[137] See H. Brinkhaus, 'Harihariharivāhana [*sic*] Lokeśvara in Nepal', in: *ZDMG Supplement VI* (XXII. Deutscher Orientalistentag [Tübingen 1983], Stuttgart, 1985), pp. 422–9.

(Auseinandersetzung, p. 426) between deities of different origin. And the same scholar has suggested that the icon expresses an act of political self-assertion on the part of Buddhism against the Hindu god Viṣṇu (p. 429).[138] In the two *sādhana*s of the *Sādhanamālā* (nos. 33–34) devoted to this form of Lokeśvara, however, it has to be noted that there is no reference to confrontation or hostility between him and his *vāhana*s. And the fact that this icon is honoured at the important Vaiṣṇava shrine of Cāṅgu Nārāyaṇa in Nepal would seem to suggest that no such hostility or

---

[138] See H. Brinkhaus, *loc. cit.* Already in his article 'References to Buddhism in the Nepāla-māhātmya' *JNRC* 4 (1980), pp. 274-86, Brinkhaus had discussed the appropriateness of the concept of syncretism, preferring the idea of inclusivism. (See also his article 'Tolerance and syncretism in the religious history of the Kathmandu Valley', contributed to the Nepal-Tagung held in Stockholm in June 1987.)

In this way, the Harihariharivāhanodbhava icon has been interpreted by Brinkhaus as what, in the parlance of Hindu iconography, is termed a *saṃhāramūrti* (as opposed to an *anugrahamūrti*). Following this interpretation, the message of the Buddhist icon in question would be in part parallel morphologically to that of the Śarabha icon, which represents this terrible manifestation of Śiva in the composite (therianthropomorphic) form of a man-bird-beast destroying Narasiṃha, himself a hybrid man-lion who annihilates the impious Daitya-king Hiraṇyakaśipu. (It is, however, true that in a certain soteriological perspective there can exist a convergence of *anugraha/upakāra* with *saṃhāra*.)

Concerning the truncated form Harihariharivāhana, it is found also in B. Bhattacharyya, *Indian Buddhist iconography*, pp. 136–37. It has in addition been used by A. Foucher, *Étude sur l'iconographie de l'Inde*, ii (Paris, 1905), p. 36 (beside the full form Harihariharivāhanodbhava on pp. 34, 39); by P. Pal, *Vaiṣṇava iconology in Nepal* (Calcutta, n.d.), p. 71; and by A. Gail, 'Nepalica iconographica', in: B. Kölver, *Aspects of Nepalese traditions* (Stuttgart, 1992), p. 85. This shortened form of the name is attested in a passage of the *Svayambhūpurāṇa* cited by Brinkhaus (p. 425). The full, and probably more correct, form of the name, which is found in the *Sādhanamālā* (nos. 33–34), has been adopted by M.-T. de Mallmann, *Introduction à l'iconographie du tântrisme bouddhique*, p.109. The form Harihariväāhana in S. Lévi, *Le Népal*, i (Paris, 1905), p. 324, is perhaps a slip; Brinkhaus has, however, posited (p. 426) a 'Hariharivāhana' (or a 'Harivāhana') on the basis of a Newari version of the *Svayambhūpurāṇa*.

As for the Harihara Lokeśvara included in B. Bhattacharyya's list entitled '108 manifestations of Avalokiteśvara' in the Appendix to his *Indian Buddhist iconography*, p. 429, it is, apparently, a different form. But see H. Brinkhaus, *loc. cit.*, pp. 426–7, on Hariharavāhana.

For what Lamotte once called 'the Viṣṇuite danger', see his *Histoire du bouddhisme indien*, i, pp. 431–8.

subordination was necessarily felt to exist. On the contrary, and very significantly, in the relevant passage of the *Svayambhūpurāṇa* (cited by Brinkhaus, p. 425) in which Harihariharivāhana is said to be a name of Viṣṇu, the chief deity is described as the protector (*rakṣakṛt*) of the three entities on whom he is mounted.

The interpretation proposed by Brinkhaus moreover takes practically no notice of the compositional member *°udbhava* (or *°udbhūta*) in the name Harihariharivāhanodbhava (and °udbhūta) which would appear to underscore the difference between this polymorphic and accretive figure rising from/over his mounts from those representations which – although they may superficially resemble it[139] – serve, on the contrary, to express a structured opposition of different levels where the superordination of the chief tutelary deity to the entity mounted and danced, or trodden, upon is expressed by words such as *ākrānta* and (*praty*)*ālīḍha*. Being founded on Hacker's idea of inclusivism as subjugation, the interpretation advanced by Brinkhaus may therefore not be altogether appropriate; for, interesting and stimulating though Hacker's notion of inclusivism was, its applicability in Buddhist thought remains problematic, as indicated in the previous section of this study.

---

139 B. Bhattacharyya, *Sādhanamālā*, ii, p. cxxxi, lumped together the Harihariharivāhanodbhava-Lokeśvara figure with those representations which, according to his hypothesis of hostile confrontation and antagonism between Hinduism and Buddhism, expressed the Vajrayānist's 'great hatred towards the gods of the Hindu religion'.

19. Borrowing and substratum models for religious syncretism and/or symbiosis

In seeking to account for certain close intertextual links between Hindu and Buddhist Tantrism, Alexis Sanderson has postulated a form of BORROWING from the former by the latter that appears to exclude (according to his own definition of it) the existence of a common Indian religious SUBSTRATUM. In his article entitled 'Vajrayāna: Origin and function',[140] Sanderson has written (p. 92): 'The problem with the concept of a "religious substratum" or "common cultic stock" is that they are by their very nature entities inferred but never perceived. Whatever we perceive is always Śaiva or Buddhist, or Vaiṣṇava, or something else specific.' He does not further explain this assertion, which it is difficult to reconcile with what has long been supposed to be known concerning the close cultural, religious and philosophical links between Buddhism and Brahmanism/Hinduism and the abundant materials shared in large part by both traditions within the overall frame of Indian civilization. The common ground between the two traditions is in fact so rich as to be overwhelmingly abundant and, indeed, perceptible to the Indologist, and thus anything but 'redundant' (as asserted by Sanderson on p. 87). It might perhaps be that a misunderstanding has arisen concerning the term 'substratum', which (as already remarked above, p. 89.) is not intended to refer to some independent, stand-alone, element (perhaps to be described as 'pre-Aryan' or 'non-Aryan') alongside Brahmanism/Hinduism and Buddhism. Nor should the term be understood as referring only to some 'hidden source' (p. 92). On the contrary, the kind of common ground or substratum here envisaged is a heritage shared by both Brahmanism/Hinduism and Buddhism, and also by Jainism.

In the same article Sanderson has gone on to argue that the expression *gr̥hadevatā* – employed in an entirely meaningful and appropriate manner in the Śaiva *Tantrasādhana* in connexion with a list of both divinities and places (*pīṭha*) sacred to these divinities – has been inappropriately

---

[140] A. Sanderson, 'Vajrayāna: Origin and function' in: *Buddhism into the year 2000* (Proceedings of an international conference held in Bangkok in 1990, and published by the Dhammakaya Foundation, Bangkok, 1994), pp. 87–102.

introduced into the Buddhist *Śaṃvarodaya*'s list of *pīṭhas*. His argument was that this inclusion in the Buddhist text of the divinity *gṛhadevatā* in what is otherwise a list of sacred places is anomalous and unwarranted given that the rest of the list in the Buddhist text is confined solely to *pīṭhas*.[141] And on the basis of this piece of evidence – which could in principle be held to establish the dependence of one text on another – Sanderson has maintained that the Buddhist text borrowed from the Śaiva one without, however, correctly understanding it. According to his opinion as expressed in the same article, then, this example of ill-informed or uncomprehending borrowing makes unsustainable the postulation of a common substratum – or 'cultic stock' as he has termed it – shared in part by both Buddhism and Hinduism.

It is not clear just how conclusive is the case of *gṛhadevatā* observed by Sanderson in his publication of 1990/1994, and further analysis is required to supply a satisfactory answer.[142] For, as is well known, a close and sometimes indissoluble association exists between a sacred place and its presiding divinity. (In Tibet this close association was to amount to virtual equivalence inasmuch as a sacred place and its resident divinity – known in Tibetan as the *yul lha*, *gži bdag*, etc. (*deus/genius loci*) – may there appear as identical. In the Tibetan case of A myes rma chen (rMa chen spom ra), for example, the mountain (*gnas ri*, etc.) and the divinity (*yul lha*, etc.) are practically one.[143])

---

141 See *Saṃvarodayatantra* (ed. Tsuda), vii.12 and ix.18. On *pīṭhas* as possible cross-over points between Hindus and Buddhists see below, p. 111.

142 A bibliography of relevant work by A. Sanderson and his followers has been compiled by E. English, *Vajrayoginī* (Boston, 2002). Amongst the most recent seems to be his 'History through textual criticism in the study of Śaivism, the Pañcarātra and the Buddhist Yoginītantras', in: F. Grimal (ed.), *Les sources et le temps* (Pondicherry, 2001, being the proceedings of a Colloquiuum held there in 1997), pp. 1–47.

143 On Tibetan mountain-deities see A.-M. Blondeau and E. Steinkellner (ed.), *Reflections of the mountain* (Vienna, 1996); and A.-M. Blondeau (ed.), *Tibetan mountain deities, their cults and representations* (Vienna, 1998). The figure of the *sa bdag*, etc., was already noticed by R. de Nebesky-Wojkowitz, *Oracles and demons of Tibet*, and by Tucci in G. Tucci and W. Heissig, *Die Religionen Tibets und der Mongolei* (Stuttgart, 1970). For A myes rma chen in particular see K. Buffetrille, 'The great pilgrimage of A-myes rma-chen: Written tradition, living realities', in: A. W. Macdonald (ed.), *Maṇḍala and landscapes* (New Delhi, 1997), pp. 75–132; and *Pèlerins, lamas et visionnaires: Sources orales et écrites sur les pèlerinages tibetains* (Vienna, 2000).

Now, the general conclusion drawn by Sanderson was not only that the hypothesis of a common substratum is 'redundant' (p. 87), and that no such substratum is ever actually 'perceived' (p. 92), but also that the origin of Buddhist Yoginī Tantras lay specifically in derivative textual borrowing from Śaivism as evidenced by a Buddhist author-redactor's failure to apprehend the true sense of what he was borrowing. This is what he has termed the 'direction of redaction', or 'text-flow', in his article of 1997/2001. In sum, from the tenor of Sanderson's discussion in his article of 1990/1994 it appears that, in order to account for components held in common between Buddhism and Brahmanism/Hinduism, he would operate with a BORROWING PARADIGM/MODEL to the exclusion of a SUBSTRATUM PARADIGM/MODEL which, according to him, is both redundant in theory and unperceived in fact.

It is, however, anything but evident how such a generalized conclusion is to be drawn from the kind of evidence adduced by Sanderson in his article of 1990/1994, or indeed from an accumulation of similar pieces of such evidence.[144] Mere quantity of evidence of this kind can scarcely cancel out the view that Buddhism, having arisen in an Indian matrix and milieu, already shared common ground with Brahmanism/Hinduism.

For Yar lha šam po see below, Appendix I.

Concerning Gr̥hadeva(tā), Sanderson's article does not take account of R. A. Steins's researches, summed up in his article 'La mythologie hindouiste au Tibet', in: R. Gnoli and L. Lanciotti (ed.), *Orientalia Iosephi Tucci memoriae dicata*, iii (Rome, 1988), p. 1410.

144 This is not to deny that the authenticity of a Tantric text has not sometimes been questioned by Buddhist writers. For example, in Tibet, rṄog Ñi ma seṅ ge, a disciple of 'Gos Khug pa lhas btsas, contested the Hevajratantra (a *ma rgyud*); see A khu's *Tho yig* (ed. Lokesh Chandra), no. 12442. On the complex question of Śaiva contamination of Buddhist Vajrayāna practice, see D. Seyfort Ruegg, 'Deux problèmes d'exégèse et de pratique tantriques', in *Tantric and Taoist studies* (R.A. Stein Felicitation Vol., *MCB* 20, 1981), p. 212 ff.

By a student of Sanderson's we are informed that, 'so far', for a quarter of the verses of the *Laghuśaṃvara* it has been possible to demonstrate dependence on Śaiva sources. See R. Mayer, *A scripture of the Ancient Tantra Collection: The Phur-pa bcu-gnyis* (Oxford, 1996), p. 60. In his 'History through textual crticism', in: F. Grimal (ed.), *Les sources et le temps*, p. 41 ff., Sanderson has published further material intended to demonstrate the dependence of the *Laghuśaṃvara* on Śaiva sources.

Equally importantly, the question must arise as to why, in the absence of any shared religious and cultural ground or substratum between them, a Buddhist author or redactor would in the first place have wished to engage in 'pious plagiarism' (as Sanderson called it in 1995) by borrowing from a Śaiva source.[145] For an interaction such as borrowing by Buddhists from Hinduism to have taken place at all, it might be thought that there must have existed a common ground to make such borrowing meaningful to the borrower. Failing this, it is hard to understand what could have motivated the Buddhist to borrow from the Śaiva. In short, *if* (as Sanderson has claimed) it were the case that no common substratum existed between them, why did Buddhists borrow freely from the Śaivas (as he also avers, and as may in fact have been the case in some instances)? Are we perhaps to believe that the Buddhist somehow felt so inferior to the Śaiva that he felt impelled, or indeed compelled, to take over from the latter what he considered a prestige item? (This sort of reasoning is sometimes found in discussions of this kind, but seldom has it been adequately substantiated.) But the sort of uncomprehending and inappropriate borrowing postulated by Sanderson's hypothesis would, it seems, confer little prestige on the borrower, whom it would instead make appear ridiculous. Was Sanderson perhaps thinking of some kind of inclusivism in Hacker's sense (possibly the first form, on which see p. 97 above)? This important, and indeed crucial, question he has unfortunately not attempted to elucidate, or even to pose, in his published article.[146] In order to be able to discover whether his view concerning the redundancy of an Indian substratum/ground bears on a matter of substance and content, or at least of methodology, or whether it turns on a mere difference about terms and labels, it will be necessary to await the

---

[145] The expression 'pious plagiarism' was used by Sanderson in a lecture entitled 'Pious plagiarism: Evidence of the dependence of the Buddhist Yogatantras on Śaiva scriptural sources' cited by Mayer, *op. cit.*, p. 452. But if, *ex hypothesi*, there has existed no common substratum shared by Buddhists and Śaivas that could induce Buddhists to look up to Śaivas, the sense in which this supposed plagiarism would be 'pious' is by no means evident. (In the frame of a substratum model, on the contrary, there will be no reason to postulate 'plagiarism', pious or otherwise.)

[146] Nor did he refer to C. Regamey's 'Motifs vichnouïtes et śivaïtes dans le Kāraṇḍavyūha' already cited several times above.

full publication of his views, which seem to have mainly circulated hitherto in unpublished form.

As things at present stand with Sanderson's view of the matter in its published form – where from postulated instances of borrowing there is deduced a generalized borrowing hypothesis that explicitly sets aside the possibility of an Indian religious and cultural substratum common to Buddhism and Hinduism –, Buddhists are made to appear something like beachcombers fortuitously picking up what came into their hands without understanding its significance, or as indulging more or less randomly in a kind of cargo-cult. (Is this perhaps some form of Lévi-Straussian *bricolage*?).[147]

If, as stated above (p. 90), a BORROWING MODEL and a SUBSTRATUM MODEL are not, automatically and necessarily, totally exclusive of each other – one or the other model being applicable according to the particular case in question, and the two being compatible to the extent that it is precisely a common substratum that could provide the shared ground and required conditions for borrowing to take place meaningfully – it is also clear that 'beachcomber' and 'cargo-cult' variants of the borrowing model are hardly compatible at all with any substratum model that posits a religious and cultural heritage genuinely and meaningfully shared in large part between two (or more) communities.

In sum, the kinds of religious and cultural interactions and linkages that have been at issue here in the case of Tantra and the Vajrayāna are, in principle, to be found not between closed, and hence essentialistically independent, cultural forms, practices and communities but, rather, between related ones which, in their SYMBIOSIS, remain open to processes of INTERCHANGE and OSMOSIS. It is precisely the existence of an Indian religious and cultural substratum, (back)ground or heritage which – very far from being 'redundant'– would have provided common ground and some of the required conditions for such interaction to take place.[148]

---

147 See D. Seyfort Ruegg, 'A note on the relationship between Buddhist and "Hindu" divinities in Buddhist literature and iconology: The laukika/lokottara contrast and the notion of an Indian "religious substratum"', in R. Torella *et al.* (ed.), *Le parole e i marmi* (R. Gnoli Felicitation Volume, Rome, 2001), pp. 735–42.

148 An example of this from later times is the idea of the Buddha as the true Śaṃkara/Śiva which is attested in the **Sarvajñamaheśvarastotra* by Udbhaṭasiddhasvāmin,

In modern times, a common civilization linking Buddhism and Hinduism may still be observed in Nepal, amonst the Newars, where a *b(a)uddhamārgī* and a *śivamārgī* religious and social organization exists juxtaposed in parallel. What might be called a cross-over relation, often described as syncretism, between the two traditions is also found there (see above).[149]

Borrowing in the reverse direction, namely from Buddhism to Hinduism, has been postulated by a number of scholars. Reference can be made to a study in which Gudrun Bühnemann has described Vajrayoginī (Chinnamuṇḍā, accompanied by Vajravarṇanī and Vajravairocanī) as the prototype of the Hindu goddess Chinnamastā (accompanied by Ḍākinī and Varṇinī), and where it has been noted that forms of Ekajaṭā and Mañjughoṣa were also adopted into the Hindu pantheon. In the same article it has been shown how the description of a Hindu divinity found in the *Phetkāriṇītantra*, and in later parallel texts of Hindu Tantra, depends on that of Mahācīnakrama-Tārā which is found in the Buddhist *Sādhanaśatapañcāśikā* and *Sādhanamālā*. In the Hindu Tantras there are also found references to Vasiṣṭha's having received the *mahācīna* tradition of the goddess from Viṣṇu-Buddha in the country of Mahācīna. Bühnemann's conclusion is (p. 479): '... Śāśvatavajra's *sādhana* [no. 101 in B. Bhattacharyya's edition of the *Sādhanamālā*] of Mahācīnakrama-Tārā/Ugra-Tārā (eleventh century) was almost completely incorporated in the Hindu *Phetkāriṇītantra* (thirteenth century?), including not only the iconographical description of the goddess but also the typically

already referred to above, nn. 63, 111, 121. It is also to be noted that this phenomenon is not confined to the relation between Buddhism and Hinduism and that it extends also to Jainism. Thus, in Jinasena's *Ādipurāṇa* (ed. Jain, Chap. 25, v. 66 f.) and in Mānatuṅga's *Bhaktāmarastotra* (25, ed. Jacobi, *Indische Studien* 14 [1876] p. 370), the Tīrthaṃkara Vṛṣabha is addressed by the epithet Śiva or Śaṃkara (and other epithets that are the names of Hindu deities). Cf. J. Schneider, 'Der Buddha als der wahre Śiva', *BIS* 8 (1995), p. 155.

[149] For references see D. Gellner, *Monk, householder, and Tantric priest*; A. Vergati, 'Bouddhisme et caste dans la vallée de Kathmandou', in: F. Fukui and G. Fussman (ed.), *Bouddhisme et cultures locales* (Paris, 1994), p. 53–67; and S. Lienhard, *Diamantmeister und Hausväter* (Vienna, 1999). The situation existing among the Newars is no doubt not all that simple to analyse and characterize in a few words, and some writers have spoken of 'syncretism'. The situation sometimes found in Sri Lanka also is probably no simpler to characterize.

Buddhist Tantric visualization pattern. The goddess's description was adopted by a large number of Hindu texts from the *Phetkāriṇītantra*'s version.'[150]

R. K. van Kooij has on the other hand argued that it is not necessary to think that Ekajaṭā came first to be adopted in Buddhism and thence in Hinduism.[151]

It would seem that a most fertile cross-over point favouring and facilitating such interchange (and borrowing, if such be the correct term here) may have been those *pīṭhas* or sacred sites where both Hindus and Buddhist encountered each other when celebrating their respective rituals of worship and propitiation.[152]

Cases of close contact between Buddhists and Brahmanists/Hindus are, of course, not confined to the area of religion and Tantric ritual alone. An interesting example of sustained interchange and philosophical argument between the two coming from quite another area of activity is to be found in the field of logic and epistemology (*pramāṇa*). It is well known that, from the early centuries of the common era onwards, discussions, polemics and also influences took place between them in this important area of Indian thought. The methods and themes of the Buddhist *pramāṇa* school are known to have very much in common with those of

---

[150] See G. Bühnemann, 'The goddess Mahācīnakrama (Ugra-Tārā) in Buddhist and Hindu Tantrism', *BSOAS* 59 (1996), pp. 472–93. Cf. id., 'Buddhist deities and mantras in the Hindu Tantras I: The *Tantrasārasaṃgraha* and the *Īśānaśivagurudevapaddhati*', *IIJ* 42 (1999), pp. 303–34. See also E. Benard, *Chinnamastā, the aweful Buddhist and Hindu Tantric goddess* (Delhi, 1994), with the review by G. Orofino, *Tibet Journal* 23 (1998), pp. 114–18; and E. English, *Vajrayoginī* (Boston, 2002).

[151] See R. K. van Kooij, 'Some iconographical data from the Kālikāpurāṇa with special reference to Heruka and Ekajaṭā', in: J. E. van Lohuizen-de Leeuw *et al.* (ed.), *South Asian archaeology 1973: Papers from the Second International Conference of South Asia Archaeologists held in the University of Amsterdam* (Leiden, 1974), pp. 161–70. – In a paper on Vajrapūtanā (Vajrayakṣiṇī), who corresponds to Chinnanāsā in the Trilokavijaya *maṇḍala* of the *Tattvasaṃgraha* (ed. Yamada, p. 173), M. Nihom has also postulated a borrowing of Hindu divinities 'inducted into a Buddhist system'; see his article 'Vajrapūtanā, Śītapūtanā and Chinnanāsā: A mantra and its meaning', *BIS* 11/12 (1998), p. 219.

[152] For the geography of several *pīṭhas*, see D. C. Sircar, *The Śākta pīṭhas* (Delhi, 1973).

the Brahmanical schools, which in turn received impulses from Buddhist thinkers. Links in the ninth-tenth centuries between the logical-epistemological school of Dharmakīrti and the Pratyabhijñā school of Kashmir (where Dharmottara, *c.* 740–800, had settled at the invitation of King Jayāpīḍa) have been examined by Raffaele Torella. According to Abhinavagupta's (*c.* 950–1020) *Locana* on Ānandavardhana's *Dhvanyāloka* iii.47, a major treatise on the *dhvani* theory in poetics and semantics, the latter master composed a *Vivṛti* (now lost) on Dharmottara's commentary on Dharmakīrti's *Pramāṇaviniścaya*. Another very significant and indeed pivotal figure with respect to the interaction between Buddhism and Brahmanism was Śaṃkaranandana, to whom Abhinavagupta has referred.[153]

Mention may finally be made here of research which has concluded that the *Yogavāsiṣṭha-Rāmāyaṇa* was a remake of the *Mokṣopāyaśāstra* achieved, *inter alia*, by editing out certain Buddhist features that characterize the older work.[154]

*

To the present writer it seems that this religious and cultural situation described above can perhaps be most appropriately described as SYMBIOSIS, and that the latter may be best understood as existing on the ground of a partly shared religio-cultural heritage. It is no doubt true that, in the course of the long and complex history of Buddhism in South Asia, BORROWING and ENCULTURATION of Brahmanical/Hindu elements in

---

[153] See R. Torella, 'The Pratyabhijñā and the logical-epistemological school of Buddhism', in: T. Goudriaan (ed.), *Ritual and speculation in early Tantrism* (Studies in honor of André Padoux, Albany, 1992), pp. 327–45. See also the same scholar's *The Īśvarapratyabhijñākārikā of Utpaladeva with the author's Vṛtti* (Rome, 1994), Introduction, pp. xv, xxi f.; and 'The Word in Abhinavagupta's *Bṛhad-Vimarśinī*', in R. Torella *et al.* (ed.), *Le parole et i marmi*, ii, p. 867 ff. – On Śaṃkaranandana, the author of a critique of theism (the *Īśvarāpākaraṇasaṃkṣepa*), see nn. 121 and 62 above. For Abhinavagupta's references to him, see R. Gnoli, *Pramāṇavārttikam of Dharmakīrti* (Rome, 1960), pp. xxiii–xxiv. – It is to be noted that a critical discussion of the Pratyabhijñā doctrine is ascribed to the logician and epistemologist Jitāri, a teacher of Atiša Dīpaṃkaraśrījñāna and Durvekamiśra.

[154] See W. Slaje, 'Observations on the making of the *Yogavāsiṣṭha* (*caitta*, *naňartha* and *vaḥ*)', in R. Torella *et al.* (ed.), *Le parole e i marmi*, ii. pp. 771–81.

Indian Buddhism did take place from time to time; but it would nonetheless seem preferable to consider that when it happened this process took place against a partly common background, and in the frame of SYMBIOSIS.

In summary, the matter thus engages the fundamental socio-religious problem of the interrelationships existing between Brahmanism/Hinduism and Buddhism which has been discussed earlier in the present study. To speak of a characterized borrowing by the latter from the former – or, indeed, by the former from the latter – without recognizing the existence of a certain ground shared by both would appear to posit each as a free-standing, fixed, and isolated entity, an essentialization of the two traditions that would tend to minimize their participation in a common historico-social process in South Asia. This view of the matter does not appear to correspond to the situation that actually existed in ancient and mediaeval India. And it seems hardly credible simply to invoke here a Buddhist need, or desire, to emulate, to legitimate itself, and somehow to gain prestige, by borrowing from Hinduism. If the two did not partly share a common heritage and religio-cultural (back)ground, it is hard to understand why Buddhists would have been motivated to emulate Hinduism and why they would have felt that the latter would bring them legitimation and prestige.

Our questioning of a generalized, and exclusive, borrowing model that sets aside the existence of a common Indian substratum by no means commits us, however, to the kind of reductionism that would simply regard Indian Buddhists as Hindus (see above, pp. 1–2 on the notion of 'Hindutva', and p. 89).

In the areas of iconography and aesthetics, the existence of an artistic idiom that was shared, at least in large part, by both Buddhists and Hindus (and other Indian religions) is attested in Indian art history. This is supported by the observation made by scholars that from the same artists' workshops there have sometimes emerged images to be used by both of these religions (and also by the Jainas).[155] For its explanation this

[155] See e.g. Debala Mitra, *Bronzes from Achutrajpur* (Delhi, 1978), pp. 145–50; and R. C. Sharma, *Buddhist art, Mathura school* (New Delhi, 1995), pp. 14–15. On finds of Buddhist, Hindu and Jaina images all at the same site (or on the absence of such finds), and possibly (but not necessarily) from the same workshops, see, e.g., S.

fact does not necessarily presuppose the BORROWING MODEL in any generalized and exclusive sense, and it can equally well be accounted for in terms of SYMBIOSIS in the frame of a SUBSTRATUM MODEL.

Huntington, *The "Pāla-Sena" schools of sculpture*, pp. 97 and 104 (Bodh Gayā); pp. 24, 111 (Nālandā); pp. 161 n. 30 and 193 (Pāhāṛpur); pp. 53, 104 (Kurkihār); and S. K. Sarasvati and K. C. Sarkar, *Kurkihar, Gaya and Bodh-Gaya* (Rajshahi, 1936), p. 18 (on Kurkihār). But on the different artistic styles belonging to Buddhism and Hinduism see, e.g., S. Huntington, *op. cit.*, p. 133.

20. Vaiṣṇava and Śaiva elements in the Kālacakra

In the Kālacakra – a current of Vajrayānist Yoga, ritual and thought which took final shape in the tenth and early eleventh centuries and is classified among the *rnal 'byor bla med kyi rgyud* (*yogānuttara/yoganir-uttara-tantra*), specified sometimes as a *gñis med kyi rgyud* 'Advaya-tantra' and sometimes as a *ma rgyud* 'Mother Tantra' (Yoginītantra) – we find a universalist outlook showing awareness of Indian Tīrthika (i.e. non-Buddhist) ideas and even of Islam. The Kālacakra was indeed well on the way to developing a Buddhist xenology in addition to an eschatology that envisages, on the exoteric level, a kind of apocalyptic Armageddon in which the twenty-fifth and last Kalkin-king of Sambhala/Śambhala, Raudra (Mahā)Cakrin, is pitted against irreligious Tāyins in a great struggle against barbarians (*mlecchayuddha*), a *raudra-yuddha*, at the close of the Age of Discord (*kaliyuga* = *rtsod pa'i dus*) (i.160).[156]

In a verse of the Abhiṣeka-chapter of the *(Laghu)Kālacakratantra*, mention is made of the virtuous and learned Yogin of pure heart who, in his behaviour and practice (*caryā*), appears not only as a Buddhist but also as a follower of other religious practices (iii.169):

bauddhaḥ śaivo 'tha nagno bhagava iti tathā snātako brāhmaṇo vā
kāpālī luptakeśo bhavatu sitapaṭaḥ kṣetrapālas tu kaulaḥ/
maunī cônmattarūpo 'py akaluṣahṛdayaḥ paṇḍitaś chātra eva
yogī siddhyarthahetoḥ sakalaguṇanidhir labdhatattvo narendra//

---

[156] Diachronically, the word *tāyin* (Tib. *stag gzig*) employed to denote peoples of western Asia may well derive from the Arabic *ṭayyi*, as proposed by J. Newman (*JIABS* 21 [1998], pp. 316–19, 333). Synchronically, within the semantic system of Indo-Aryan, it seems in effect to enter into a paronomastic and, indeed, antiphrastic relation (by 'enantiosis') with its homonym, and virtual antonym, *tāyin* (Tib. *skyob pa*) denoting the Tathāgata or Buddha. The use of *tāyin* as an ethnonym appears to have been reinforced by the ethnonym *tājika* 'Tajik' (cf. Pahlavī *tāzig*, Parthian *tāžīg*) – i.e. Arab –, as is suggested by its Tibetan equivalent *stag gzig/ta zig*. (Cf. W. Sundermann, 'An early attestation of the name Tajiks', *Orientalia Lovanensia Analecta* 47 [1993], p. 163 ff.) (In Middle Indo-Aryan, not only does initial *y*(*a*) become *j*(*a*) but intervocalic *-y-* > *-yy-/-jj-*; and in Gāndhārī Prakrit *-y-* > *-ś-* = [ž]; see O. von Hinüber, *Das ältere Mittelindisch im Überblick*, § 213; on the letter *ysa* = [za] see *ibid.* § 193.)

(*saṅs rgyas pa daṅ ži ba pa'am gcer bu skal ldan žes daṅ de bžin gtsaṅ gnas bram ze'am//*
thod pa can daṅ skra 'bal daṅ ni gos dkar dag daṅ žiṅ skyoṅ rigs can dag daṅ thub pa daṅ//
bsñon pa'i gzugs can dag daṅ sdig pa med pa'i sems ldan mkhas pa daṅ ni slob gñer ba yaṅ ruṅ//
rnal 'byor pa ni dṅos grub don slad mtha' dag yon tan gter te de ñid thob pa'o mi yi dbaṅ//)

A Buddhist he may be, or a Śaiva, a naked [Paramahaṃsa], one called 'fortunate'(?), as well as one having completed his Vedic studies, a Brahman, a Kāpālin, a shaven-headed [?, Kṣapaṇaka], one dressed in white, a Kṣetrapāla, a Kaula, one who observes silence, also one appearing intoxicated: having an unsullied heart, a scholar, a student even, for the sake of spiritual realization the Yogin is a receptacle of all qualities, one who has attained the true, O king.

The Kālacakra is, indeed, very much aware of Brahmanism/Hinduism. In its Lokadhātu-chapter the *LKT* describes the Jina's *jñānakāya* as the source of many religious concepts, including even the Veda and the Tarkaśāstra (i.156). And the whole of the end of this chapter (i.150–170, a section not commented upon, however, in Śrī Puṇḍarīka's *Vimalaprabhāṭīkā*), reference is made to eight of Viṣṇu's Avatāras (from Matsya to Kṛṣṇa inclusive, and thus excluding both the Buddhāvatāra and Kalki[n]) (i.153, 168). In *LKT* ii.161 ff. reference is made to the Veda and the teachings of Brahmā, Viṣṇu, Śiva, the Jainas, etc.; the *Vimalaprabhā* (p. 256.2) comments interestingly that, when considered as *lokasaṃvṛti*, *sarvadarśanasiddhānta* serves worldly success (*laukikasiddhi*) (compare p. 139 below).

The Kālacakra takes notice in addition of the religion of its neighbours to the (north)west. Reference is thus made to a list of personages and prophets recognized in Islam (i.154).[157] In (*Laghu*)*Kālacakratantra* i.26–27, moreover, Mecca (Skt. Makha-viṣaya) is mentioned specifically (see also i.160 and ii.50), as is the date (622) of the *hijra* of Muhammad (Madhumati = sBraṅ rtsi'i blo gros ~ Madhupati = sBraṅ bdag). In the Kālacakra reckoning, this event took place 403 years previous to the last year of the sexagenary cycle ending in 1026 and, thus,

[157] On this subject see G. Orofino, 'Apropos of some foreign elements in the Kālacakratantra', in E. Steinkellner *et al.* (ed.), *Proceedings of the 7th Seminar of the International Association for Tibetan Studies* (Vienna 1997), pp. 714–24; and J. Newman, 'Islam in the Kālacakra Tantra', *JIABS* 21 (1998), pp. 320–3.

some 1400 years after the Buddha's preaching of the *Kālacakra-Mūla-tantra* (also according to the chronology of the Kālacakra).[158] Reference is also made to Baghdad (i.154).

In the very extended explanation, entitled *Paramākṣarajñānasiddhi*, on verse 127 of the Jñāna-chapter of the *Laghukālacakratantra* and included in Śrī-Puṇḍarīka's *Vimalaprabhā*, we find a discussion of the doctrines of various non-Buddhist schools, and thus of doxography and even a kind of xenology.

The Kālacakra has sometimes been linked in particular with the Madhyamaka school of Buddhist thought (see for example *VP* ii.173, and the *Paramākṣarajñānasiddhi* in *VP* v.127 [III, pp. 86–87]. And at *VP* ii. 177 we are told that the Madhyamaka rejects (*nirākr̥-*) the position (*siddhānta*) of the heterodox Tīrthika. Yet what is equivalent, on the surface-level (*saṃvr̥tyā*) or on the explicit level (*vivr̥tyā*), to the Word of the Fully Awakened One (*sambuddhavacanasama*) is not to be refuted (*dūṣaṇīya*). The *LKT* ii.177 indeed states:

ityādi jñānahetoḥ prakaṭayati mahau deśanāṃ kālacakraḥ

---

[158] Beside Makha(viṣaya) (Mecca) found in the Sanskrit (and Ma kha in the corresponding Tibetan), (the Tibetan translation of) the *Padminī* on *LKT* i.160 reads Ma ga. It is not impossible that in the tradition a certain confusion or conflation has on occasion arisen between this land of Makha/Maga and the Iranian magus-priests known in Sanskrit as Maga (Tib. Ma ga). The Maga are mentioned in the Mīmāṃsā-chapter of Bhāviveka's sixth-century *Madhyamakahr̥dayakārikā* (ix.31) with the *Tarkajvālā* (D, f. 281b–284a, which speaks of both Ma ga and Par sig = Pārasika) (cf. C. Lindtner, 'Buddhist references to old Iranian religion', *Acta Iranica* 12 [1988], pp. 433–44); the 'Dru bā na' of the Par sig is mentioned in Avalokitavrata's comment on Bhāviveka's *Prajñāpradīpa* (D, wa, f. 114a5). On Indian sun-priests in the Purāṇas, see H. von Stietencron, *Indische Sonnenpriester: Sāmba und die Śākadvipīya-Brāhmaṇa* (Wiesbaden, 1966); A. Gail, 'Der Sonnenkult im alten Indian – Eigengewächs oder Import?', *ZDMG*128 (1978), pp. 333–48; and F. Chenet, 'Les Saura de l'Inde: le brillant échec d'une identité religieuse inclusiviste', *JA* 281 (1993), pp. 317–92.

Concerning the Kālacakra's 403-year calculation, see D. Seyfort Ruegg, 'Notes on some Indian and Tibetan reckonings of the Buddha's Nirvāṇa and the duration of his Teaching', in: H. Bechert (ed.), *The dating of the historical Buddha*, Part 2 (Göttingen, 1992), p. 271 f.; G. Orofino, *Sekoddeśa* (Rome, 1994), p. 15 f.; J. Newman, 'The epoch of the Kālacakra Tantra', *IIJ* 41 (1998), pp. 319–49; id., *JIABS* 21 (1998), p. 337; and D. Pingree, 'Ravikās in Indian astronomy and the Kālacakra', in: R. Torella *et al.* (ed.), *Le parole e i marmi* (R. Gnoli Felicitation Volume, Rome, 2001), pp. 659–60.

puṃsāṃ cittānusārāṃ mṛdukaṭhinaparāṃ vāsanāyā balena/
cittaṃ vai bhāvarāgaiḥ sphaṭikavad upadhād rāgatāṃ yāti yasmāt
tasmād dharmo na kaścit svaparakulagato yoginā dūṣaṇīyaḥ//

(*žes pa la sogs bstan pa dus kyi 'khor los sa la rab tu gsal mdzad ye šes slad du ste//*
'jam daṅ sra daṅ gžan pa'i bag chags stobs kyis skyes bu rnams kyi sems kyi rjes su 'braṅ ba ste//
sems ni ṅes par dṅos po'i tshon gyis ñe bar bžag pa dag las šel bžin tshon ldan ñid 'gyur ba//
gaṅ yin de phyir raṅ gžan rigs su gyur pa'i chos ni 'ga' yaṅ rnal 'byor pa yis sun mi dbyuṅ//)

According to this [teaching], for the sake of knowledge, in the world [the Lord] Kālacakra expounds to men a teaching in accord with [their] minds, concerned as it is with the gentle, hard and the other in virtue of [their] mental impregnations. Like a crystal, the mind through conditioning indeed becomes coloured by the colorations of things. Hence the Yogin should refute no *dharma* whatever belonging to his own or to another's spiritual family (*kula*).

This view does not appear to represent a mere unreflective syncretism, any more than it is clearly an example of Paul Hacker's inclusivism. Nor does it seem to be either simple tolerance or mere relativism and indifferentism. The criterion here, a quite pragmatic one, is soteriological salutariness and usefulness, at least provisionally and for a given stage of development. As the *VP* (iii.169) has observed, one may adopt various forms of behaviour (*caryā*) until spiritual realization (*siddhi*) is achieved. This would apply to traditions with which Buddhism shared some common ground or substratum. On the contrary, a tradition with which Buddhism shared no common ground is rejected as a barbarian one (*mlecchadharma*), a bad one (*kudharma*).

It is no simple and straightforward matter precisely and unambiguously to characterize the Kālacakra with respect, synchronically, to its attitude towards and, diachronically, to its historical relationship to Brahmanism/Hinduism.

In the iconography of the Ādibuddha Śrī-Kālacakra, one of whose feet rests on Maheśvara/Rudra, we find an example of a SUPERORDINATION schema along the lines of the *laukika* : *lokottara* model discussed earlier. And in the *maṇḍala* of Kālacakra we find the DECENTRING, OF PERIPHERALIZATION, of certain inferior, mundane divinities, a procedure which was also discussed earlier.[159] But neither the process of SUPERORDINATION nor that of PERIPHERALIZATION evoked in this study seems fully to account for the various features of Kālacakra thought just described, any more than do the concepts of SYNCRETISM (with its connotation of the lumping together of heterogeneous elements), ENCULTURATION (implying importation from an exogenous source), and either TOLERANCE or INDIFFERENTISM. And whereas the Kālacakra does indeed include within itself materials from Brahmanism/Hinduism in a sort of universalist, and so to say cosmopolitan, SYMBIOSIS, the concept of an interreligious INCLUSIVISM as defined by Paul Hacker does not seem appropriate either; for while indeed UTILIZING, and even INTERNALIZING, them, at the same time, in its own particular xenology, the Kālacakra 'parallelizes' these Brahmanical/Hindu materials, which it continues to regard as 'other', and no doubt as subordinate, from its own Buddhist view of things.

In the Kālacakra (as elsewhere in Buddhism) there is found a soteriological UNIVERSALISM that is closely associated with the deployment, by a Buddha or Bodhisattva, of salvific expedient devices (*upāya*), and with an EMANATIONIST and DOCETIC view involving ectypal *nirmāṇa*s, etc., that is characteristic of the Mahāyāna and Vajrayāna. Whether 'syncretism' or 'symbiosis' is better suited to describe this complex situation is perhaps a matter of definition of terms. At all events, historically and analytically distinguishable models and paradigms have not necessarily been kept clearly apart in the sources under discussion.

---

[159] See above, p. 77; and below, Appendix I.

21. Kalkin in the Kālacakra

Kalki mentioned above (p. 77) is as a proper name very well known from Hindu literature, where the name designates the tenth Avatāra of Viṣṇu.[160] An Upapurāṇa, the *Kalkipurāṇa*, is devoted to this emanation of Viṣṇu.[161] In this text Kalki is incarnated as the son of Viṣṇuyaśas and

---

160 The etymon of the word *kalki(n)* is uncertain, as is its declension. The nominative singular form *kalkiḥ* is not uncommon in Hindu texts, whilst in Buddhist sources the nom. sing. form *kalkī* is usual. *Kalkī*, from the stem *kalkin*, is seemingly derived (with the possessive suffix *-in-*) from *kalka* 'paste; dirt, filth'. And E. Abegg has suggested that the name may be dysphemistic; see his *Der Messiasglaube in Indien und Iran* (Berlin, 1928), p. 57 n. 3. The word is, however, translated into Tibetan by *rigs ldan* (*rigs* = *kula/gotra*, which has then led to the inappropriate Sanskritization 'Kulika', which applies rather to the Nāgarāja Kulika); this lends no support to the supposition that the person concerned was named so to say by enantiosis or antiphrasis. (Could the translation of *kalkin* by Tib. *rigs ldan* have been somehow induced by the references to the *kalkigotra* at *LKT* i.160 and *VP* i, I, p 22.8–9 and p. 25.17?) But in view of the alternation *r/l* in Indo-Aryan languages, M. Mayrhofer (*Kurzgefaßtes etymologisches Wörterbuch des Altindischen* [Heidelberg, 1956], p. 183) has pointed out that the word may be derived from *karka* 'white horse', a white horse being in fact the mount of Kalki(n). In Kṣemendra's *Daśāvatāracarita* the form *karkyavatāra* is in fact found. As for *karki/karkin* < *karka* 'crab', it is the sign cancer in the zodiac which does not seem to be relevant here. For the Kālacakra, R. Gnoli (see R. Gnoli and G. Orofino, *Nāropā, Iniziazione* [Milan, 1994], p. 63; and R. Gnoli, 'La realizzazione della conoscenza del Supremo immoto', Supplemento No. 1 alla *Rivista degli Studi Orientali* [Rome, 1997], p. 70) has suggested that Kalkin means something like cement-possessor by reason of Kalkin's uniting ('cementing together') the castes; Gnoli refers to *VP* v.127 [III, p. 96.25]) where we read: *kalko nāma varṇāvarṇānām ekīkaraṇam/ sa kalko 'syâstîti kalkī, na kalkena vinā, sa eva kalkī.* See also *VP* i (I, p. 22.8–9): *kalaśaguhyaprajñājñānābhiṣekataḥ sarvavarṇānām ekakalko bhavati, sa kalko 'syâstîti kalkī, tasya gotraṃ kalkigotram.* On the importance of the association with the horse see below.

Whilst in Hinduism Kalki(ḥ) is the proper name of the tenth Avatāra of Viṣṇu, in the Kālacakra the appellative is an epithet common to twenty-five rulers of Sambhala.

As for the ninth Avatāra, the *buddhāvatāra*, he is found in the *Daśāvatāracarita* of Kṣemendra (eleventh c.) and the *Gītagovinda* of Jayadeva (twelfth c.).

161 See E. Abegg, *Der Messiasglaube in Indien und Iran.* For this Purāṇa, which is presented as a continuation of the *Bhāgavata*, see L. Rocher, *The Purāṇas* (Wiesbaden, 1986), p. 183.

Sumati in Sambhala/Śambhala-grāma. His rôle is to conquer the barbarians (*mleccha*) at the end of the aeon, restore the Vedic Dharma and annihilate the Buddhist Dharma (propagated, in the Kaliyuga, by the Buddhāvatāra, Viṣṇu's ninth Avatāra, as a stratagem employed by this great god in order to destroy the irreligious). Kalki's mount is a (winged) white horse. A minor Avatāra of Viṣṇu linked with the horse (and sometimes showing a theriomorphic, or hippocephalic, form), but who is kept quite separate from Kalki, is Hayagrīva – the 'Horse-necked' (or 'Horse-headed') –, in which manifestation, and in order to rescue the Veda, this great god vanquishes a Daitya. In Buddhist Vajrayāna, Hayagrīva (Tib. rTa mgrin, identified with Padmāntaka), whose human head is surmounted by that of a horse, is a prominent figure often considered a *nirmāṇa* of Avalokiteśvara, who in turn is associated with his horse, the king of horses (*aśvarāja*) Bālāha/Valāha(ka) (also the name of a horse of Viṣṇu's).[162]

Now, the Buddhist Kālacakra in particular shares certain noteworthy features with Viṣṇuism. In it (see *[Laghu)]Kālacakratantra* i.158 f. and ii.48, and *Vimalaprabhā* v.127 [III, pp. 96–97]), the Kalkin Raudra Cakrin (Rigs ldan drag po 'khor lo can) is connected with Sambhala, and its capital Kalāpa, as its twenty-fifth Kalkin-ruler.[163] His predecessor as first Kalkin-ruler (and eighth Dharma-king of Sambhala counting from King Sucandra [Zla ba bzaṅ po], the Buddha's interlocutor in the *Kālacakratantra*) was Mañjuśrī-Yaśas ('Jam dpal grags pa), the promulgator (*saṃgītikāra*, *VP* I, p. 25) of the (*Laghu*)*Kālacakratantra*, who is consid-

---

[162] See R. van Gulik, *Hayagrīva, the Mantrayānic aspect of horse-cult in China and Japan* (Leiden, 1935). Hayaśīrṣa/Hayaśiras/Hayāsya/Aśvaśiras, the 'Horse-headed', is also a form of Viṣṇu. Hayagrīva is in addition the name of a Daitya vanquished by the Matsyāvatāra of Viṣṇu. – On the horse Bālāha (etc.) see also n. 240 below.

[163] In the Kālacakra, Sambhala is generally situated to the north of the Śītā/Sītānādī, a river often identified as the Tarim in Central Asia. In Hindu literature Sambhala/Śambhala has been placed in India itself.
On the perhaps not totally unrelated idea of Śvetadvīpa, the abode of Viṣṇu/Nārāyaṇa and the hyperborean 'Isle of the Blest' located in the 'far north', or to the north-west of Meru, see W. E. Clark, 'Śvetadvīpa and Śākadvīpa', *JAOS* 39 (1919), pp. 209–42; K. Rönnow, 'Some remarks on Śvetadvīpa', *BSOS* 5 (1928–30), pp. 253–84; and T. Oberlies, 'Die Textgeschichte der Śvetadvīpa-Episode des Nārāyaṇīya (Mbh 12, 321–326)', in: P. Schreiner (ed.), *Nārāyaṇīya-Studien* (Wiesbaden, 1997), pp. 75–118.

ered an emanation of Mañju(śrī)ghoṣa, a Bodhisattva of the tenth stage. The second Kalkin-ruler of Sambhala, Śrī-Puṇḍarīka (Padma dkar po), the author of the *Vimalaprabhā* (*ṭīkākāra*), is an emanation of Lokeśvara the lotus-holder.[164] In the Kālacakra, Kalkin is less a proper name than an epithet or title of the twenty-five rulers of Sambhala.

Kalkin Raudra Cakrin is associated with what are called *śailāśva*s (*LKT* i.161; *VP* v.127 [III, pp. 96–97]) (*śailāśva* is rendered in Tibetan sometimes as *ri'i rta* 'mountain horse' and sometimes as *rdo'i rta* 'stone horse'). This scenario is associated with Mount Kailāsa (i.161). At the time of the great Armageddon at the end of the Age of Discord (*kali-yuga*), after having entered into the supreme 'equine concentration' (*paramāśvasāmādhi*), and after having thereby radiated forth *paramāśva*s with which he will melt the minds of the *mleccha*s, he will, unshakeable like a mountain (*śailavan niṣkampaḥ*), fix the irreligious in his Dharma (*VP* v.127 [p. 96.26–28]). The Kalkin Raudra will thus usher in the Golden Age of perfection and truth (*kṛdyuga*, i.e. the *kṛtayuga/satya-yuga*).

In his great struggle against his foe, the Kalkin Raudra Cakrin will be accompanied by a multitude of *brahmarṣi*s from Kalāpa (*VP* i [I, p. 22.4], as opposed to the *duṣṭarṣi*s, *VP* v.127 [III, pp. 94–96]) headed by the sage Sūryaratha (*VP* i [I, pp. 26–28]). Raudra will be assisted in this struggle by Hari (i.e. Viṣṇu), Rudra or Hara (i.e. Śiva), by Skanda and Gaṇendra (*LKT* i.161–3), and also by Hanumant (i.163; ii.48). Finally, in the Golden Age he will be succeeded as ruler by eight Avatāras of Viṣṇu, or at least by eight kings having the names of Matsya, Kūrma, etc., down to Kṛṣṇa (i.168).

Whilst in the Lokadhātu-chapter of the Tantra (*LKT* i) the struggle in question, including Raudra Cakrin's epic battle, is described as due to take place in the external world – the macrocosm or *bāhya* = *phyi* level of Kālacakra hermeneutics –, its Adhyātma-chapter (*LKT* ii) interiorizes the battle with the barbarians, making it take place within the exercitant-Yogin's own body (*svadeha*) (ii.48–50) – the microcosm or *adhyātman* =

---

164 The list of the kings and Kalkin-rulers of Sambhala is given at *VP* i, pp. 25–26. See D. Reigle, 'The lost Kālacakra Mūla Tantra on the kings of Śambhala', *Kālacakra Research Publications* i (Talent, 1986); and J. Newman, 'A brief history of the Kālacakra', in: Geshe Lhundub Sopa *et al.* (ed.), *The wheel of Time* (Ithaca, 1985).

naṅ level of the Tantra's hermeneutics.[165] We are in fact told explicitly that the *mlecchayuddha* located in the Makha-viṣaya – a battle compared with a magical show (*māyārūpa*) – is in fact no ordinary war, for it takes place within the Yogin (*dehamadhye*, ii. 50). At the same time it is probably not without significance that, as a common noun, the word *raudra* designates the last of the four kinds of ritual activity (*[']phrin las*, *karman*) employed by an enlightened and compassionate being for the benefit of sentient beings (namely *śānti* = *ži ba*, *puṣṭi* = *rgyas pa*, *vaśī-karaṇa* = *dbaṅ [byed]*, and *raudra[karman]* = *drag po['i las]*, the *dgra las* or *abhicāra* = *mṅon spyod*). These procedures might then be thought of as forming part of the salvific 'mesocosm' of ritual and practice placed between microcosm and macrocosm, and corresponding to the Yogic and mystical (*gžan*) level of Kālacakra hermeneutics.

At *LKT* i.163 and ii.48 Raudra Cakrin's foe, the king of the *mleccha*s and lord of the demons (*danupati*), has received the enigmatic name Kr̥nmati (Tib. Byed pa'i blo, Byas/Byis pa'i blo).[166] According to *LKT* ii.48-50 and to the accompanying *VP* (see also *VP* v.127 [p. 97]), allegorically speaking – and within the Yogin's own body (*svadeha*) in the Kālacakra's homology between microcosm and macrocosm –, the counterpart of Cakrin (that is, the Kalkin Raudra) is *vajrin* (i.e. the *cittavajra*); the counterparts of the Twelve Gods (*surapati*, i.e. Īśvara, etc.) are the stopped *aṅga*s (i.e. the twelve members of production in dependence, *pratītyasamutpāda*);[167] the counterpart of the Kalkin is exact Gnosis (*samyagjñāna*); the counterparts of the serving foot-soldiers, elephants, horses, and chariots of the Kalkin's (i.e. Raudra's) four-fold host are the Immeasurables (viz. the four *brahmavihāra*s *maitrī*, *karuṇā*, *muditā*, and *upekṣā*); the counterpart of the Kalkin's helper Rudra is the *pratyeka*(*buddhajñāna*); the counterpart of his helper Hanumant is the

---

[165] The parallel with the inner and external *jihad* of Islam is noteworthy. But there is of course no need to assume a dependence, and interiorization is a regular and not infrequent process in Indian and Buddhist thought. A kind of parallel seems to be provided by the 'secular' epic of the warrior king Ge sar which, at the hands of a 'Ju Mi pham or a Ka lu Rin po che, has undergone a sort of sublimation and interiorization in hamony with religio-philosophical principles of Buddhism.

[166] On this personage cf. J. Newman, *JIABS* 21 (1998), p. 329.

[167] Twelve Lords of the Gods are mentioned also in Bu ston's comment on *LKT* i.161, but without further detailed specification.

śrāvaka(jñāna); the counterpart of the evil barbarian lord (*mlecchendra-duṣṭa*) is one's sullied mind (*pāpacitta*); and the counterpart of Kr̥nmati, the purveyor of Ill (*duḥkhadātr̥*), are the unsalutary factors (*akuśala-[karma]patha*). Yogic identifications of Mañjuśrī and Lokanātha (Puṇḍarīka), the first two Kalkin-rulers, are also supplied (ii.50).

Curiously, in its account of Viṣṇu's Avatāras found in Purāṇa-literature, the *Paramākṣarajñānasiddhi* (in the *Vimalaprabhā* v.127 [III, p. 95. 27–28]) has alluded to Buddha/Vāsudeva as the ninth Avatāra (whilst in the standard lists Kr̥ṣṇa/Vāsudeva is the eighth Avatāra, as he is also in *LKT* i.153), Kalki being the tenth.[168] (Does this rather enigmatic allusion perhaps point to an attempt at the unification of the figures of Kr̥ṣṇa-Vāsudeva and Buddha?[169]) At *Vimalaprabhā* v.127 (III, p. 96.10), where views of Paurāṇikas are recorded, Kalkin, the son of Yaśas, is even referred to as Vāsudeva.[170]

Notwithstanding its considerable knowledge and, indeed, internalization of a very large body of Brahmanical/Hindu materials, the Kālacakra school of thought remains well aware of its own difference from the Hindu Tīrthikas. This becomes clear, for example, from *LKT* ii.162-171 (cf. the *VP ad loc.*) where the views of Hindu Tīrthikas are discussed,[171]

---

[168] On the Avatāras, see L. Rocher, *The Purāṇas* , p. 106 ff., with P. Hacker, 'Zur Entwicklung der Avatāralehre', *WZKSO* 4 (1960), pp. 47–70.

[169] No doubt – a fact sometimes overlooked – it is not without significance that several Buddhist masters and translators into Tibetan have borne the name Kr̥ṣṇa, and that Kāṇha/Kr̥ṣṇa is the name of the author of Buddhist *Dohā*s and of the author of the *Yogaratnamālā* on the Hevajratantra. On Viṣṇuism and the place of Nārāyaṇa within Buddhism, for example in the *Kāraṇḍavyūha* and the *Ratnagotravibhāga*, see above, p. 23. Cf. C. Regamey, 'Motifs vichnouites et śivaïtes dans le Kāraṇḍavyūha', in: *Études tibétaines dédiées à la mémoire de Marcelle Lalou*, pp. 411–32.

[170] It is perhaps not altogether clear whether Yaśas here is Viṣṇuyaśas, i.e. Kalki himself, or the father of the Kalki of the Paurāṇikas – who have been quoted in this passage of the Paramākṣarajñānasiddhi included in the *Vimalaprabhā* –, or Mañjuśrī-Yāsas, the predecessor of the Kalkin Raudra of the Kālacakra. R. Gnoli in his translation (cited above in n. 160), p. 70, takes this Yaśas to be the father of the Kalkin Puṇḍarīka of the Kālacakra.

[171] See also *Vimalaprabhā* i, p. 41: *iha prādeśikī hariharādīnāṃ dharmadeśanā bauddhair nânumodanīyā sarvasattvakr̥payā rahitā saṃsāraduḥkhadāyinī mithyāhaṃkārakāriṇī jātivādābhimāninī*; and v.127 (*Paramākṣarajñānasiddhi*, pp. 91–100).

together with those of the Lokāyatas and Cārvākas (ii.164ab, 175), the Tāyins/Mlecchas (ii.164cd, 174), the Kṣapaṇakas (ii.165), and certain other Buddhist schools of thought (Vaibhāṣika, Sautrāntika, and Yogācāra, ii.173; cf. *VP* v.127 [pp. 86–87). And when the Buddha is said to be the source of both Veda and Tarkaśāstra (*LKT* i.156), this is no doubt to be understood as an expression of ectypal EMANATIONISM in its DOCETIC form. The supramundane beings of Buddhism are indeed said to emanate docetically as *nirmāṇa*s the sages and teachers of other systems beneficial to living beings.[172]

As observed above (p. 119), whether this complex situation, found in sources belonging to the end of the first millennium and the beginning of the second millennium of the common era, is best described as SYNCRETISM OR SYMBIOSIS is perhaps a matter of definitions and terminology. In any case, it appears sometimes to reflect a kind of COSMOPOLITANISM in keeping with an aspiration towards soteriological UNIVERSALISM that operates DOCETICALLY through emanations (*nirmāṇa*s, etc.). Analytically, and also historically, these models and paradigms are no doubt distinguishable, but here they appear to converge and to complement and reinforce each other.

It is to be observed finally that, within Buddhist thought, the *laukika* is correlated in Naḍapāda/Nāropā's *Paramārthasaṃgraha* (the *Sekoddeśaṭīkā*) with realization of divinities through the generative phase, and the *lokottara* with realization of supramundane reality through the consummate phase: *devatāsādhanam utpattikrameṇa pūrvoktaṃ laukikam/lokottaratattvasādhanam utpannakrameṇa/* (ad *Sekoddeśa* 24, ed. Sferra, p. 121).

For the criticism of Brahmanical systems in the Kālacakra, see G. Grönbold, 'Heterodoxe Lehren und ihre Widerlegung im Kālacakra-Tantra', *IIJ* 35 (1992), p. 273 ff.

[172] In Buddhism docetism is, of course, not solely (or even mainly) an interreligious phenomenon, it being a characteristic feature of the Mahāyāna and its doctrine of the Buddha's three Bodies (*trikāya*) including the *nirmāṇakāya*. See above.

22. On syncretism in the borderlands of Northwestern India and the western Himalaya

In the geographical area covering the northwest of the Indian subcontinent (Gandhāra), the western Himalaya, Kaśmīr, present-day Afghanistan (Bactria), and part of the Iranian world, there evidently existed at the turn of the second millennium a remarkable religious and cultural symbiosis in which Buddhism and Śivaism had some share.[173]

References to the existence of syncretistic movements in the vicinity of and in western Tibet (mṄa' ris skor gsum, Žaṅ žuṅ; [s]Pu [h]raṅs and Gu ge) at the time of *lha bla ma* Ye šes 'od, *pho braṅ* Ži ba 'od and his brother *lha btsun* Byaṅ chub 'od[174] are found in connexion with the controversies that surrounded a certain teacher known as the 'Blue-clad one' (*šam thabs sṅon po can*; cf. *nīlāmbara-dhara*) and another teacher called the 'Red Master' (Ācārya/Atsarya dmar po). Some Tibetan authorities have considered that the latter figure at least might have been an authentic Buddhist. But others strongly disagreed with this view and held them both to be heterodox (*mu stegs pa* = *tīrthika*) teachers from whom the transgressive (and perhaps antinomian) and anomistic practices of ritual sexual union and mactation (*sbyor sgrol*) crept into the Buddhist fold. They were then associated with the so-called Ar tsho Bande (or A ra mo Band[h]e). To counter such practices considered a serious threat to Buddhism, the great Indian Buddhist master Dīpaṃkaraśrījñāna (Atiša of Vikramaśīla, c. 982–1054) was invited by its abovementioned rulers to their kingdom of western Tibet, where he arrived in 1042. There, following the request of Byaṅ chub 'od, he composed at

---

[173] On symbiosis, etc., in Gandhāra, see G. Fussman, '*Upāya-kauśalya*: L'implantation du bouddhisme au Gandhāra', in: *Bouddhisme et cultures locales* (Paris, 1994), pp. 17–51.

[174] On the political history of this area, and on the identification of Ye šes 'od with either 'Khor re or Sroṅ ṅe, see L. Petech, 'Western Tibet: historical introduction', in: D. Klimburg-Salter, *Tabo, a Lamp for the Kingdom* (Milan, 1997), p. 232 ff.; and R. Vitali, *The kingdoms of Gu.ge Pu.hrang* (Dharamsala, 1996); id., *Records of Tho.ling* (Dharamsala, 1999) (who identifies Ye šes 'od with Sroṅ ṅe).

Žaṅ žuṅ Tho l(d)iṅ his renowned *Bodhipathapradīpa* in the commentary (*pañjikā*) to which allusion is made to such practices.[175]

This was also the general geographical area in which there earlier lived the famous Indian adept and thaumaturge Padmasambhava of Uḍḍiyāna/Udyāna (U rgyan/O rgyan, Swāt), who contributed to the propagation of Buddhism in Tibet in the late eighth century. In Afghanistan, besides Buddhist rulers Hindu rulers of the Ṣāhi dynasty were established. In addition, scholars have speculated about the existence at a still earlier time, in the Kushan period, of some kind of convergence between Buddhism and Śivaism in the borderlands between Indian and Iranian civilization.[176]

There exist, then, several suggestive pieces of evidence susceptible of being interpreted as indicating the presence from fairly early times of a Buddhist-Śaiva symbiosis, or syncretism, in these areas of intercultural contact (often referred to by the term 'Indo-Tibetan interface'). This matter remains, however, a topic in which the utmost scholarly caution has to be exercised, and where much research still needs to be carried out before any of these movements can be freed from the realm of conjecture and speculation and brought clearly to light. At all events, the attitude

---

[175] On the two rather enigmatic figures of the 'Blue-clad one' and the 'Red Ācārya', and on the *sbyor sgrol* practices associated with them, see D. Seyfort Ruegg, 'Deux problèmes d'exégèse et de pratique tantriques', in: M. Strickmann (ed.), *Tantric and Taoist studies in honour of R. A. Stein* (*MCB* 20, Brussels, 1981), pp. 212–26; and id., 'Problems in the transmission of Vajrayāna Buddhism in the western Himalaya about the year 1000', in: *Studies of mysticism in honor of the 1150th anniversary of Kobo Daishi's Nirvāṇam* (*Acta Indologica* 6, Narita, 1984), pp. 369–81. On the Red Master see also J.-U. Sobisch, *Three-Vow theories in Tibetan Buddhism* (Wiesbaden, 2002), pp. 13 f., 324 f. In accordance with the negative evaluation of these teachers, they might perhaps be compared with the so-called Aris in Burma. On related matters see C. Scherrer-Schaub, 'Contre le libertinage: Un opuscule de Tabo adressé aux tantristes hérétiques?', in R. Torella *et al.* (ed.), *Le parole e i marmi* (R. Gnoli Felicitation Volume, Rome, 2001), pp. 693–733.

[176] For a brief discussion see M. Bussagli, *L'art du Gandhāra* (Paris, 1984), pp. 456–8. See also D. Snellgrove, *Indo-Tibetan Buddhism* (London, 1987), p. 473 ff. – In connexion with this 'syncretism' there arises the question of the identity of Klu sKar rgyal (cf. D. Martin, 'The Star King and the four children of Pehar', *AOH* 49 [1996], pp. 171–95), as well as of the form of earlier Bon that was perhaps quite close to the Buddhism that first reached Tibet (see below, Appendix I).

adopted by Buddhist authorities concerning the ‘Blue-clad one’, and by certain ones among them with regard also to the ‘Red Ācārya’, demonstrates that Buddhist traditions have been well aware of the problems involved of interchange and possible contamination, and they have therefore sought to establish a clear line of demarcation between authentic Buddhist masters and other teachers who were only on the fringes of Buddhism and seem to represent some kind of Śaiva-Buddhist syncretism.

23. The *laukika* : *lokottara* opposition in relation to the oppositions sacred : profane and spiritual : temporal

In 1964 the present writer proposed employing the concept of a SUBSTRATUM alongside the structured contrastive and complementary opposition *laukika* : *lokottara* when studying the relations between Buddhism and the ambient religions and civilizations of India and Tibet.[177] It appeared that the idea of a partly common religious and cultural substratum, (back)ground or heritage might significantly help in accounting for common features, and indeed sometimes a certain INTERTEXTUALITY, which we encounter when studying Buddhism in the context of the religions of India. In many cases the substratum model appears to be of greater usefulness than the BORROWING paradigm (which itself seems to presuppose the existence of common ground between borrower and lender). As observed above (pp. 83, 93), the pair *laukika* : *lokottara* is DYNAMIC rather than DUALISTICALLY STATIC since it does not comprise two frozen, and reified, levels that are hermetically sealed off from each other, and since it allows for passage from the one to the other.

Also in 1964 the anthropologist Michael Ames made use of the Pali Buddhist categories *lokika/lokiya* : *lokuttara*.[178] Ames did so largely in

---

177 D. Seyfort Ruegg, 'Sur les rapports entre le bouddhisme et le "substrat religieux" indien et tibétain', *JA* 1964, pp. 77–95; cf. also our *Ordre spirituel et ordre temporel dans la pensée bouddhique de l'Inde et du Tibet*, p. 135 ff. See also id., 'A recent work on the religions of Tibet and Mongolia', *TP* 61 (1975), p. 314; review of M.-T. de Mallmann, *Introduction à l'iconographie du tântrisme bouddhique* in: *JAOS* 98 (1978), pp. 544–5; and 'A note on the relationship between Buddhist and "Hindu" divinities in Buddhist literature and iconology: The *laukika* : *lokottara* contrast and the notion of an Indian religious substratum', in: R. Torella (ed.), *Le parole e i marmi* (R. Gnoli Felicitation Volume, Rome, 2001), pp. 735–42.

178 'Magical animism and Buddhism: A structural analysis', in: E. B. Harper (ed.), *Religion in South Asia* (Seattle, 1964), pp. 21–52; id., 'Ritual prestations in the structure of the Sinhalese pantheon', in: M. Nash (ed.), *Anthropological studies in Theravāda Buddhism* (Detroit, 1966), p. 37. See the discussion in H. Bechert, 'On the popular religion of the Sinhalese', in: H. Bechert (ed.), *Buddhism in Ceylon...* (as in n. 44), p. 217 ff., who in addition refers (p. 218) to a review by G. Obeyesekere in the *Ceylon Journal of Historical and Social Studies* 2 (1958), pp. 259–62, which argued

terms of Durkheim's dichotomy of the PROFANE and the SACRED. But since, in Buddhism, the *laukika* covers a significant portion of the area describable as sacred (and divine) whilst the *lokottara* extends beyond what is usually regarded as the sacred, the applicability of the Buddhist categories *laukika* and *lokottara* to Ames's analysis seems problematical. Indeed, it is anything but clear how the religious phenomena in question in his article, and which are characteristic of Buddhism in Sri Lanka and elsewhere, can be made to fit the familiar, but rather over-tidy and rigid, dichotomy sacred : profane.[179]

It is noteworthy that, in Sri Lanka, the contrastive and complementary opposition transmundane : mundane finds a linguistic counterpart in the employment of Pali and Sanskrit, the first being used in texts relating to what may be described as the *lokottara* level whilst the second has largely been reserved for secular literature belonging to the *laukika* level.[180] (By contrast, in Tibet where both types of works are normally in Tibetan, either as a result of translation or from the outset, the Tibetan language has been used for both levels and both types of literature.)

It has been suggested by Heinz Bechert that, in the contrastive pair *laukika* : *lokottara*, the mundane level covers in large part the space of royal political power, and the supramundane the sphere of the Buddhist Saṃgha and Sāsana which is ultimately directed towards liberation from rebirth in *saṃsāra*. This dichotomy, it was further suggested by him, has been employed by the political authority to justify and legitimate the way in which the Saṃgha has been integrated into the political system placed

---

'against the separation of "Buddhist" and "non-Buddhist" beliefs and described both as parts of "one interconnected system which may profitably be studied as Sinhalese religion"'. Concerning the Sinhalese *laukika/lokottara* distinction, compare J. Holt, *Buddha in the crown*: *Avalokiteśvara in the Buddhist tradition of Sri Lanka* (New York, 1991); id., *The Buddhist Viṣṇu* (New York, 2004), pp. 28, 177–8, 191 (interpreting the two as 'two ends of a temporal continuum', i.e. the contemporary and the future).

[179] cf. D. Seyfort Ruegg, *Ordre spirituel et ordre temporel dans la pensée bouddhique de l'Inde et du Tibet*, pp. 139–40.

[180] cf. H. Bechert, *Eine regionale hochsprachliche Tradition in Südasien*: *Sanskrit-Literatur bei den buddhistischen Singhalesen* (Vienna, 2005).

under the control of the state by keeping it from meddling in the mundane domain.[181]

This last interpretation would seemingly amount to making the pair *laukika* : *lokottara* co-extensive with the two categories constituted in the Pali Buddhist tradition by the temporal Wheel of Rule (*āṇācakka*) and the spiritual Wheel of Dharma (*dhammacakka*), and incidentally with the two Mahāyānist systems of governance represented in Tibet by the *lugs gñis/tshul gñis/khrims gñis* and in Mongolia by the *qoyar yosun*. In other words, this contrastive pair would be coterminous with the twin categories of the TEMPORAL and SPIRITUAL. However, while it is perhaps true that there exists a certain isomorphism between the pair *laukika* : *lokottara* and the two Wheels (or the two Systems) the two binary sets can scarcely be treated as equivalent. For the theory of the two *cakka*s (and the two Systems) finds its application within the sphere of rulership and religio-political theory, whilst the pair *laukika* : *lokottara* has been employed more widely in both religious and philosophical contexts.[182] Bechert has himself observed (*loc. cit.*, p. 220): 'Though in theory Theravāda Buddhists have always accepted the dualism of a "mundane" and a "supramundane" sphere, in practice they only applied it to a limited degree'.

Were it furthermore to be suggested that *lokottara* corresponds to Buddhism in the sense of Buddhist 'orthodoxy', and *laukika* to the not strictly Buddhist sphere of the temporal, this again could be begging the question or displacing it without clarifying it. For, as seen in preceding parts of this study, the *laukika* has been integrated into the Buddhist world-view and cosmos; and it could even be regarded as in part directed towards liberation even if, *per se*, it is not directly and immediately salvific in the ultimate sense.

Nor does it seem possible to regard the pair *laukika* : *lokottara* as equivalent to the familiar Hindu distinction between *bhukti* and *mukti*, for the category *laukika* is not co-extensive with the idea of prosperity and its enjoyment.

---

[181] See H. Bechert, 'Introduction", p. 19 ff., and 'On the popular religion of the Sinhalese', pp. 218–21, in: H. Bechert (ed.), *Buddhism in Ceylon and Studies on religious syncretism in Buddhist countries* (as in n. 44).

[182] See above, p. 69 f.; and D. Seyfort Ruegg, *Ordre spirituel et ordre temporel dans la pensée bouddhique de l'Inde et du Tibet*, pp. 55, 77; and *passim*.

With the exception of the last, the above-mentioned pairs (sacred : profane and spiritual : temporal) which have been compared by scholars with the *laukika* : *lokottara* are of course more or less 'etic' ones, like those listed above (p. 95). This fact may help to explain why they do not fully fit the categories expressed by the Buddhist contrastive and complementary pair under discussion. An 'etic' opposition coming a little closer is perhaps that of 'Little Tradition' : 'Great Tradition' (see above, pp. 11, 95).

24. 'Emic' expressions relevant to the substratum model

In the search for indigenous concepts employed by Buddhists themselves which may correspond to the SUBSTRATUM concept – that is, when looking for 'emic' categories rooted in the very dynamics of Buddhist thinking –, the question arises as to whether Indian Buddhists ever developed a theory together with a corresponding terminology that would serve to represent and explain the religious processes involved when mundane gods, godlings, etc., are integrated in the world-view of Buddhists, and are included in a Tantric clan (*kula*), in ritual and meditative cosmograms (*maṇḍala*), and elsewhere in Mahāyānist and Vajrayānist thought, albeit in a subordinate position relative to the transmundane protective divinities of Buddhism.

On the Indian side, and also on the Tibetan side, apart from the contrastive pair *laukika* = *'jig rten pa* : *lokottara* = *'jig rten las 'das pa* discussed above and certain terminologies descriptive of sectors of the Mahāyānist and Vajrayānist Paths (*mārga*; see pp. 43, 69 above), the nearest thing we find may be the DOCETIC EMANATIONISM whereby a Buddha or Bodhisattva projects a phantom *nirmāṇa* (Tib. *sprul pa*) the function of which is, *inter alia*, to assume the appearance of divinities and *daemons*, local or otherwise, of the Indian, or Tibetan, religious substratum. As for the *laukika* term in the contrastive pair *laukika* : *lokottara*, it is not unrelated to the concept of a religious SUBSTRATUM.

Japanese Buddhism has, moreover, adopted a remarkable theory with a corresponding terminology that describes the process by which a Buddha or high Bodhisattva may manifest as a Shintō god (for example Hachiman). The Japanese expression employed is *honji suijaku*, where *honji* 'fundamental nature'[183] designates an original ground – i.e. the transmundane *dharmakāya* of a *buddha* – from which there emanates the *suijaku*, a 'trace', 'imprint' or 'manifestation' that is a Kami, or Shintō deity, according to this doctrine. The system whereby a Kami, or Shintō deity, is connected with a Buddha or Bodhisattva, and thus so to say co-opted into Buddhism, is known as the *shinbutsu shūgō* ('unification of gods and

---

[183] Japanese *hon* 本 = Chinese *pên* (Mathews no. 5025).

Buddhas').[184] The expression *honji suijaku* is, however, of wider application and is not restricted to the relationship between Buddhism and Shintō. Thus, within Japanese Buddhism, the *suijaku* may represent a 'mundane' emanation of an underlying transmundane archetype, be the latter a Buddha or Bodhisattva. The Japanese system is evidently emanational, but subtending it is the implicit structured opposition between what in Indian parlance is known as the *laukika* and the *lokottara*.

A treatment of the relationship existing between two categories – one SUPERORDINATE and 'transmundane' and the other SUBORDINATE and 'mundane' – which takes account of original Buddhist categories would seem to be at least as pertinent and useful for our understanding of the issues raised in the present study as analyses based solely on such categories as SYNCRETISM, INCLUSIVISM or BORROWING between Hinduism and Buddhism, or even on such familiar oppositions as SACRED : PROFANE, OTHER-WORLDLY : THIS-WORLDLY, etc. The search for such categories is satisfied by the 'emic' concept of a Buddha's or high Bodhisattva's emanation by *nirmāṇa* as an entity operating in the world, and by the structurally opposed categories *laukika* : *lokottara*. Whether in principle one accepts or not that 'emic' categories require to be identified alongside western theoretical and metatheoretical, and also 'etic', ones when we set out to analyse a religious phenomenon, excluding the use of the catgories of the *nirmāṇa* and *laukika* : *lokottara* simply because they are indigenous to Buddhist thought would constitute extremely fastidious methodological abstinence for which no need or justification is evident. In the study of Buddhist religion and thought, this set of Indian (and Tibetan) 'emic' concepts and terms can thus occupy a very useful place beside the no less significant concept and terminology attested in Japan in the form of the *honji suijaku* theory.[185]

*

---

[184] Mathews characters nos. 5716+1982, 2499+2117: 神佛習合. For a bibliography of studies on the *honji suijaku* paradigm, see above, n. 69.

[185] Two further 'emic' categories of importance for the study of Buddhist thought which have been mentioned above are the two Wheels (*āṇācakka* and *dhammacakka*) of the Buddha's rule and the two Systems (*lugs gñis*, *tshul gñis*, etc.) of worldly governance embodied in Inner Asia by the conjunction of the religious preceptor-donee (*mchod gnas*, *yon gnas*) and the donor-prince (*yon bdag*), i.e. the Dharmarāja (*chos rgyal*).

On the Brahmanical/Hindu side there have also existed concepts and terms which require attention in an examination of the question of the Indian substratum or (back)ground shared, at least in part, by Buddhism and Brahmanism, and the matter of the SYMBIOSIS and CONCORD of India's religious traditions and scriptures.

One very noteworthy concept is that of the normative quality – the validity/authority – of all traditions (*sarvāgamaprāmāṇya*) that has been discussed by Jayantabhaṭṭa in his *Nyāyamañjarī*.[186] There this important Kaśmīri philosopher has introduced the ideas of congruence or concord (*saṃvāda*), absence of conflict (*avivāda*) and discord (*avipratipatti*), and confluence (*sam-pat-*) in one higher good (*śreyas*) of many streams each issuing from a reliable (*āpta*) initiator in the form of expedient means (*abhyupāya*). The notion of common (back)ground or milieu perhaps approaches this author's notion of *tulyakakṣyatva* – literally the possession of an equivalent enclosure or orbit – even if the latter has been described in Jayanta's text as resting on the criterion of each tradition having been promulgated by a reliable initiator (*āptapraṇītatva*).[187] In

---

[186] Jayanta has been placed in the second half of the ninth century by P. Hacker, 'Jayantabhaṭṭa und Vācaspatimiśra', *Beiträge zur indischen Philologie und Altertumskunde* (Festschrift W. Schubring, Hamburg, 1951), pp. 160–9. (W. Slaje, 'Untersuchungen zur Chronologie einiger Nyāya-Philosophen', *StII* 11/12 (1986), pp. 245–78 placed Jayanta *c.* 900.) He was a contemporary and adviser of King Śaṃkaravarman of Kaśmīr (883–902).

[187] *Nyāyamañjarī*, Pramāṇaprakaraṇa 4 (Kāśī Sanskrit series, p. 244 f.). Reference can also be made to the same author's *Āgamaḍambara* (*Ṣaṇmatanāṭaka*), a play in which Jayanta has, however, portrayed and satirized a clashing hubbub of religious traditions including the Buddhist. Farcical representations of Buddhists are also to be found already in the Pallava king Mahendravikrama-varman's *Mattavilāsa-prahasana* (early seventh c.) and in Bodhāyana's *Bhagavadajjukīya*.

For a discussion of this particular notion of *prāmāṇya*, see A. Wezler, 'Zur Proklamation religiös-weltanschaulicher Toleranz bei dem indischen Philosophen Jayantabhaṭṭa', *Saeculum* 27 (1976), pp. 329–47. In connexion with the reference of the expression of 'all traditions', Wezler has also taken up the question of the *nīlapaṭas* and the *nīlāmbaravrata*, which Jayanta opposed (on this subject see also the present writer's two articles cited in n. 175 above'), and the matter of the *saṃsāramocaka* (on which see also A. Wezler, 'On the quadruple division of the Yogaśāstra ...', *IT* 12 [1984], p. 316 n. 74 and p. 317 n. 81; and W. Halbfass, *Tradition and reflection* [Albany, 1991], p. 97 ff.). A *saṃsāramocaka* (Tib. *'khor ba sgrol byed pa*) is mentioned earlier in Bhāviveka's *Madhyamakahṛdayakārikās* (Mīmāṃsā-chapter,

this passage, then, there clearly appears neither straightforward eirenicism nor out-and-out subordinating inclusivism in Hacker's sense; instead there are invoked in it the idea of competence (*adhikāra*) and of the person possessing ritual and spiritual competence in a given area (*adhikārin*).

A parallel idea of very considerable interest in the present context is *śāstrāṇāṃ melanam*, the subject of Chapter xxxv of Abhinavagupta's *Tantrāloka*. The expression employed by this very important Kashmiri thinker of the tenth-eleventh century can be rendered as the 'meeting (i.e. mingling or confluence) of traditions'.[188] In a harmonious hierarchy of traditions, both *laukika* and *vaidika*, expressed by this phrase are included a number of Brahmanical/Hindu traditions, and also Buddhism and Jainism. As a major source for this notion Abhinavagupta cites the *Svacchandatantra*, and his commentator Jayaratha quotes relevant passages from this text. This idea of a harmonious meeting of traditions has, however, not prevented Abhinavagupta from considering the Śaiva Āgamas as primary and supreme (xxxv.23–25). The various traditions are stated by him to come forth from Brahmā's several heads (xxxv.26–27). And to account for this 'meeting', Abhinavagupta also invokes the principle that different people have various competences (*adhikārin*) (xxxv.35). Instead of using the word *śāstra*, Jayaratha refers in his comment to these traditions as *āgama*, the term we have already met in Jayantabhaṭṭa's *Nyāyamañjarī*. In his comment on *Tantrāloka* xxxv.1, Jayaratha observes also that the theme of *sarvāgamaprāmāṇya* is to be

ix.35; D, f. 32b) and in the *Tarkajvālā* (D, f. 284b).

188 The expression has been translated as 'incontro delle scritture' by R. Gnoli, *Luce delle sacre scritture* (Turin, 1972). On this idea see also W. Halbfass, *India and Europe*, p. 360. (The etymologically possible causative sense of *melana* may be conveyed by rendering it 'bringing together', but the standard meaning of the word, 'junction, union', is not causative.)

On Abhinavagupta's position with regard to the standardness and validity of *āgamas*, see P. Granoff, 'Tolerance in the Tantras: its form and function', *JOR* 56–62 (1986–92), p. 288 ff., who has called attention to Abhinava's understanding of *āgama* as *jñāna* and as a *vimarśa* 'reflection' that is verbal in nature (*śabdātman*). Granoff has further compared Abhinava's view with the Jaina *nayavāda*, and has referred in particular to his *Mālinīvijayavārttika* (641, p. 59).

set forth by Abhinavagupta through the idea of the oneness of purport of all systems (*sarvaśāstraikavākyatā*).

In the area of philosophy, as an example of agreement between Brahmanical and Buddhist thought, historians have regularly pointed to to Gauḍapāda's *Āgamaśāstra* (*Māṇḍūkyakārikās*), and in particular to Chapter iv of this text on *ajātivāda* as a case of synthesis of Buddhism and Vedānta.[189] On the other hand, by an opponent the great Vedāntic master Śaṃkara has been called a crypto-Buddhist (*pracchanna-bauddha*),[190] a description that would seem to exclude the possibility of any true synthesis of the traditions.

Attention may finally be drawn to the concept of *sarvasiddhānta-siddhānta* found in the *Yogavāsiṣṭha*. This work too has referred to the *prāmāṇya* of all recognized *śāstras* (vii.100.15cd–16ab); but it has relativized this validity of traditions by showing each to depend on some philosopher's unilateral ascertainment (*niścaya*) of it in terms of concepts constructed (*kalpita*) by his own philosophical postulates (*svavikalpa*). This relative, and subjective, *prāmāṇya* of other *śāstras* is then subsumed in, and transcended, by the *Yogavāsiṣṭha*'s own *sarvasiddhāntasiddhānta* (vii.100.16cd) – that is, the underlying principle of consciousness (*saṃvid*, *cit*) – which, as the ultimate philosophical doctrine (*siddhānta*), resumes in itself all provisionally valid doctrinal positions.[191]

---

[189] See V. Bhattacharya, *The Āgamaśāstra of Gauḍapāda* (Calcutta, 1943). Cf. T. Vetter, 'Die Gauḍapādīya-Kārikās', *WZKS* 22 (1978), pp. 95–131. But this is not the view of Śāntarakṣita, *Madhyamakālaṃkāra* 93 ff.

[190] cf. H. Nakamura, *A history of early Vedānta philosophy*, i (Delhi, 1983), p. 120 f. Compare also P. Hacker, 'Vedānta-Studien', in: *Kleine Schriften*, p. 59; W. Halbfass, *Tradition and reflection*, p. 217 f.

[191] See W. Slaje, 'Sarvasiddhāntasiddhānta: On "tolerance" and "syncretism" in the Yogavāsiṣṭha', *WZKS* 36 (1992, Supplementband), pp. 307–22. At p. 316 of this article Slaje has concluded that the intention of the *YV* is 'to falsify all the other Śāstras by reducing their *siddhāntas* to mere subjective mind-constructions based on consciousness'. The question remains whether, for the procedure at issue here, relativization might not be a better description than falsification. Slaje has contrasted (p. 317) the position of the *YV* with the perspectivism (*anekāntavāda*) of the Jainas. But do not the Jainas also claim a superior and overarching truth for their philosophy of non-absolutism (*anekāntavāda*)? It would seem that, in this respect, the view of the *YV* and the perspectivism of the Jainas are formally close, despite the fact that, as to

The notion of an essentially harmonious array of traditions and doctrines seems to have been especially well represented in Kaśmīr around the year 1000. But as seen above (p. 13), the idea of concord between Buddhism and Brahmanical tradition is attested much earlier in Bhāviveka's *Madhyamakahṛdayakārikā*s (sixth century). That Bhāviveka's idea of religio-philosophical CONCORD cannot, however, be simply equated with religious SYNCRETISM and philosophical RELATIVISM or INDIFFERENTISM should be clear from the central position he occupied in the history of Buddhism and of the Madhyamaka school, and from the fact that his *Madhyamakahṛayakārikā*s contain a critical examination of various schools of Indian philosophy, Buddhist and non-Buddhist.

Bhāviveka defended a further very remarkable principle which is also relevant to the relationship between Buddhism and a Brahmanical tradition when he wrote that whatever has been well-formulated in the Vedānta is entirely 'Buddha-word' (*Madhyamakahṛdayakārikā* iv.56ab):

vedānte ca hi yat sūktaṃ tat sarvaṃ buddhabhāṣitam/[192]

Clearly, much more than syncretism, or even symbiosis, this statement seems to be based on the idea of a latent CONCORD between traditions and systems. It might, indeed, even be seen as an instance of a particular kind of inclusivism. His statement is perhaps best understood as expressing the idea of the equivalence of the whole of the 'well-formed' with the Word of the Awakened: whatever is well-formed is, Buddhistically speaking, Buddha-word. In the *Adhyāśayasaṃcodanasūtra* this concept has been expressed in the words: *yat kiṃcin maitreya subhāṣitaṃ sarvaṃ tad buddhabhāṣitam.*[193] It should be noted that the converse affirmation

---

content, the former teaches a monism of consciousness while the latter maintains the principle of non-absolutism without engaging overtly in subordination of views which it instead juxtaposes. Whether either case in fact amounts to an example of Paul Hacker's inclusivism – as Slaje has concluded (p. 319) for the view of the *YV* – is a separate question which depends on whether one considers every case of the hierarchic ordering of views to be also a case of subordinating inclusivism. This is certainly not the case for the hierarchic ordering of *siddhānta*s in ascending order as found in much of the Indian and Tibetan doxographical literature (see below).

For *sarvadarśanasiddhānta* in the *Vimalaprabhā* of the Kālacakra, see p. 116 above.

[192] cf. V. V. Gokhale, 'The Vedānta philosophy described by Bhavya in his *Madhyamakahṛdaya*', *IIJ* 2 (1958), p. 179.

[193] Quoted in Śāntideva's *Sikṣāsamuccaya* (ed. Bendall), p. 15, and in Prajñākaramati's

that whatever the Buddha has spoken is well-said – 'well-formulated' – is also attested in Buddhist tradition.[194]

On the other hand, in the sequence of chapters in Mādhava-Vidyāraṇya's Brahmanical *Sarvadarśanasaṃgraha* (fourteenth century) – where the order of doctrines treated begins with the Cārvāka, the Bauddha, and the Jaina, passes on through the Rāmānuja, Śaiva, Pratyabhijñā, Vaiśeṣika, Naiyāyika, Jaimini, Pāṇinīya, Sāṃkhya, Yoga, etc., and finally culminates in the Śāṃkara (i.e. the Advaita-Vedānta) – the subordination of Buddhism to other doctrines, in particular the authors' own, is expressed through the progressive, and in general hierarchically ascending, arrangement of the doctrines treated.[195] On the contrary, in Bhāviveka's *Madhyamakahṛdayakārikā*s no such progressive, scalar and 'gradualistic', arrangement of non-Buddhist in relation to Buddhist doctrines is perceptible, although a scalar arrangement of *siddhānta*s has indeed been widely used in the later Buddhist doxographical literature of the Tibetan *Grub mtha'*s.[196]

Bodhicaryāvatārapañjikā ix.43ab. On the Buddha's *subhāṣita* (and its comparison with a *sūkta*) see further Mātṛceṭa, *Varṇārhavarṇastotra* vii (Brahmānuvāda) 17–22.

194 See the *Subhāsitasutta* in *Suttanipāta* iii.3 (pp. 78–79), with the *Āmagandhasutta* in *Suttanipāta* ii.2.14 (verse 252, p. 45) and the *Kiṃsīlasutta* in ii.9.2 (verse 325, p. 56); Aṅguttaranikāya IV 164; Saṃyuttanikāya IV, 188–9. The idea is attested also in Asoka's Calcutta-Bairāṭ/Bhabra inscription (ed. J. Bloch, p. 154): *e keci bhaṃte bhagavatā buddhena bhāsite savve se subhāsitevā*. On the value of *subhāṣita*, see also the present writer's remarks in *JIABS* 18 (1995), p. 180.

195 On the authorship of this work, see A. Thakur, *ALB* 25 (1961), pp. 524–38). On Mādhava, see P. V. Kane, *History of Dharmaśāstra*, i/2² (Poona, 1975), p. 778 ff. – On the other hand, in the *Ṣaḍdarśanasamuccaya* by the Jaina Haribhadrasūri (eighth century), the order of treatment is: Bauddha, Naiyāyika, Sāṃkhya, Jaina, Vaiśeṣika, and Jaiminīya, with a chapter on the Lokāyatamata at the end. Comparison may be made with Haribhadra's treatment of other doctrines in his *Anekāntajayapatākā*. Cf. O. Quarnström, 'Haribhadra and the beginnings of doxography in India', in: *Approaches to Jaina studies: philosophy, logic, rituals and symbols* (Toronto, 1999), pp. 169–210. – On these doxographical treatises cf. W. Halbfass, *India and Europe*, p. 349 ff.

196 The use of the expression 'gradualism' in the sense of the hierarchical subordination of one member in a progressive series to another is found in P. Hacker, *Grundlagen indischer Dichtung und indischen Denkens* (ed. K. Rüping,Vienna, 1985), p. 132 ff. But the gradualistic and hierarchical arrangement of non-Buddhist and then Buddhist doctrines found in Buddhist doxographical literature does not seem inclusivistic in

Hacker's sense. For the non-Buddhist doctrines (when they are treated) are not embraced inclusivistically; and even though the Buddhist doctrines are recognized as based on the progressively graded teachings of the Buddha – who taught them in accordance with the different and graded capacities of his auditors – they are usually carefully delineated and distinguished in the doxographical literature.

25. Concluding remarks

In the present study an attempt has been made to investigate the need for theoretically grounded and historically broad-based concepts and terms that take account of the specific character of the complex we know as Buddhism with a view to understanding and describing it in relation both to the cultural matrix in which it arose and developed and to the ambient religions of South Asia (and, incidentally, of Central, Inner and East Asia also). Whilst the concepts and terms investigated here should be appropriate to and closely fit Buddhism and the Indian (and Tibetan) situation, it is nonetheless hoped that they are not so culture-bound and parochial as not to be more universally intelligible. In the past, a number of terms, concepts, paradigms, and models – usually more 'etic' than 'emic' – have been employed by scholars when studying Buddhism in its historical milieu. But being so often rooted in western categories, many have proved to be overly culture-bound and parochial. The limitations, and some also of the Procrustean presuppositions and implications, of several of them have been noted above.

Three concepts in particular – those of docetic emanation (an 'emic' concept), of a substratum (which is 'emic' to the extent that it is largely co-extensive with the Buddhist concept of the *laukika*), and of the contrastive pair *laukika* : *lokottara* (which is of course 'emic') – have been considered above in regard to their capacity for providing, singly or jointly, useful approaches to the issues and questions raised. It is of course necessary to ensure that the concepts of emanation and substratum, and of the subordination of the *laukika* to the *lokottara* level, are not misunderstood as just artful, or more or less polite, ways of giving expression to either religious antagonism (as seems to have been assumed by Benoytosh Bhattacharyya and those scholars who followed him regarding the subordination of the *laukika* level) or superiority of the inclusivist variety (under Paul Hacker's particular definition of inclusivism). This is not, however, to assert that an icon depicting an entity dancing upon another was *never* in any circumstance intended to express, or at least suggest, the victory of one deity, or tradition, over another. (Compare also above, note 2, as well as notes 68, 70, 138 on the *śarabha* icon, note 87 on the *brahmahatyā* theme, and the Tibetan source cited on pp. 75–76.)

Now, it has to be freely recognized from the outset that there probably exists no single universal category or tool, no single 'etic' or 'emic' model or paradigm, suitable for organizing and interpreting the totality of the evidence available from our sources relating to the issues and questions discussed here. (It indeed appears that Indian modes of categorization have sometimes been set up without theorization, and case by case rather than systematically.) Also, in its structures, classical Indian thought has often tended to be polythetic rather than monothetic, so that thinking was in terms of so-called 'family resemblances' rather than reified essences.[197] This observation largely holds also for the procedures of Buddhist thought in India (and Tibet) studied in the present work. Hence, whilst the *laukika* : *lokottara* contrastive opposition considered here indeed possesses far-reaching relevance for the understanding of Buddhist thought, it is not being asserted that this model can be expected, of and by itself, to provide a single universal key for opening up all our materials and resolving the totality of issues they pose. Nevertheless, this contrastive opposition has very frequently served as an ordering principle for organizing and elucidating a complex world of religious and cultural representations.

In order fully to address the task before us, it is no doubt necessary to go beyond the division between indigenous, and in-built, 'emic' and imported, and superimposed, 'etic' concepts and categories. It is necessary to develop what one might call a methodology and anthropology – religious and more – drawing on the traditional twin disciplines of philology and history as well as on ethnography, linguistics and philosophy.[198] Only thus, it seems, is it possible to approach and describe the complex phenomena which we study under the names of Buddhism and Brahmanism/Hinduism.

---

[197] For observations on this point, see D. Seyfort Ruegg, *Buddha-nature, Mind and the problem of gradualism in a comparative perspective* (London, 1989), p. 2; and 'Aspects of the study of the (early) Indian Mahāyāna', *JIABS* 27 (2004), p. 59.

[198] For some observations on the 'emic' and the 'etic' in the present connexion, see also D. Seyfort Ruegg, *Ordre spirituel et ordre temporel*, pp. 11–12, 140 f. Clearly, the emic and etic methods can be complementary, and employed alternately, and they should not be regarded as necessarily exclusive of each other.

The structured contrastive opposition *laukika* : *lokottara* differs from the familiar opposition sacred : profane because the Buddhist concept does not readily reduce to the latter tidy, and perhaps somewhat rigid, dichotomy. The category 'sacred' or 'sacral' is wider than *lokottara*, and it impinges on the *laukika* inasmuch as the latter includes a large number of divinities, *numina*, etc., recognized in practice by Buddhism – possibly in some cases even by the Buddha himself – in conformity with the usage of the world (*lokānuvartana*). Indeed, on the conventional level of discursive practice, the Buddha is reported to have once declared that it is not he who disputes with the world but the world that disputes with him: he acknowledges what is acknowledged in the world but not what is not acknowledged in the world (*loko mayā sārdhaṃ vivadati nâhaṃ lokena sārdhaṃ vivadāmi/ yal loke 'sti sammataṃ tan mamâpy asti sammatam/ yal loke nâsti sammataṃ mamâpi tan nâsti sammatam/*, quoted in Candrakīrti's *Prasannapadā* xviii.8; cf. Saṃyuttanikāya III.138). As for the 'profane', it is not even clear to what Sanskrit (or Tibetan) category, concept and term it might precisely correspond.[199] Moreover, the opposition *laukika* : *lokottara* is not a frozen and essentialized one; and Buddhist thought in fact holds that it is possible to pass from the former to the latter, even to reach the latter through treating the former as an expedient, i.e. salvific, device.

Approaches that are based on SUBSTRATUM and SYMBIOSIS paradigms on the one side, and on the other side on COMPROMISE or on BORROWING paradigms – including SYNCRETISM and ENCULTURATION – are not necessarily and automatically incompatible throughout the entire range of our source materials. In the course of history they have not been entirely exclusive of each other.

Historically attested instances of borrowing from Brahmanism/Hinduism would, presumably, have arisen precisely when Buddhism was developing on the basis of a common ground or inherited substratum which it largely shared with its religious ambience. Even advocates of the strongest version of the intracultural borrowing hypothesis would

---

199 The English-Sanskrit dictionaries by Monier Williams and Apte are of no real assistance in this regard (although for 'profane' = 'secular' they give *laukika*), nor are Dawasamdup's and Dhongthog's English-Tibetan dictionaries. Goldstein's English-Tibetan dictionary gives *'jig rten* for 'profane', and *chos* for 'sacred'.

probably concede that, to begin with, Buddhism was an Indian movement having much in common with other Indian movements. And historians of (intercultural) borrowing and enculturation between India and Tibet would no doubt acknowledge that Tibetan Buddhism has constituted a specific religious system (or, rather, set of systems), yet one which through (intracultural) perfusion or osmosis embraced elements held in common with pre-Buddhist, or para-Buddhist, forms of Tibetan religion (cf. pp. 168–172 below). In the first case, that of Indian Buddhism, what was taken over was presumably not totally foreign and alien (otherwise why would it have been 'borrowed' in the first place?). And in the second case, that of Tibetan Buddhism, any borrowed pre-Buddhist or para-Buddhist component would, by definition, be historically (if perhaps not typologically) allogenic to the Buddhism being newly propagated in Tibet.[200]

A further problem needs to be mentioned in this connexion. This is the fact that, for the reason that Buddhism ostensibly disappeared from India about a millennium ago, it has tended – unlike the other Śramaṇa tradition of Jainism – to be regarded as something dispensable, and hence non-essential and extraneous, within the body of Indian civilization (see below, p. 151 ff.). On this assumption certain academic programmes have even been constructed which in effect excluded Buddhist studies from mainline Indology. As far as Buddhism in India is concerned, such compartmentalization may well have favoured the generalized form of borrowing paradigm that has been in question here. Similarly, some Sinologists (more Confucean perhaps than the Chinese themselves), Japanologists and Tibetologists have regarded Buddhism as a foreign body – as a 'xeno-transplant' – throughout all periods of East Asian and Inner Asian cultures. In this way a problem in the history of religions that concerns the relationship of Buddhism either with the religion and culture of the land of its origin or with the lands of its adoption is to be found impinging on – and potentially being in its turn influenced by – academic

---

200 See Appendix I below. On the possibility of distinguishing conceptually, and even historically, between a Buddhism in Tibet and a Tibetan Buddhism, see D. Seyfort Ruegg, 'The Indian and the Indic in Tibetan cultural history, and Tsoṅ kha pa's achievement as a scholar and thinker: An essay on the concepts of Buddhism in Tibet and Tibetan Buddhism', *JIP* 32 (2004), pp. 321–43. On the 'exogenous' and 'allogenic' see n. 239 below.

structures that have become prevalent either deliberately or accidentally. This form of compartmentalization has contributed to the formation of a somewhat distorted picture of Asian civilizations.

As observed above, no single theory or hypothesis can be expected to provide a universal key, or an 'ideologeme', for resolving all the issues and questions that may arise in connexion with the problems under discussion here. In some cases philological and historical evidence may point to the dependence of a Buddhist document or icon on a Hindu one; whilst in other cases the reverse may be true. This holds not only for religion and Tantrism but for other areas of thought, the case of Indian logic and epistemology (*pramāṇa*) being a well-documented example. It seems that the idea of a partly shared (back)ground or common Indian substratum is highly useful, indeed necessary, when seeking to account for instances of historical dependence, as well as of characterized INTERTEXTUALITY, in order to understand the cultural circumstances in which borrowing of any kind could have taken place. Alexis Sanderson's notion of unidirectional 'text-flow' will be a specific case of intertextuality between Buddhist and Hindu sources where the direction of influence can be clearly and securely determined; whereas instances of intertextuality where this determination cannot be made might be grounded in a partly shared SUBSTRATUM.

In addition, the concept of a common ground or substratum is pertinent in cases where the available evidence is insufficient to demonstrate direct borrowing, and where we meet instead with somewhat more diffuse cultural, religious and philosophical features, structures and procedures broadly shared by both Buddhism and Hinduism. The precise nature and modalities of the relationship between Buddhist and Hindu culture – i.e. whether they are based on a common source, (back)ground or substratum or whether they are due rather to a particular historical borrowing at a given time – needs, therefore, to be investigated case by case.

At all events, neither Buddhism nor Hinduism is a totally monolithic entity, and account will have to be taken of the existence of variables – and possibly (given the imperfect nature of our documentation) of indeterminables. Variation in both time and space between the regions of India as well as distinct social, family and school traditions may be expected to have been in operation, and the possible impact of these forces has to be kept in mind in order to avoid unwarranted generalization.

Viewed diachronically with respect to their development over time, such variations assume diatopic and diastratic dimensions.

In sum, a substratum model may in fact not fit all cases. But at the same time it is exceedingly difficult to understand how it can be simply dismissed as 'redundant' (as A. Sanderson once did). A borrowing hypothesis that completely rules out the substratum model cannot account for the entirety of the very rich evidence available. In particular, its postulation requires a satisfactory explanation as to why one group (the Buddhists) felt either the need or the desire to borrow – to 'plagiarize' even 'piously' (as Sanderson put it in 1995) – from another group (e.g. the Śaivas or Vaiṣṇavas) *if* at the same time it is assumed that there existed no common religious and cultural ground between them, and that, for them, what they borrowed was, *ex hypothesi*, exogenous and alien. To invoke rivalry or emulation would seem to explain very little indeed. For in what circumstances, and for what reason, would Buddhists have felt Brahmanism/Hinduism to be so prestigious were it in fact the case that Buddhism did not share common ground with it? Emulation surely presupposes some existing common ground. Competition too would seem to imply the existence of some shared background.[201]

In other words, whilst a substratum model may of course be marked by a certain under-extension, or *avyāpti*, in so far as it does not pretend to offer a universal key and solution to all issues and questions arising in respect to the relationship between Hinduism and Buddhism, the claim of any borrowing model that rejects the substratum model as redundant is gravely vitiated by generalizing over-extension and over-application – in Indian parlance by *ativyāpti* and *atiprasaṅga*.

*

On the one side, looking at the relationship between Buddhism and Brahmanism/Hinduism HISTORICALLY, i.e. along a DIACHRONIC axis, three conclusions can be drawn.

---

201 cf. D. Seyfort Ruegg, 'A note on the relationship between Buddhist and 'Hindu' divinities in Buddhist literature and iconology: the *laukika/lokottara* contrast and the notion of an Indian 'religious substratum' (as in n. 53).

First, because in its Indian homeland Buddhism arose in an Indian matrix, it is there that the SUBSTRATUM MODEL for their relationship finds an appropriate application. Yet, given more or less frequent and regular contacts over time between Buddhists, Hindus, Jains, etc., this model allows also for influences on Buddhism from its ambient religious and social milieu, and for borrowing from this milieu in the course of the historical development of Buddhism. In other words, within the overall frame of the SUBSTRATUM MODEL there is room for ACCOMMODATION and BORROWING.

Secondly, it seems difficult to account for conscious borrowing by Buddhism from Brahmanism/Hinduism, etc., when it is not admitted that such borrowing took place against the background of a common substratum. Why indeed would Buddhists have wished to borrow, or to 'plagiarize', from non-Buddhists if they did not share, at least to a significant degree, a common background with them? But, as already stated, the very idea of a monolithic, and monothetic, Brahmanism/Hinduism neatly demarcated and set off from a monolithic, and monothetic, Buddhism appears more than questionable. Discussion no doubt needs to proceed with reference to smaller or larger groups of Buddhists and Hindus, and eventually to individual masters (along with their disciples). According to the particular circumstances of each case, the conditions in which accommodation and borrowing took place may have been eirenic, or they may have been confrontational.

Thirdly, there thus exists the probability of instances of historical CONFRONTATION, and even of secular ANTAGONISMS, expressible by the formula 'Buddhism *vs.* Hinduism' (or 'Hinduism *vs.* Buddhism'). But for the reasons given above – and however great its value and explanatory power might be in other contexts – INCLUSIVISM as defined by Paul Hacker cannot fully account for the the incorporation of the the *laukika* level into Buddhism and its subordination to the *lokottara* level.

On the other side, looked at SYSTEMICALLY, and along a SYNCHRONIC axis, the relationship between Buddhism and Brahmanism/Hinduism (and Jainism) takes on a somewhat different aspect, the perspective here being no longer spread out over time but structural. At this level of analysis in particular the contrastive opposition WORLDLY/MUNDANE (*laukika*) : SUPRAMUNDANE/TRANSMUNDANE (*lokottara*) takes on its full significance. And it is at this level that the historical, and eventually secular, opposition 'Buddhism *vs.* Hinduism' proves to be problematic.

In some cases an analysis based on its postulation appears indeed to be quite inappropriate, for example in the case of icons representing a SUPERORDINATE, and transmundane, divinity treading on a SUBORDINATE, and mundane, one (although, as noted above at pp. 49–50, the mere fact that a protector divinity is described and iconographically depicted as treading on an inferior figure does not automatically show that the divinity must belong to the *lokottara* level).

In the last analysis, then, the choice for the historian of religion will not lie between two clear-cut and mutually exclusive alternatives, i.e. between a substratum model and a borrowing model.[202] Rather, it will often be necessary to have recourse to more than one model, each being appropriate to distinct aspects or levels of analysis, and without one relevant model necessarily excluding another relevant one. If neither a sub-

---

202 As the matter has been starkly formulated by an advocate of the latter model in accordance with his understanding of Sanderson's views on the subject; see R. Mayer's statement on p. 272 of his article 'The figure of Maheśvara/ Rudra in the rÑiṅ-ma-pa Tantric tradition', *JIABS* 21 (1998) (pp. 271–310): 'For specialists in Tantric Buddhism, the most significant result of Sanderson's work has been to seriously call into question the previously dominant view accepted by a majority of Buddhological scholars, who had suggested that any such observable parallels between the specifically *kāpālika* or "cemetery" strands within the Buddhist Vajrayāna and a number of very similar Śaiva systems, were primarily the result of both traditions arising from a common Indic cultural substrate. While Martin Kalff since the 1970's and David Snellgrove since the mid-1980's had already begun to question the validity of this unsatisfactorily vague position on the grounds of common sense and more generalised observation, it was only with the presentation of Sanderson's minutely detailed and substantially documented philological analysis that we have finally been able to conclude with a reasonable degree of certainty that such similarities are much better explained as a result of direct Buddhist borrowings from the Śaiva sources.' This statement of the matter appears unsatisfactory in several respects. First, it is far from clear that a 'substrate' explanation has been accepted by 'a majority' of 'Buddhological scholars'; numerically the majority would seem to have taken a borrowing model as a given. Secondly, and more importantly, the very abundant evidence – which has not in fact, so far, been set out in a 'minutely detailed and substantially documented philological analysis' – is far from being unilateral and unequivocal, and from lending itself universally, in 'generalised observation', to a single form of analysis. Thirdly, it is by no means evident whose (and what) 'common sense' is being invoked here as normative (that of the various authors of the Vajrayānist sources or that of the individual modern analyst?): in these matters claims invoking so-called common sense are all too often subjective and doubtful.

stratum model – which is an 'etic' and historical one except to the extent that it corresponds to the *laukika* level in Buddhist thought, which is an 'emic' as well as a synchronic category – nor even an 'emic', and synchronic, form of the substratum model corresponding to the contrastive opposition *laukika* : *lokottara* can, alone and by itself, fully account for the entirety of the very complex religious and doctrinal evidence available to us, neither can a generalized borrowing model do so alone. Explanation and hermeneutical understanding both need to be refined and made context-sensitive. And analysis and interpretation need also to operate on more than a single level and, sometimes, with more than a single model or paradigm.

*

It has also to be kept clearly in mind that, in the Buddhism of the Mahāyāna and Vajrayāna, the dichotomy *laukika* : *lokottara* is resolvable, and as it were deconstructible, in the Emptiness of self-existence (*svabhāva-śūnyatā* or *niḥsvabhāvatā*) and essencelessness (*nairātmya*) that characterizes all things (*dharma*) and entities (*bhāva*). Thus, neither of the two terms of this pair, nor of course even the pair itself, is to be essentialized and reified. This is indeed a fundamental point in Prajñāpāramitā and Madhyamaka thought that subtends Mahāyāna and Vajrayāna. Hence, while beings of the *laukika* level are all regarded as subject to the conditioned (*saṃskr̥ta*) processes of the round of existences (*saṃsāra*), and while gods make up one of the recognized five or six states of existence (*gati*), the divinities belonging to the *lokottara* level are not to be hypostatized as ultimately real entities. Rather, the tutelaries of the *lokottara* level are so to say symbols of yogic and intellectual attainment (see Appendix II below). The gods of the *laukika* level largely correspond to the Pali category of *sammutideva*s and *upapattideva*s, whilst divinities of the *lokottara* level parallel the Pali category of *visuddhideva*s.

*

Topics discussed above touch on an old, and very vexed, issue in Indian studies, namely the question why Buddhism did not survive as a distinct entity in India and why it practically disappeared in the land of its birth as a distinct religious movement.

The fact that Buddhism arose in an Indian matrix and developed in an Indian ambience, and that it has many features in common with Brahmanism/Hinduism and also Jainism, can scarcely justify the view that it was somehow fated to recede back into its milieu at some point in its history and then practically disappear from view. As pointed out above, the substratum model discussed in the present work does not imply that Buddhism was nothing but a version of what is now called 'Hindutva'.[203] Both Buddhists and Brahmanists/Hindus have in fact been aware of their distinctiveness and their mutual differences, and they did not fail to discuss and dispute with each other on matters of religion and philosophy. An interesting piece of evidence is furnished by the *Prabodhacandrodaya*, an allegorical drama by Kṛṣṇamiśra, a contemporary of the Candella king Kīrtivarman of Jejākabhukti (Bundelkhand) who advocated at the end of the eleventh century a form of Vishnuite Vedānta, where Buddhism has been depicted in a conventional, and polemical, light. (The Pālas, who had reigned a little earlier, were the last major Buddhist dynasty of India.)

Yet it is a historical fact that – unlike Jainism, another Śramaṇa movement – Buddhism did not live on in the Indian heartlands as a distinct and discrete entity. This may have to do at least in part with the fact that, unlike Jainism, Buddhism did not cultivate the kind of socio-religious organization necessary to ensure its survival as a distinct institution.[204]

It could of course be maintained that Buddhism has survived in India in a diffuse and non-institutional form in the sense that, by cross-fertilization or osmosis, it has contributed much to the historical development of Brahmanism/Hinduism (and Jainism). The Buddha was for example adopted as an *avatāra* of Viṣṇu (the motive for this acceptance being, however, double; see above, pp. 14, 122). Since the nineteenth century, moreover, many educated Indians have felt a keen interest in, sometimes

---

203 See pp. 1–2, 113 above.

204 See P. Jaini, 'The disappearance of Buddhism and the survival of Jainism' (as in n. 28 above). And on the Jaina *śramaṇopāsaka* helping to guarantee the separate survival of Jainism, see P. Jaini, 'Śramaṇas: their conflict with Brahmanical society' (as in n. 3 above), p. 65. Cf. K. R. Norman, 'The role of the layman according to the Jain canon', in M. Carrithers and C. Humphrey (ed.), *The Assembly of Listeners, Jains in society* (Cambridge, 1991), pp. 31–39.

even an affinity to, Buddhism (without in most cases ceasing to consider themselves true Hindus). The Mahābodhi Society arose at that time. And Hindus are quite prepared to give alms and hospitality to a Buddhist monk or nun, whom they recognize as a religious and renunciant. Also, since the middle of the twentieth century, there have existed the so-called Neo-Buddhists inspired by B. R. Ambedkar. Furthermore, on the periphery of the Indian subcontinent – in Ladak, Nepal, Sikkim, Bhutan, Bangladesh,[205] Burma, and Sri Lanka – Buddhism has continued to live on in various forms. But the fact remains that, for many centuries, Buddhism has for all practical purposes been barely present in the Indian heartlands – in the Āryāvarta or Madhyadeśa of old – and in India south of the Vindhya mountains at least until the twentieth century.[206]

By scholars this fact has been explained in various ways. Some explanations have simply displaced the problem without resolving it. And sometimes what was hypothetical, and still in need of demonstration, was taken as the premiss of a further argument, so that questions were simply begged.

Several considerations cited in the past in order to account for the disappearance of Buddhism in India can be seen not to be specific to Buddhism alone and to apply *mutatis mutandis* also to other surviving Indian religions.

Thus the view that seeks to explain the disappearance of Buddhism on the ground that Hinduism was 'always predominant' in India fails to tell us why it was that Buddhism's numerical inferiority – which presumably was its demographic situation in much of India during most if not all of its history there – caused it to decline at one point rather than at another in this history. Above all, it fails to explain how it came about that, unlike Jainism, Buddhism was unable to survive in a position of numeri-

---

[205] On historical and cultural problems posed by this presence in the east of the Indian subcontinent, see H. Bechert, 'Zur Geschichte des Theravāda-Buddhismus in Ostbengalen', in: H. Härtel (ed.), *Beiträge zur Indienforschung* (Festschrift E. Waldschmidt, Berlin, 1977), pp. 45–66, who distinguishes between true survival from earlier times, more or less recent migration and conversion, and Hindu-Buddhist syncretism.

[206] For South India, see recently J. Guy, 'Southern Buddhism – Traces and transmissions', in: C. Jarrige and V. Lefevre (eds.), *Proceedings of the 16th European Association of South Asian archaeology* (Paris, 2005), pp. 495–504.

cal inferiority. But does 'predominance' here include other factors such as royal preference, or at least support? Questions then arise as to what caused Buddhism sometimes to be preferred by a king (or perhaps a queen) over other religions, and when it was being supported by royal patronage alongside other religions. Following this line of thinking, it seems that the reverse of royal preference or favour – i.e. prolonged persecution and radical extirpation – might account for its disappearance. Shrouded as they are in the mists of time, however, the historical developments in question often remain uncertain if not undeterminable for us. (In the case of the emperor Aśoka, we do have extensive independent and contemporary documentation – namely this king's inscriptions – that contribute to clarifying his relation to Buddhism. For Harṣavardhana of Kanauj in the first part of the seventh century, available evidence connects this king with both Buddhism and Śaivism (*'paramamāheśvara'*), and his drama *Nāgānanda* includes both Buddhist and Śākta features; in the Sonpat seal of Harṣa, his elder brother Rājyavardhana is called a *paramasaugata*. Examples of such complex religious affiliation could of course be multiplied easily.[207])

The transition from earlier Brahmanism – with currents within which Buddhism has indeed had numerous points of contact and relationship – to what is known as Hinduism with its strong theistic orientation, and its caste- and 'class'-oriented *varṇāśramadharma*, must have been a very significant factor in the disappearance of Buddhism. Yet Buddhism too has had its devotional or *bhakti* currents; and as is clear from material discussed in the present work the presence of the divine, and of gods, is well attested in it. And although Buddhism did not accept the external-

---

[207] To Harṣa is also ascribed the *Aṣṭamahāśrīcaityastotra*. The prologues of two other plays attributed to him, the *Ratnāvalī* and the *Priyadarśikā*, bear the imprint of Śaivism.

An inscription on a bronze image of the Buddha from Central India dedicated by an anonymous 'queen' of a certain 'king' Hari of the Gupta dynasty includes the curious formula *sarvasattvānāṃ ... anuttarapadajñānāvāptaye* (the more usual formula being: *...anuttara(buddha)jñāna...*); see O. von Hinüber, *Die Palola Ṣāhis* (Antiquities of Northern Pakistan 5, Mainz, 2004), pp. 126–7. The inscriptional (and also numismatic) materials of course yield much suggestive information concerning Buddhist-Hindu symbioses. In the history of Buddhism, queens sometimes appear to have been more closely linked with Buddhism than were their husbands.

ities of Hindu *varṇāśramadharma*, it did recognize a class of Āryas and successive stages in religious life. In Buddhism, the Āryan person was determined and defined not by birth and family but by inner qualities and by that person's spiritual 'family' and stage of development. In this respect, as well as in regard to monachism and monasticism, Brahmanism/Hinduism – where renunciation (*saṃnyāsa*, as distinct from restraint), even though prized, has nevertheless been a somewhat problematic category – can be described as being in a certain sense both more societally oriented, and somewhat more lay or 'secular' (as opposed to monachal or monastic), than Buddhism tended to be in India.[208] But, of course, in such matters generalization can be dangerous, and the concept of the secular is slippery in a civilization that does not in fact oppose the secular and the religious, the temporal and the spiritual, in the way this has usually been done in the modern West. In Hinduism, the *varṇāśramadharma* is of course considered an eminently religious value.

A further weighty factor in the present context may well have been the fact that, in India, Buddhism was so closely associated with the monk's (and eventually the nun's) code of discipline (*vinaya*), and that it came to be bound up to a high degree with its monastic institutions. Institutional monasticism with populous and costly monasteries (as distinct from temples) evidently weighed less, generally speaking, in Hinduism, and in Jainism, than in Buddhism. (In this connexion it is interesting to note that, in Tibet, the survival of Buddhism in times of troubles – and notably at the time of its persecution there in the ninth century – has been linked with the action of lay [*khyim pa* = *gṛhin*]

---

[208] The high proportion of 'secular' literature – poetry (albeit regularly with Hindu religious themes), poetics and of course grammar – in the traditional Sanskrit education of the *paṇḍit* in India has been pointed out in E. Gerow, 'Primary education in Sanskrit: Methods and goals', *JAOS* 122 (2002), p. 661 f.; see also A. Michaels (ed.), *The pandit* (New Delhi, 2001). This situation may be compared and contrasted with the traditional Tibetan curriculum – beginning with the class of logic-epistemology and ending with the class of Abhidharma or Vinaya – largely dispensed in monastic seminaries. Even in Tibet 'secular' literature including *belles lettres* was not always entirely neglected; see Part II of our *Ordre spirituel et ordre temporel dans la pensée bouddhique de l'Inde et du Tibet*.

On *saṃnyāsa* with Śaṃkara, see R. Marcaurelle, *Freedom through inner renunciation* (Albany, 2000) with the review by J. Taber, *JAOS* 123 (2003), pp. 692–5.

religious – i.e. the Tibetan category of the white-clad [*skya bo*, *dkar po*] religious and married Mantrin [*sṅags pa*] – in particular among the rÑiṅ ma pas for whom vast monastic implantations, as distinct from temples, were for long of limited importance, but also among other Tibetan orders and schools [*chos lugs*]. During difficult times in Tibet, Buddhism could survive, and remain alive, with proportionally few monastics [*grva pa*, etc.], and even fewer fully ordained monks [*dge sloṅ = bhikṣu; btsun pa = bhadanta*], relatively to the population compared with other periods in that country's history.)

Very significant must also be the fact that Hinduism has situated itself as 'Vedic' – and hence as of non-human (*apauruṣeya*) and timeless origin – and as the *sanātanadharma*, whereas Buddhism has been a movement that regarded itself as originating from a human Sage and Awakened One (*[sam]buddha*; that is, it is classed as *pauruṣeya*). Yet even this important difference can be overstated. Although also a Śramaṇa movement, Jainism has survived in India. And, beside the 'Vedic', non-Vedic (Āgamic and Tantric) strands have flourished in abundance within Hinduism. These non-Vedic traditions claimed to have their source not in a human teacher but in god (*īśvara*, i.e. Śiva, Viṣṇu, etc.).

Another factor traditionally regarded as having favoured the disappearance of Buddhism in India was the 'universal conquest' (*digvijaya*) of India by Śaṃkarācārya and his Śāṃkara-Vedānta.[209] Yet, interestingly, it is in his tradition that monasticism came to play a considerable rôle. And in its essence Śaṃkara's Vedānta is highly 'intellectual', and anything but 'popular'. It also includes certain features reminiscent of Buddhism; indeed, by opponents, Śaṃkara was considered a 'secret Buddhist' (*pracchannabauddha*; see above, p. 139). Except through its being largely represented in society by Smārtas with their *pañcāyatanapūjā* (directed to Śiva, Viṣṇu, Durgā, Sūrya, and Gaṇeśa), the Advaita-Vedānta is in itself scarcely more theistic than Buddhism.[210] As for Mīmāṃsā,

---

[209] *Śaṃkaravijaya* is the title of a hagiography of Śaṃkarācārya ascribed to his disciple Ānandagiri, *Śaṃkaradigvijaya* being the title of a later hagiography attributed to Mādhava-Vidyāraṇya.

[210] Some aspects of this question have been reviewed by P. Stephan, 'Göttliche Gnade in Śaṅkaras Soteriologie?", *ZDMG* 154 (2004), pp. 397–416 (discussing B. Malkovsky, *The role of divine grace in the soteriology of Śaṅkarācārya* [Leiden 2001]). See also

also non-theistic, its great representative Kumārila (seventh century) was a strong critic of Buddhism.

It is certain that Buddhists were engaged in organized debates with Brahmanical/Hindu opponents, by whom they were no doubt sometimes defeated and may eventually have been compelled publicly to renounce their religio-philosophical position. Moreover, that Buddhists were on occasion the targets of religio-political or sectarian attacks and persecution by Hindu rulers and Brahmans also seems clear.[211] Perhaps the threat of persecution came less from Vedāntin or Mīmāṃsaka thinkers than from sectarian followers of the Indian theistic religions (Śaivas, Vaiṣṇavas, etc.) claiming *āstika*, and eventually 'Vedic' (*vaidika*), affiliations. In so far as they were philosophers, by the time of the decline of Buddhism in India its opponents appear to have been linked closely with the Nyāya school (Udayana of Mithalā, a Śaiva, was a leading example in the eleventh century).

An impression of hostility to the point of persecution may sometimes be conveyed by the highly polemical style of debate traditionally practised in India (and Tibet), which could go so far as to include mockery, obloquy and invective. It should be remembered, however, that extreme forms of language could on occasion be adopted even by debaters belonging to different traditions within the same school – and also by fellow students in school debates (for example in a Tibetan seminary or *grva tshaṅ*) – and that this conventionalized, and even highly ritualized, style became a sort of formalized hortatory or admonitory procedure having paraenetic as well as intimidatory uses.

A further cause of the decline of Buddhism in India is credibly stated to have been Muslim (Turuṣka, etc.) invasions and depredations, in particular the destruction of its great monastic centres.[212] This, however,

---

P. Hacker, *Kleine Schriften*, ed. L. Schmithausen, Index s. u. 'Gott'; and M. Comans, *The method of early Advaita Vedānta* (Delhi, 2000), pp. 184 ff., 215 ff.

211 Evidence for the persecution of Buddhism in India has recently been studied by G. Verardi; see n. 2 above). The question of both persecution and tolerance was reviewed by R. C. Mitra, *The decline of Buddhism in India* (Santiniketan, 1954), p. 125 ff.

212 For a later Buddhist view of the situation then prevailing see, e.g., Tāranātha, *rGya gar chos 'byuṅ* (ed. Schiefner), pp. 193–4. A contemporary account is provided in the

leaves intact the question as to the extent to which the survival of Buddhism in India was in fact dependent on the continued existence of these monastic centres, and also on the extent to which there existed Buddhist householder-religious (of whom a Vimalakīrti was doubtless an idealized instance) and non-monastic *gomins* (such as Candragomin). In principle, in times of trouble, these would have been in a position to ensure the continued existence of the Buddhist traditions in the lay setting of a family and lineage.[213]

What is noteworthy is the fact that Buddhism has remained alive around the periphery of India – in Sri Lanka, in sub-Himalayan, Himalayan and trans-Himalayan regions, and in Southeast Asia – and also in distant Japan. Even in China it survived in a much more visible and palpable form than it did in the Indian heartland. It was in 'exterior India' that Buddhism has lived on, whereas in most of India proper it more or less disappeared as a distinct and discrete entity.

None of the aforementioned factors can, it seems, fully account for the vicissitudes that have marked the history of Buddhism in India. They can at best elucidate some individual cases, but without comprehensively explaining the fate there of Buddhism as a whole. The Indian plant that was Buddhism apparently somehow came to be felt to be exotic and exceptional (even alien) in the Indian heartlands in spite of the fact that it had sprung from Indian soil and had long shared a multitude of features with Brahmanism/Hinduism. Something in the nature of a paradigm gap seems to have developed. And meaningful dialogue appears to have become difficult between Buddhists and most 'orthodox' Brahmanists, who often found themselves simply talking past each other. Notwithstanding the fact that there has existed a wide range of shared ritual behaviour, mental categories, even linguistic expression – and, indeed, also a commonality of ends (i.e. liberation or *mokṣa*) –, a certain discontinuity, even

---

biography of the Tibetan pilgrim-student Chag Lo tsā ba Chos rje dpal (1197–1264), as well as in the biographies of Śākyaśrībhadra (1140–1225) and his associates.

213 See the remarks made above. On the matter of the *gomin*, and on the non-monastic Mahāyānist, see the observations in D. Seyfort Ruegg, 'Aspects of the study of the (earlier) Indian Mahāyāna', *JIABS* 27 (2004), p. 25. As observed above, Buddhism in Tibet is said to have been in a position to survive catastrophe and persecution by reason of its having been transmitted by householder religious and lay *sṅags pa*s who were able to preserve it in a family and lineage structure.

a rupture, evidently came to be felt to exist as regards attitudes and approaches, and the religious and philosophical organization and mapping of life. Then, in the time of upheaval through which large parts of India were passing at the turn of the millennium, the close links between these two traditions were largely lost sight of (except, in part, in so-called 'Tantrism' and hence in areas deeply marked by 'Tantric' culture).

The old 'religious-cultural code' of Buddhism would appear for instance to have come to be regarded as somewhat alien in a time when theism had prevailed in India. But it does not seem that the decisive factor in its virtual disappearance there could have been so-called Buddhist atheism alone; for, as seen in our sources, whatever the subordinate place it may have assigned to gods and celestials, Buddhism not only very clearly included them on one level but it embraced a distinctive sense of the divine. In particular – and contrary to an often-expressed opinion – it does not appear to be the case that it was Buddhist recognition of the mundane level of the *laukika* – inclusive of the religious and also temporal substratum which it largely shared with Brahmanism/Hinduism – that was inexorably to result in Buddhism's receding, and in effect being absorbed, into the matrix from which it had sprung, and in which it had flourished over many centuries. Even though the *laukika* was acknowledged by Buddhists, this was balanced by the recognition of a distinctively Buddhist *lokottara* level: the two levels are indeed linked terms in a structured opposition. How decisive the argument could be that this *lokottara* level had become less and less perceptible and significant, at least to ordinary followers of the Buddhist religion, is a matter of conjecture. Inclusivism under Hacker's definition does not in any case seem to have been responsible. In Japan too, dividing lines between Buddhism and other traditional religion have on occasion been blurred, doubtless leading sometimes to a marginalization of Buddhism, but not to its disappearance. In Tibet, such marginalization did not take place, even though there too lines of demarcation have on occasion been obscured.

The exploration of these and related issues will constitute a major task for further study and research in the history of Buddhism.[214]

---

214 This is not the place to pursue any parallelism or isomorphism between the absorptive integration (docetic or otherwise) of the *laukika* level into the *lokottara* with Indian polities and state-formation that have been variously described as

*

To sum up, in the source materials surveyed in the present study, the relationship between the two levels of the worldly/mundane and the transmundane/supramundane has been conceived of mainly in terms of three paradigms: 1) the idea of a *laukika* divinity as phantom projection or docctic emanation (*nirmāṇa* = *sprul pa*) of a being (or symbol) belonging to the *lokottara* level, 2) the idea of a *laukika* divinity's respectful submission to this being (or symbol) of the *lokottara*, and 3) the idea of the forcible subjugation of a *laukika* divinity to the *lokottara* deity, either directly by the latter or through the agency of Vajrapāṇi. The last two paradigms are frequently associated with the idea that the *laukika* divinity offers a vow (*saṃvara* = *sdom pa*) or promise (*pratijñā* = *dam bca'*) to protect the Teaching and enters into a convention (*samaya* = *dam tshig*) with the transmundane level. Essential here is the theme of training (*vi-nī-* = *'dul ba*) on the Path of liberation. And the idea of a solemn predictive declaration (*vyākaraṇa* = *luṅ bstan*) for Awakening and future buddhahood may also be present, especially in the context of paradigm 2.

Iconographically, these modes could be variously depicted. The integration of a worldly divinity in the *kula* 'clan' of a *lokottara* deity can be represented by the image of the latter placed vertically above the head, or

---

integrative (H. Kulke), segmentary (B. Stein), galactic (S. Tambiah), or feudal. The fact that *maṇḍala*-structure has been prominent in both areas may have provided a link. Characteristic of Indian polity and state-formation was the absorption or integration of neigbouring, peripheral chiefs or 'little kings' – *sāmanta*(*rāja*)s exercising effective political control locally – into a larger, central realm of a 'great king' possessing *inter alia* extended ritual sovereignty or suzerainty. There exists then a certain comparability between *sāmanta* rulers and regional or local divinities (along with their temples and sacred places) who are integated into the myth, ritual and ideology of a central and superordinate deity (and his sacred centre). A great transmundane protector (*dharmapāla*) may even be represented as placed in the centre of his *maṇḍala*, surrounded by his entourage or court consisting of ministers, generals, warriors, messengers, etc. But although there may indeed exist parallels or echoes, any reductionism that would seek to derive the religious from the political or societal, or to explain the former by the latter, cannot be postulated *a priori*. The political and historical issues have been surveyed in, e.g., H. Kulke (ed.), *The state in India 1000–1700* (Delhi, 1995); see also the same scholar's *Kings and cults*: *State formation and legitimation in India and Southeast Asia* (New Delhi, 1993).

in the headdress, of the the former, a depiction that corresponds in particular to paradigm 2. Such incorporation can also be depicted horizontally by placing the *laukika* in a subordinate field of the *maṇḍala* of the main, central, deity. The forcible subjugation of a *laukika* divinity can be depicted by the figure representing the *lokottara* shown dancing, or treading, upon the the *laukika* divinity, a depiction corresponding to paradigm 3. Paradigm 2 may be more or less closely associated with the docetism characteristic of paradigm 1. This is exemplified also in the Japanese *honji suijaku* concept.

It is important to observe that, in a soteriological perspective, the *laukika* level may be transformed, or trans-valued, on to the *lokottara* level. Conversely, the noumenal (*ye šes pa*) of the *lokottara* level may be 'invited', by ritual and yogic means, to 'descend' on to the phenomenal, and conventional (*dam tshig pa*), level of the practiser (see Appendix II below). In terms of religion, soteriology and even gnoseology, then, the *laukika* and *lokottara* levels are not thought of as fixed and frozen reified entities between which there is no possibility of transfigurative communication. And their relation involves very much more than infiltration, borrowing, syncretism, or inclusivism (under Paul Hacker's definition). Pertinent, rather, are the ideas of symbiosis and a common ground, or substratum, one on the basis of which intertextuality and intericonographicity (and indeed borrowing) may have operated in certain cases.

Appendix I

Hinduistic elements in Tibetan Buddhist and Bon po sources, and the terms 'Buddhistic', 'Hinduistic', and 'Indic'

As is well known, much use has been made in Tibet of myths and legends found in the Indian Epics and Purāṇas which are, therefore, not specifically Buddhist even though they have been adopted by Tibetan Buddhist mythographers, story-tellers and literati.[215] Texts of later Indian Buddhist origin that include this kind of material, and which were much favoured as sources by the Tibetans, are notably Śaṃkarasvāmin's **Devātiśayastotra/Devatāvimarśastuti* and Udbhaṭasiddhasvāmin's **Viśeṣa/Viśiṣṭa-stava* and **Sarvajñamaheśvarastotra* together with Prajñāvarman's commentaries on the first two of these works. The Vinaya of the Mūlasarvāstivādins, Ārya-Śūra's *Jātakamāla* and Kṣemendra's *Bodhisattvāvadānakalpalatā* can also be mentioned here. Abundant relevant materials are to be found in addition in Tantras and their commentaries, for example in the *Ḍākinī-agnijihvājvālātantra* (*mKha' 'gro ma me lce 'bar ba'i rgyud*; P 466, D 842) discussed already many years ago by Tucci and Stein.[216]

In Tibetan as well as in Indian Buddhist tradition, the first human king was Mahāsammata (Tib. Maṅ pos bkur ba['i rgyal po]), the 'Honoured One' or 'Approved One' often mentioned in our sources. Generations later, Rupati – an Indian prince regarded by some writers as the the son of Śatānīka (dMag brgya pa, identifiable as the son of the Pāṇḍava Nakula and Draupadī) but by others as one of the Pāṇḍava brothers (sKya seṅ gi bu lṅa) who survived the great fratricidal Mahābhārata war between the descendants of Pāṇḍu (sKya [bo] seṅ), the Pāṇḍavas, and the Kauravas (sGra ṅan) – is said to have taken refuge in Tibet disguised as a

---

[215] Once they came to be recognized as forming part of Tibetan culture, such elements of Brahmanical/Hindu origin might be referred to as 'Hinduistic'; on the usefulness of this conceptualisation and its terminology, see below, pp. 173 f.

[216] See G. Tucci, *Tibetan painted scrolls*, p. 218; and R. A. Stein, 'La mythologie hindouiste au Tibet', in: G. Gnoli and L. Lanciotti (ed.), *Orientalia Iosephi Tucci memoriae dicata*, iii (Rome, 1988), pp. 1407–26. On the Kālacakra in particular see above.

woman after the defeat of his clan. This Rupati has been identified by some authorities with the first Tibetan king gÑa' khri btsan po, who descended on top of a mountain in Tibet, was carried by the inhabitants on their shoulders as a mark of honour, and was adopted by the Tibetans as their king. The Tibetan tradition concerning such a 'king come from elsewhere' (*glo bur*, as opposed to an 'Approved One', *bskos pa*, and to one belonging to a [Tibetan] lineage, *gduṅ brgyud*) has been known under the name of *gsaṅ ba chos lugs* 'the hidden tradition of Dharma'.[217] But the legend identifying the Indian Pāṇḍava prince Rupati with the Tibetan king gÑa' khri btsan po has been firmly rejected by some writers, for example by the historian Nel/Ne'u pa paṇḍi ta, who ascribed its propagation in Tibet to the scholar Rig pa'i ral gri of sNar thaṅ (second part of the thirteenth century).[218]

---

217 On this *gsaṅ ba chos lugs* – which in, e.g., the *bKa' thaṅ sde lṅa* stands beside the *bsgrags pa bon lugs* and, curiously, the *yaṅ gsaṅ mu stegs lugs* 'the particularly hidden tradition of the Tīrthikas' – see A. Macdonald, 'Une lecture des Pelliot tibétain 1286, 1287, 1038, 1047, et 1290', in: *Études tibétaines dédiées à la mémoire de Marcelle Lalou*, pp. 193, 206; and A. M. Blondeau, 'Identification de la tradition appelée bsGrags-pa bon-lugs', in: T. Skorupski (ed.), *Indo-Tibetan Studies* (D. Snellgrove Felicitation Volume, Tring, 1990), p. 37 f.

For the above-mentioned three types of king, see, e.g., mKhas pa lDe'u, *rGya bod kyi chos 'byuṅ* (Lhasa, 1987), p. 191 ff. In this context, *glo bur* (Skt. *āgantuka*) means not 'sudden' (as it has frequently been mistranslated) but 'from elsewhere, external, extrinsic' (the spelling *blo bur* is also found).

That the Pāṇḍava brothers repaired to the Himālaya (Kedāra) to expiate as ascetics their sin of having killed their Kuru kinsmen is a familiar theme in Hindu sources.

218 See Nel pa, *Me tog phreṅ ba* (of 1283) (ed. Uebach), p. 54; related stories have also been criticized by dPa' bo gTsug lag phreṅ ba, *Chos 'byuṅ mKhas pa'i dga' ston*, ja, f. 5b–6a. The story in question is found already in the *bKa' chems ka khol ma* (Lanzhou, 1989), {p. 77 f.}; see Tsering Gyalbo, G. Hazod and P. Sørensen, *Civilization at the foot of Mount Sham-po* (Vienna, 2000), p. 58 n. 70, where further sources are listed.

For the legend of the Pāṇḍavas in Tibet, in addition to several standard Tibetan historical works, see lHa smon dza sag Ye šes tshul khrims, *sKya seṅ bu lṅa'i byuṅ ba brjod pa* in: *Rare Tibetan historical and literary texts from the library of Tsepon W. D. Shakabpa*, published by T. Tsepal Taikhang (New Delhi, 1974). In Tibet, the story of the Pāṇḍava Rupati's coming there may go back to Prajñāvarman's commentary on Śaṃkarasvāmin's **Devātiśayastotra/Devatāvimarśastuti* (verse 3), perhaps through commentaries on Sa paṇ's *Legs par bšad pa rin po che'i gter* such as dMar ston Chos

The link between Indian and Tibetan mythology is of course by no means confined to the 'national' royal line, and it extends further to include princely lineages of regional and local significance. To take an example: Yar lha šam po – a famous *gnas ri* which is simultaneously conceived of as a mountain, its protective divinity, and the latter's residence – is known also as the divinity Šam bu (classified in Tibet as a *gnod sbyin* = *yakṣa*). It/he appears as the protector of the land of gYa' bzaṅ, and of its myriarchs (*khri dpon*). This mountain-cum-divinity, classifiable as a mundane protector (*'jig rten pa'i sruṅ ma*), has then been sometimes assimilated to the Indian Śambhu (i.e. Śaṃkara/Śiva/Mahādeva/Maheśvara, who is associated with Mount Kailāsa). While Yar lha šam po's mount is a great white yak, Śiva's is the white bull Nandi(n). Also found as the protectress of the gYa' bzaṅ pa lineage is lHa mo Tsaṇḍi ka (i.e. Caṇḍikā = Durgā, the *śakti* of Śiva), regarded also as the consort of Ye šes mgon po (Jñānanātha-Mahākāla, an emanation of Lokeśvara/Avalokiteśvara). Śiva's seat of Mount Kailāsa, the Tibetan Gaṅs Ti se, is also the palace of bDe mchog (Śaṃvara)/'Khor lo sdom pa (Cakrasaṃvara). In the gYa' bzaṅ tradition, the *gza' bdud* Draṅ sroṅ Rāhu(la) also fulfils the function of a protector (sGra gcan [Rāhu] being there regarded as an emanation of Mahākāruṇika-Avalokiteśvara). And Laṅka mGrin bcu – i.e. Daśagrīva/Daśakaṇṭha (Rāvaṇa) of the Rāma epic – figures in the mythology of gYa' bzaṅ, as do Rāmaṇa/'Ra ma pha la' (i.e. Rāma) himself and Hanumant (described there as a Bodhisattva).[219] As for Šam bu and Tsaṇḍi ka, in Tibet they are regarded in this

---

kyi rgyal po's. Cf. U. Roesler, 'The great Indian epics in the version of dMar ston Chos kyi rgyal po', in H. Blezer (ed.), *Religion and secular culture in Tibet* (Tibetan Studies II, PIATS 2000, Leiden, 2002), pp. 431–50.

[219] See the *gYa' bzaṅ chos 'byuṅ*, ff. 9b–10a, reproduced in T. Gyalbo *et al.*, *Civilization at the foot of Mount Sham-po*, pp. 119–20. On the mountain-divinity Yar lha šam po see also R. de Nebesky-Wojkowitz, *Oracles and demons of Tibet*, Index *s. u.*; and S. Karmay, 'The Tibetan cult of mountain deities and its political significance', in : A.-M. Blondeau and E. Steinkellner (ed.), *Reflections on the mountain* (Vienna, 1996), pp. 59–75.

It may be noted that in the Khotanese Rāmāyaṇa Rāma has been identified, in a Jātaka-like passage, with Śākyamuni, and is apparently (?) said to have defeated Viṣṇu and Śiva; see R. Emmerick, 'Polyandry in the Khotanese Rāmāyaṇa', in: C. Chojnacki *et al.* (ed.), *Vividharatnakaraṇḍaka* (Festschrift A. Mette [Swisttal-Odendorf, 2000], p. 234.

context as salvific emanations of, respectively, Avalokiteśvara/Lokeśvara and Tārā.[220] We find here a Tibetan counterpart of the Japanese *honji suijaku* concept described above.[221]

A further example of the same idea is provided by the *sku žaṅ* princes of Ža lu, Grags pa rgyal mtshan (first half of the 14th c.) being considered an emanation (*sprul pa = nirmāṇa*) of rNam thos sras (Vaiśravaṇa/Kubera, the Mahārāja-guardian of the North whose seat is Mount Kailāsa), who is classifiable as a supramundane protector (*'jig rten las 'das pa'i sruṅ ma*).[222] And among the rulers of the myriarchy (*khri skor*) of gYas ru Byaṅ (i.e. La stod byaṅ) with its centre at Byaṅ Ṅam riṅ, some of whom cultivated a special interest in the Kālacakra, one Byaṅ bdag was considered to be the 'returning' (*slar byon pa*) of the second Kalkin Puṇḍarīka, whilst an earlier Byaṅ bdag was held to be an emanation of Mahākāruṇika-Avalokiteśvara.[223] Similarly, in Šel dkar in La stod lho district, lHo bdag Chos kyi rin chen (d. 1402) – the son-in-law of a Byaṅ bdag whose land had previously been at war with La stod lho – was held

---

220 See T. Gyalbo *et al.*, *Civilization at the foot of Mount Sham-po*, pp. 10 ff., 29 n. 28, 46, 61 ff., 90 f., 166 ff., 208 ff. The equivalence Šam bu = bDe byuṅ is given in the *gYa' bzaṅ chos 'byuṅ*, f. 14b, reproduced on p. 122 of the same publication.

221 For the *honji suijaku* concept, see above, pp. 135–136 with n. 69. On the *nirmāṇa* see above.

It should be noted, nevertheless, that N. Iyanaga has distinguished the conceptual schema adopted in Tibet from that familiar to us from China and Japan; see his article 'Récits de la soumission de Maheśvara par Trailokyavijaya', in M. Strickmann (ed.), *Tantric and Taoist studies in honour of R. A. Stein* (*Mélanges chinois et bouddhiques* 22 [Brussels, 1985]), p. 732 n. 16 ('... ni en Chine ni au Japon, les divinités de la (ou des) religions indigènes n'ont à peu près jamais été assimilées aux "Dieux hérétiques" (ou, plus précisément, les Dieux *laukika*) du bouddhisme indien (du moins en tant qu'objets de soumission par les Vénérés bouddhiques) – alors qu'il semble bien que cela ait été le cas au Tibet').

222 See *Bu ston rnam thar*, f. 14a, with D. Seyfort Ruegg, *The Life of Bu ston Rin po che* (Rome, 1966), p. 89. Compare pp. 50, 70 above.

223 See Dalai Lama V, *Bod kyi deb ther dpyid kyi rgyal mo'i glu dbyaṅs* (Beijing, 1988), pp. 113–14; and Rag ra Ṅag dbaṅ bstan pa'i rgyal mtshan, *rGyal rabs chos 'byuṅ šel dkar me loṅ* (in: *Bod kyi lo rgyus deb ther khag lṅa*, Lhasa, 1990), pp. 225–6. A *sDe pa gYas ru byaṅ pa'i rgyal rabs* has been published by T. Tsepal Taikhang in the collection *Rare historical and literary texts from the library of Tsepon W. D. Shakabpa* (New Delhi, 1974).

to be the *rnam 'phrul* or manifestation of King Zla ba bzaṅ po (presumably Sucandra, the interlocutor of the Buddha in the preaching of the *Kālacakratantra*).[224] Very numerous additional examples of emanationism could of course be cited from the Tibetan cultural area, but for our present purpose the cases just referred to may suffice.[225]

Concerning the distinction between the protectors (*sruṅ ma*) who are *'jig rten las 'das pa* 'supramundane' and those who are *'jig rten pa* 'mundane', according to Kloṅ rdol bla ma's *bsTan sruṅ dam can rgya mtsho'i miṅ gi graṅs* the former have attained the higher Paths of the Ārya or 'Noble' (*'phags lam = āryamārga*, starting with the *mthoṅ lam = darśanamārga*), whilst the latter are classified as ordinary worldlings (*so so'i skye bo = pr̥thagjana*). The latter are subdivided into those who have entered the Path (*lam*, i.e. the *tshogs lam = sambhāramārga* and the *sbyor lam = prayogamārga*); as beings having accepted a convention (*dam tshig = samaya*) and bound themselves by an oath (*dam bcas pa*) to guard the 'White Side' (*dkar phyogs*), they protect *upāsaka*s/*upāsikā*s (*dge bsñen pha ma*) and *bhikṣu*s/*bhikṣuṇī*s (*dge sloṅ pha ma*), and those who have entered the Path. The latter may even belong to the 'Black Side' (*nag phyogs*) of the Paranirmitavaśavartin divinities whose chief is Māra in the Kāmadhātu.

---

224 See Ṅag dbaṅ skal ldan rgya mtsho, *Šel dkar chos 'byuṅ*, ff. 11b–12a. Cf. P. Wangdu and H. Diemberger, G. Hazod, *History of "White Crystal"* (Vienna, 1996).

225 An extensive Tibetan account of protective deities (*bstan sruṅ*, *sruṅ ma*) of the supramundane (*'jig rten las 'das pa*) and mundane (*'jig rten pa*) classes who are bound by an oath (*dam can*) to guard the Dharma-Teaching is to be found in sLe luṅ rje druṅ bŽad pa'i rdo rje (b. 1697), *Dam can bstan sruṅ rgya mtsho'i rnam par thar pa cha šas tsam brjod pa sṅon med legs bšad* (reprinted in two volumes at Paro in 1978, and in one volume at Beijing in 2003). A shorter list has been given by Kloṅ rdol bla ma Ṅag dbaṅ blo bzaṅ (b. 1719) in his *bsTan sruṅ dam can rgya mtsho'i miṅ gi graṅs* (section ya of the gSuṅ 'bum). Cf. R. de Nebesky-Wojkowitz, *Oracles and demons of Tibet*; and R. Kaschewsky and Padma Tsering, *sDe-dpon sum-cu* (Wiesbaden, 1998) based on the *'Jig rten mchod bstod sgrub pa rtsa ba'i rgyud* (see above, n. 93).

For Indian ideas in the legend of the foundation of the state of Nan-chao – which became subordinated to Tibet at the end of the eighth century (see P. Demiéville, *Contributions aux études sur Touen-houang* [Geneva, 1979], p. 5) – see E. Rosner and K. Wille, 'Indische Elemente in der Gründungslegende des Königreiches Nan-chao', *ZDMG* 131 (1981), pp. 374–83.

*

The incorporation into Tibetan legend and mythography of Hindu elements can be viewed in the light of the allowance made, in the Abhiṣeka-chapter of the *(Laghu)Kālacakratantra* (iii.169), for the virtuous and learned Yogin-practiser to make use, in his behaviour and praxis (*caryā*), of various cults, including the Śaiva (see above, pp. 115 f). Perhaps more than in any other Buddhist system, the universalist viewpoint of the Kālacakra, finalized in the tenth-eleventh century, evidently reflects an attitude not so much of interreligious TOLERANCE – or alternatively of interreligious INCLUSIVISM (as defined by P. Hacker) – as of a certain SYMBIOSIS (and religious 'cosmopolitanism' ?) founded in the deployment, by a Buddha or Bodhisattva, of soteriological and ritualistic expedient devices (*upāya*) of the DOCETIC type (*nirmāṇa*s, etc.).

The question arises, however, as to why and in just what circumstances such mythical-religious elements of Indian origin came to be adopted in Tibet, where they became current and indeed enculturated. Until more conclusive evidence is available (cf. below), it is no doubt not possible confidently to postulate the existence of some over-arching religio-cultural substratum between Hindu India and Buddhist (or Bon po) Tibet – even if it is true that Tibetans did take over from Buddhist Indians a large part of the common heritage the latter shared with non-Buddhist Indians to such a degree that it becomes possible to speak of a shared Indo-Tibetan cultural background.[226] By itself, this fact will hardly be sufficient satisfactorily to explain the presence, under consideration here, of Hindu or Tīrthika (*mu stegs pa*, *mu stegs can*) elements in indigenous Tibetan writings, and we still have to look for further factors possibly determining this process.

It would appear that a highly important factor here may be the 'emic' model, considered above, of the *'jig rten las 'das pa = lokottara* : *'jig rten pa = laukika*. The latter, structurally subordinate, category is, it should be recalled, susceptible of being integrated into the Buddhist cosmos and, eventually, raised to the level of the superordinate *lokottara* either through a process of 'conversion' or 'training' (*'dul ba = vi-nī-*) –

---

[226] See D. Seyfort Ruegg, *Ordre spirituel et ordre temporel dans la pensée bouddhique de l'Inde et du Tibet* (Paris, 1995), Part II.

i.e. of TRANS-VALUATION – once a mundane divinity is bound by solemn oath (*dam la btags pa*) or by agreed 'convention' (*dam tshig = samaya*) – making a vow (*sdom pa = saṃvara*) to guard the Dharma as a so-called Upāsaka (*dge bsñen gyi sdom pa 'bogs pa*),[227] or undertaking to produce the Thought of Awakening (*sems bskyed = cittotpāda*) – or through regarding the *laukika* divinity as a docetic, ectypal, emanation (*sprul pa*) of a *lokottara*, archetypal, Bodhisattva (such as Avalokiteśvara/Lokeśvara).[228]

The *'jig rten pa = laukika* deities such as Maheśvara/Rudra have, furthermore, been included in the category of the *dregs pa* (*dregs ldan*), i.e. beings whose overweening pride (*dregs pa = māna*, etc.) as to their superior power binds them to the cycle of rebirth (*saṃsāra*) and needs to be humbled before they can be 'trained' and occupy a place in the Buddhist cosmos.[229]

In Tibet the primordial structured function and ideological significance of the *'jig rten pa : 'jig rten las 'das pa* opposition has come acutely and dramatically to the fore in the case of the religious protector rDo rje šugs ldan, whose rôle has been the subject of much controversy. The ambivalence of this figure is mapped by the important distinction between this protector regarded as a Noble (*'phags pa = ārya*) on the Path of the Bodhisattva, beginning with the *darśanamārga* (*mthoṅ lam*) which is the first stage on the *lokottara* Path, and rDo rje šugs ldan considered as an ordinary worldling (*so so skye bo = pṛthagjana*) who has not reached the higher spiritual Path.[230] In the case of rDo rje šugs ldan, the *laukika : lokottara* opposition does not serve to set apart what is

---

[227] Compare above, n. 50.

[228] On these themes, and on 'trans-valuation', see Index *s.v.* Concerning the semantics of *vi-nī-* and *vinaya*, see n. 76 above.

[229] See above, n. 110, on the category of *dregs pa/dregs ldan/dregs pa can.*

[230] For rDo rje šugs ldan see R. de Nebesky-Wojkowitz, *Oracles and demons of Tibet*, p. 134 ff.; G. Dreyfus, 'The Shuk-den affair; history and nature of a quarrel', *JIABS* 21 (1998), pp. 227–70.

For the *āryamarga* of the Bodhisattva defined as beginning with the *darśanamārga*, see above, pp. 43, 69.

considered Buddhist from what is not (such as the *tīrthika*), as in so many other cases considered in this paper; and it is here found operating within Buddhism itself.

*

It is, nevertheless, still necessary to attempt to understand why it was that Tibetan Buddhist writers chose to adopt and employ components derived originally from Tīrthika, or Hindu, myth and legend in order to fill the structural 'slot' constituted by the category of the worldly/mundane in Buddhism. This process of adoption of exogenous components may be regarded as one involving INTERNALIZATION and ENCULTURATION.

One theoretical possibility that needs to be considered is that Tīrthika myth and legend might have somehow already reached Tibet through Bon, the old non-Buddhist (or para-Buddhist) religion of Tibet. For it has been noted that such elements are to be found in Bon also.[231] And a discussion has turned round the vexed question as to whether – and, if so, to what extent – (a form of) Bon might perhaps have included earlier, and still unstandardized, Mahāyānist components from Northwestern South Asia and Central Asia – earlier, that is, and unstandardized or 'non-official', in relation to the standard and 'official' Tibetan Buddhist *Chos* predominating in Tibet starting from the end of the royal period at the close of the eighth century (that is, from the time of Padmasambhava, Śāntarakṣita and Kamalaśīla).[232]

---

[231] cf. G. Tucci and W. Heissig, *Die Religionen Tibets und der Mongolei* (Stuttgart, 1970), pp. 236 n. 3, 247, 254 n. 18; R. A. Stein, 'La mythologie hindouiste au Tibet' (as in n. 63 above), p. 1409.

[232] The relationship between Bon and Buddhism in Tibet presents some interesting parallels (if not strict similarities) to that between Buddhism and Hinduism in India. Concerning Bon, there has been a protracted discussion as to whether it was the original, i.e. primitive and autochtonous, pre-Buddhist religion of Tibet, which was then supplanted (in part) by Buddhism, or whether Bon too has non-Tibetan origins (notably, perhaps, in the North West of the South Asian subcontinent and western Asia: Žaṅ žuṅ, Ta zig/sTag gzig [Iranian area], etc.). The question of the relation between Bon and a so-called 'Padmaism' (a designation employed by H. Hoffmann to denote a major component of the Tibetan rÑiṅ ma in his book *Die Religionen Tibets* [Freiburg, 1956], p. 39 ff.) is also pertinent here, even though Hoffmann adopted the first of the above mentioned views making Bon the 'original' religion of Tibet; see his *Quellen*

Furthermore, whilst Buddhist kings in Southeast Asia do indeed seem to have employed Hindu priests (*purohita*) and ritualists at their courts –

---

zur Geschichte der tibetischen Bon-Religion [Mainz, 1950]). As is well known, rÑiṅ ma tradition and Bon both include a *rdzogs chen* theory and practice, on which see, e.g., S. Karmay, *The Great Perfection* (Leiden, 1988). But specialists on the subject now appear to give much weight to some form of the second view. See P. Kværne, *The Bon religion of Tibet* (London, 1995); id., 'The study of Bon in the West', in: S. Karmay and Y. Nagano (ed.), *New horizons in Bon studies* (Senri Ethnological Reports 15, Osaka, 2000), pp. 10–11, 16–17. In this connexion, and with regard to Bon eclecticism, Kværne refers (pp. 10–11) to D. Snellgrove, *Indo-Tibetan Buddhism* (London, 1987), p. 388 f., 399 f.

Moreover, it is known that there exist textual parallels (and borrowings) between Bon and Buddhist texts. Concerning what he terms 'Bon-Chos intertextuality', D. Martin has suggested that 'this particular type of scriptural adaptation [between Buddhism and Bon] is, at this stage of research, best attested in rNying-ma-pa adaptations of Bon scriptures (as well as perhaps in Buddhist adaptations of Shaivite tantric scriptures [...])'. See his article 'Comparing treatises: Mental states and other *mDzod phug* lists and passages with parallels in Abhidharma works ...', in: S. Karmay and Y. Nagano (ed.), *op. cit.*, p. 67. On the other hand, with respect to Abhidharma-type *mātṛkā*-lists in Bon po works, Martin's conclusion was (*ibid.*, pp. 67–68): 'My suggestion is that the *mDzod phug* is best understood, historically speaking, not only as a continuation of the general Buddhist Abhidharma tradition, but also a continuation of a traditional Buddhist technique for perpetuating and reproducing the teachings of the Buddha for different audiences. If Abhidharma treatises could be produced in Kashmir, Gandhâra, Tukhâra and Bactria, there is really no reason they could not be produced in nearby Zhang-zhung and Tibet as well. [...] I would suggest that [...] Bon probably did not "appropriate" Chos passages and lists as "a means for keeping up with the Buddhists" [...], but rather because they had already [...] come to accept the ideas contained in these passages.' For cosmology, see K. Mimaki, 'A preliminary comparison of Bonpo and Buddhist cosmology', in S. Karmay and Y. Nagano (ed.), *op. cit.*, p.p. 89–115. For mythology and theogony, see H. Blezer, 'The "Bon" *dBal-mo nyer-bdun* (*/brgyad*) and the Buddhist *dBang-phyug-ma nyer brgyad*: A brief comparison', *ibid.*, pp. 117–78. And for doxography, see K. Mimaki, 'Doxographie tibétaine et classifications indiennes', in: F. Fukui and G. Fussman, *Bouddhisme et cultures locales* (Paris, 1994), pp. 115–36.

A major difference between the relation of Buddhism in India to Brahmanism/Hinduism and that of Tibetan Buddhism to Bon lies in the fact that, whilst the traditions of Indian Buddhism were developed in an Indian milieu (and in part by Brahmans), for the most part the traditions of Tibetan Buddhism did not, of course, arise in Bon.

this being the case for instance in Thailand[233] – there seem to exist no clear records of this particular custom having been followed by rulers in the Tibetan cultural area. As just seen, however, the use of Indian mythical and legendary material is well attested in the annals of Tibetan kingdoms and principalities.

Beside the above-mentioned *laukika* : *lokottara* opposition that yields an 'emic' frame within which the relation between mundane divinities and supramundane ones may be envisaged – a frame with which the the idea of subjugation/subordination/engagement/incorporation through a 'convention' (*dam tshig*), vow (*sdom pa*) or oath (*dam bca'*) appears very closely associated – mention needs to be made of a further schema through which the mundane level was integratable within the Buddhist cosmos. This is the model according to which a subordinate divinity becomes assimilated in virtue of a promise to become a *yon bdag* 'donor' of a monastic establishment and of the Buddhist Saṃgha. According to one of the gYa' bzaṅ documents,[234] when this religious institution was being established by its founder, local divinities (*gži bdag*) and *numina* (*mi ma yin* = *amanuṣya[ka]*, *amānuṣa*), with Šam bu/Śambhu at their head, undertook to become its supporters (*yon bdag byed par dam bca' ba*). In the traditional Buddhist structure of society, the donor (*yon bdag*, an honorific form of *sbyin bdag* = *dānapati*) functions as the counterpart of the *mchod gnas* (Skt. *dakṣiṇīya*), i.e. the religious as donee.[235] Now, this particular conceptual frame which undergirds the relationship between a local – telluric and mundane – protective divinity and the world of the Buddhist Dharma seems quite distinct from the *laukika* : *lokottara* model explored above. Yet the two frames are not incompatible, and they can be seen to be linked through the idea of the 'convention', vow or oath which plays a determining part in each. Still another link between the two conceptual frames is evidently supplied by

---

233 cf. R. Lingat, *Royautés bouddhiques* (Paris, 1989), pp. 128, 137, 152 ff.

234 See T. Gyalbo *et al.*, *Civilization at the foot of Mount Sham po* (as in n. 218), p. 143.

235 See D. Seyfort Ruegg, *Ordre spirituel et ordre temporel dans la pensée bouddhique de l'Inde et du Tibet*, Part I; id., 'The preceptor-donor (*yon mchod*) relation in thirteenth-century Tibetan society and polity, its Inner Asian precursors and Indian models', in: H. Krasser *et al.* (ed.), *Tibetan studies* (Proceedings of the 7th Seminar of the International Association of Tibetan Studies, Vienna, 1997), pp. 857–872.

the figure of the lay devotee and donor, be he termed a *dge bsñen* = *upāsaka* (in the first model) or a *yon bdag* (in the second model).[236]

*

The complex relationship obtaining between Tibetan Buddhism (the *Chos*) and Bon with regard to the question of the existence of a common ground between them presents then, in certain respects, an interesting counterpart to the relationship that existed between Indian Buddhism and Hinduism/Brahmanism with reference to their common ground or substratum.

When attempting to conceptualize these relationships, attention is to be paid to the twin processes of 'Indian-izing' and 'Buddhist-izing' (in the case of historically identifiable Tibetan borrowing of exogenous elements from India), and the parallel (and distinct) processes of evolving 'Indic' features (in Tibetan Buddhist *Chos*, in the case of the endogenous development in Tibet of new, but typologically Indian, components) and evolving 'Buddhistic' features (in 'developed' Bon, i.e. the so-called *bsgyur bon*).[237]

---

[236] In his article 'Hindu-isation, Buddha-isation, then Lama-isation', in: T. Skorupski (ed.), *Indo-Tibetan studies* (D. Snellgrove Felicitation Volume, Tring, 1990), A. W. Macdonald has explored themes under discussion here with special reference to La phyi ('Godāvarī'), the border region between Nepal and Tibet, which is considered to represent the Speech-schema (*gsuṅ*) of Cakrasaṃvara. And in his article 'The lake of the Yakṣa chief', ibid., pp. 275–91, J. F. Staal has considered a related set of problems with particular reference to the mTsho ma dros pa = Anavataptahrada (: mTsho ma pham pa = Mānassarovar) and Ti se = Kailāsa, which is considered to represent the Body-schema (*sku*) of the same Cakrasaṃvara. It may be noted that, in some of its sources, the Bon tradition sets itself off from the Buddhist one by writing Ma paṅ instead of Ma pham, which is the usual orthography in Buddhist tradition. On the Kailāsa area see also Namkhai Norbu and R. Prats, *Gaṅs ti se'i dkar chag* (Rome, 1989); and T. Huber and Tsepak Rigzin, 'A Tibetan guide for pilgrimage to Ti-se (Mount Kailas) and mTsho Ma-pham (Lake Manasarovar)", in T. Huber (ed.), *Sacred spaces and powerful place in Tibetan culture* (Dharamsala, 1999), pp. 125–53.

[237] Newly created but typologically Indian components formed by Tibetans thinking along Indian lines and founded in Indian models can be termed 'Indic'. See below; and D. Seyfort Ruegg, *Ordre spirituel et ordre temporel* ..., p. 141 ff.; 'The Indian and the Indic in Tibetan cultural history ... (as in n. 200).

Concerning 'BUDDHISTIC' features found in Bon, they have to be set beside traits in the Buddhist *Chos* that may be connected with Bon (or, conceivably, with a source common to both Bon and Buddhist *Chos*). The expression 'Buddhistic' (as distinct from 'Buddhist') is employed here to refer to a component in Bon that is attested also in Buddhist sources, and is describable as typologically Buddhist, but which is nevertheless found integrated into Bon tradition (any possible common source for both or, alternatively, the direction of any possible borrowing between them, being very often undetermined in the present state of knowledge). And the expression 'HINDUISTIC' (as distinct from 'Hindu') might be used to refer to a component in Tibetan Buddhism, or in Bon, that is attested in Brahmanical/Hindu sources, and which may be determined to be of Brahmanical/Hindu origin, but which has nevertheless been fully integrated into the Tibetan Buddhist, or into the Bon po, scheme of things (either through a hypothetical Indo-Tibetan substratum, or otherwise through borrowing and enculturation).[238] As for the abovementioned expression 'INDIC' (as distinct from 'Indian'), it may be employed to denote an endogenous component in Tibetan religion and thought that is typologically Indian (and hence allogenic), but which is not actually attested in extant sources of Indian origin (in Sanskrit, Pali, etc.), and which, therefore, may not have actually been borrowed from India but was developed by Tibetans thinking creatively along lines inspired by an Indian model.[239] With regard to the presence, addressed in the present Appendix, in Tibetan myth and religion of 'Hinduistic' elements integrated in Tibetan Buddhism or in Bon, they could be said to

---

[238] For the case of the Kālacakra in particular see above.

[239] The term '*allogenic*' is employed here to refer to a cultural component that is typologically distinct without being demonstrably *exogenous* and historically imported (e.g. the 'Indic' in Tibet, given that it is unattested in an extant Indian source; but, of course, it has to be recognized than any argument *e silentio* may be inconclusive); whereas '*exogenous*' is used to refer to a component that is historically of foreign and imported origin (e.g. the Indian in Tibet when attested in Sanskrit, etc., sources). The difference between exogeneity and allogeneity thus rests on a historical (diachronic) criterion rather than on a typological (i.e. systemic and possibly synchronic) one (the Indian and the Indic being of course typologically alike). See also our remarks in the two publications cited in n. 235 above.

represent in Tibetan culture an 'INDIANIZING' component deriving from borrowing followed by internalization and enculturation.

A complex set of concepts with their corresponding terminology is required in order to conceptualize, account for and describe the intricate diachronic processes and synchronic relationships existing between Buddhism and the ambient religions and cultures of India and Tibet. These topics and processes in Indian and Tibetan religion and culture, which pose such fascinating historical, philological and theoretical (typological) problems, will no doubt continue in future to form the subject of detailed research.

*

A striking further case of the incorporation into the Tibetan Buddhist world of a figure assignable to the worldly/mundane level is that of King Ge sar (Seṅ chen, 'Great Lion'). A quasi historical layman hero accompanied – sometimes to the point of virtual identification – by his excellent horse (*rta mchog*), and a conquering warrior victorious over Hor and other outlying regions surrounding Tibet, in the Tibetan epic Ge sar is associated either with the area of Gliṅ in northeastern Tibet, or with the Far North (the so-called 'Land of horses'), with Turkic peoples (Dru gu/Gru gu), and, more vaguely, with a semi-legendary Far (North-)West – the land of Phrom/Khrom (also a name of the eastern Rome of Byzantium, or eventually Rum, the Seljuk Turkic domain of Anatolia) –, but also with Žaṅ žuṅ in the West. King Ge sar is then considered a *dgra lha/bla* (as, e.g., Ge sar rgyal po Žaṅ žuṅ gi dgra lha), a 'war god' connected with the *ver ma* and *ma saṅ*(*s*) divinities. Yet in the tradition of the Khams pa polymath 'Ju Mi pham rnam rgyal (1846–1912), Ge sar came to be regarded as a Dharma-protector and superior tutelary divinity, figuring even as the object of *guruyoga* (*bla ma'i rnal 'byor*).[240]

---

[240] See R.-A Stein, *Recherches sur l'épopée et le barde au Tibet* (Paris, 1959), p. 71 ff.; and D. Schuh, *Tibetische Handschriften*, Teil 5 (VOHD xi,5, Wiesbaden, 1973), p. 144 ff.

The form (')Phrom Ge sar is attested e.g. in the *Li'i yul luṅ bstan pa* (ed. Emmerick, p. 68), where a king of Khotan is stated to have married a daughter of Ge sar. This is of course not the place to go into the origins of Ge sar and the etymology of his name. Two points may nevertheless be briefly mentioned. First, there is the assonance be-

For Ge sar there seems to exist no direct and immediate historical trace either of properly Indian origins or of a typologically Indian prototype. And the question arises as to whether the *laukika* : *lokottara* schema, which has proved useful elsewhere in this study, may be applicable in this case. The emanationist paradigm also discussed above does, however, have a certain pertinence here. For an assimilation has actually been made of Ge sar with *rigs ldan* Drag po 'khor lo can = Kalkin Raudra Cakrin, King of Sambhala in the Far North (see above, pp. 115, 123; between these two figures there indeed exists a certain ideological and iconographic homology). Ge sar has links also with rTa mgrin = Hayagrīva, the horse-headed form of Avalokiteśvara.[241]

---

tween the name Ge sar and *caesar* as a title of the Roman emperor, and subsequently of the Byzantine emperor. Under the Kuṣāṇas *kaïsara* seems already to have been a royal title (in the Ara inscription). As for the name Phrom/Khrom, it is apparently derived from Roma/Rum, a name referring *inter alia* both to the eastern Rome of Byzantium and to Rum, the domain of the Turkic Seljuk rulers of Anatolia (cf. C. Cahen, *The formation of Turkey. The Seljukid sultanate of Rum, eleventh to fourteenth century* [London, 2001]). Other Seljuk Turks exercized influence well into what we now know as Serindia. Later, in 1277, the Great Seljuk sultanate was absorbed by the Mongol Ilkhanids of Iran, i.e. the line of Hülegü (rg. 1256–1265, who had a marital link with the Byzantine imperial family; cf. A. M. Talbot, 'Revival and decline, Voices from the Byzantine capital', in: H. C. Evans [ed.], *Byzantium: Faith and power* [New York, 2004], p. 20). Much earlier, the title 'Fromo Kēsaro' appeared in a Bactrian inscription of Turkic Ṣāhis (see H. Humbach, 'Phrom Gesar and the Bactrian Rome', in: P. Snoy [ed.], *Ethnologie und Geschichte* [Festschrift K. Jettmar, Heidelberg, 1983], pp. 303–09; id., 'New coins of Fromo Kesaro', in G. Pollet [ed.], *India and the Ancient World* [Eggermont Felicitation Vol., Leuven, 1987, pp. 81–85). Secondly, in Sanskrit, *keśara/kesara* may denote the mane of a horse (or lion), and Skt. *keśarin/kesarin* may then denote a horse (or lion). Now, concerning the homology between Ge sar and Kalkin, and the importance of the equine *motif* in their respective stories, we have already seen above (p. 121 and n. 160) that Skt. *karka/kalka* may denote a (white) horse. Keśin is furthermore the name of the equine *aśvarāja* Balāhaka/Valāha (Tib. rTa'i rgyal po sprin gyi gzugs can), found in the prose of the *Mahāvastu*. To the same world of ideas belongs the *(aśva)ājāneya* = *(rta) caṅ šes*. These two values of the name Ge sar are not mutually exclusive and could co-exist.

[241] See for example the Gliṅ manuscript version of the Ge sar epic published by R. A. Stein, *L'épopée tibétaine de Gesar* (Paris, 1956). For a discussion of some of the relevant materials, see R.-A. Stein, *Recherches sur l'épopée et le barde au Tibet*, *passim*, and especially, p. 508 ff. and p. 524 ff.

Concerning the figure of Hayagrīva, see above, p. 122.

This remarkable instance of the absorption – be it SYNCRETISTIC or OSMOTIC (?) in origin – into the Tibetan Buddhist world, as a protective divinity (*yi dam*), of a quasi historical lay hero was, however, to meet with resistance from a writer such as bsTan 'dzin mkhas mchog – an author belonging to the entourage of Pha boṅ kha pa Byams pa bsTan 'dzin 'phrin las rgya mtsho (1878–1941) during the latter's visits in Khams – in the frame of a controversy which took place in Khams in the eighteenth and nineteenth centuries and continued well into the twentieth century, and which concerned both the authenticity of certain religio-philosophical teachings and the validity, from a Buddhist point of view, of specifically Tibetan cultural traditions that were suspected of being spurious (*rdzus ma*).[242] Otherwise, however, the figure of Gliṅ Ge sar has largely become incorporated into the Buddhist culture and religion of Tibet.[243]

A remarkable example of the incorporation in a prominent position in the Tibetan religious pantheon of an avowedly foreign deity is provided by the case of Pe har, brought forcibly from the Turkic (Hor, Gru gu) Bhaṭa Hor to the north of Tibet (and studied notably by R.-A. Stein and R. de Nebesky-Wojkowitz). After his transfer to Tibet, as protector of bSam yas and then gNas chuṅ, this imported deity came to be regarded as a most important *'jig rten pa'i sruṅ ma* (one moreover destined to be-

---

[242] See bsTan 'dzin mkhas mchog, *sÑan sgron du gsol zer ba'i yig rdzus kyi dpyad don mchan bus bkrol ba, dPyod ldan bžin 'dzum pa'i thal skad ṅna chen bskul ba'i dbyu gu*, f. 51a–b, a text which refers to Pha boṅ kha pa's visit in Chab mdo dGe ldan Byams pa gliṅ in 1935 (*šiṅ phag*, f. 3b) and in its colophon gives its date of composition as 1949 (*sa mo glaṅ*). This work is a critique of the harmonizing – and probably 'œcumenical' – stand adopted in a book by a certain *chos mdzad* Thub bstan blo bzaṅ rgyal mtshan (described as a disciple of dKar 'dzin Brag dkar sprul sku). It discusses the place, in the Tibetan religio-philosophical scheme of things, of rÑiṅ ma, Jo naṅ pa and Bon, and even of the relative situation of the four classical Buddhist philosophical systems (*grub mtha'*, viz. Vaibhāṣika, Sautrāntika, Cittamātra, and Madhyamaka). Another text belonging to this period and tendency is Blo bzaṅ rdo rje, *Yig rdzus la dpyod pa'i skabs kyi phros don/ dam pa gžan gyi gsuṅ sgros ñuṅ ṅur bkod pa bsriṅs pa* (a work presented by its author to Pha boṅ kha pa).

[243] See R.-A. Stein, *Recherches ...*, Chapter ix. In addition to links with other Tibetan orders and schools, Stein has studied those with the bKa' gdams pas, and their monastic centre of Rva sgreṅ, as well as with the dGe lugs pas (pp. 111 ff., 524.).

come a *'jig rten las 'das pa*). He has sometimes been identified with Tshaṅs pa (Brahmā) or brGya byin (Indra).

For want of space we shall here have to leave aside the matter of the so-called 'nameless religion' of Tibet – that is, of R.-A. Stein's 'religion sans nom' (which this scholar has virtually identified with the Tibetan *mi chos* as opposed to *lha chos*; cf. above, n. 12) – even though it too would fit well into the Tibetan *'jig rten pa/'jig rten las 'das pa* paradigm.

*

Here it is not possible either to explore in detail the topics of symbiosis, syncretism, osmosis, and enculturation, and also of substrata (and archistrata), in the Buddhist lands of Southeast Asia – Cambodia, Thailand, etc. – and of Indonesia – Java, Śrīvijaya (Sumatra), and Bali –, where an immigrant Buddhism of Indian origin has coexisted with also imported Brahmanical rites and cults (mainly royal, such as the Devarāja assimilated to Śiva), and with an imported Indian culture and civilization in general, and where the idea of a borrowing of both Buddhism and Brahmanism seems, therefore, entirely appropriate. The cultural situation prevailing in the lands of Southeast Asia differs of course from the situation in the Indian subcontinent – where Buddhism belonged to the domain of Indian civilization and where the assumption of borrowing therefore very often appears problematic – and also with the situation found in the lands of Nepal and Sri Lanka, as well as of Afghanistan (Bactria) and Tibet, which had such protracted and intimate links with India proper that two of them at least have usually been counted as forming part of the South Asian sphere.[244]

---

[244] See, e.g., I. Mabbett's and J. Ensink's sketches, with bibliographies, of Buddhism in Southeast Asia and Indonesia in H. Bechert (ed.), *Der Buddhismus I* (Stuttgart, 2000), p. 441 ff. Cf. H. Kulke and D. Rothermund, *A history of India* (London, 1990), pp. 122 f. (Chola thalassocracy and South Indian merchants), 152 ff. Concerning the Khmer kingdom, see J. Filliozat, 'Sur le çivaïsme et le bouddhisme du Cambodge', *BEFEO* 70 (1981), pp. 59–99; and D. Snellgrove, 'The relationship of Buddhism to the royal Brahmanical cults in the Khmer empire', in: R. Torella *et al.* (ed.), *Le parole e i marmi* (R. Gnoli Felicitation Volume, Rome, 2001), ii, pp. 797–821 (rejecting, at pp. 810 and 813, the idea of an 'amalgamation' of Hinduism and Buddhism).

In short, for the study of the religions and cultures of Southeast Asia, a BORROWING MODEL seems altogether appropriate inasmuch as, historically, Buddhism and Brahmanism were both brought there from outside, whereas in South Asia, where they are both indigenous, the two have of course been so closely related that the idea of borrowing – implying as it usually does EXOGENEITY as well as ALLOGENEITY – would in very many cases appear questionable if not plainly counterfactual.[245] In ancient India, Buddhists and Brahmanists were not two independent groups so clearly demarcated culturally and religiously from each other that features shared in common can be accounted for only by postulating a borrowing *sensu stricto* by the one from the other.

In relation to India, most of the other lands just mentioned, different though each may be from the others, nevertheless share a common feature: they have all embraced Indian civilization and religion without having been conquered by, and subject to, India in the sense of being part of a sustained colonial system of prolonged military, political and economic domination (as distinct from what might be termed an Indo-Southeast Asian *oikoumene*).[246]

By way of contrast, in other parallel cases that come to mind such as the Americas that formed part of the Spanish empire – and where there unmistakably took place a very rapid assimilation of an imported culture and religion that is no less remarkable than what we know from Tibet – the absorption of an imported Spanish and European civilization, and of Catholicism, came about during their colonial period beginning in the sixteenth century.[247] Beside religious conversion, a remarkable example

---

[245] See above, p. 174 with n. 239.

[246] On the nature of the relation between Indian and Southeast Asian civilizations see H. Kulke, 'Indian colonies, Indianization or cultural convergence?', in: H. Schulte Nordholt (ed.), *Onderzoek in Zuidoost-Azië* (Leiden, 1990), pp. 8–32. On the *devarāja* cult in Cambodia, see H. Kulke, 'Der Devarāja-Kult', *Saeculum* 25 (1974), pp. 24–55, with J. Filliozat, 'Sur le çivaïsme et le bouddhisme du Cambodge', *BEFEO* 70 (1961), p. 59 ff.; C. Jacques, 'Les kamrateṅ jagat dans l'ancien Cambodge', in: F. Bizot, *Recherches nouvelles sur le Cambodge* (Paris, 1994), pp. 213–25; and B. Dagens, *Les Khmers* (Paris, 2003), pp. 27–29, 171 ff.

[247] Reference might in addition be made to the (all-too-brief) article 'Contact: Indo-

of this power of cultural assimilation is provided by the 'Mission Baroque' or 'Andean Baroque' of the Indios, including the baroque-style music composed in South America, in the Viceroyalty of Peru, in the eighteenth century by indigenous members of Jesuit 'reductions' or missions. A parallel, but of course quite distinct, example of assimilation of western culture, in this case by the upper classes, took placc in South Asia, and in Burma, under foreign hegemony and colonization from the end of the eighteenth century. But there the conversion of Hindus and Buddhists, or of Muslims, was the exception rather than the rule. An example of the the rapid assimilation of western European civilization by at least the upper classes of a land *not* conquered militarily and then colonized is provided by Russia beginning with Peter the Great (1672–1725). There too the importation of western European civilization was neither accompanied nor followed by a substantial conversion of Russians to the religions – Roman Catholicism or Protestantism – of any of the western European countries whose civilization was otherwise being taken over.

In history, we accordingly find in operation variant processes of borrowing where cultural forms have been taken over by one civilization from another either with or without an overt importation of, and conversion to, the other's religion. None of the three examples of intercultural borrowing just mentioned of course replicates the form of intracultural relationship existing in both India and Tibet between Buddhism and the ambient religions. With respect to the intercultural relation between the Buddhism of India and that of Tibet, it might appear in some respects comparable to the above-mentioned South American case; but Tibetan culture was less hybridized, Tibet never having for instance taken over an Indian language as a general means of communication in the way Spanish and Portugese were adopted in South America.[248] The extent,

---

Christian art' by Eleanor Wake in *Aztecs* (Catalogue of the Royal Academy special exhibition of Aztec art, London, 2002), where attention has been called to the elimination of Aztec/Mayan iconographical (and 'narrative') contents, but to the survival nonetheless of indigenous Mexican artistic potential, imagery and technical skills ('decoration').

[248] It could nevertheless be said that Sanskrit did have an 'archistratal' function for the Tibetan *chos skad*, which was often patterned on Sanskrit syntactically and lexically. See D. Seyfort Ruegg, 'Sanskrit-Tibetan and Tibetan-Sanskrit dictionaries and some problems in Indo-Tibetan philosophical lexicography', in B. Oguibénine (ed.), Lexi-

however, to which the ideas of 'proselytism by missionary' and 'conversion' are equivalent to the (Tibetan) Buddhist concepts expressed as (*chos lugs*) *sgyur ba* and *'dul ba* – and by syntactic constructions that include the terms *dam tshig/dam bca'/sdom pa* – no doubt requires careful reflection. At all events, culturally speaking, religious conversion from without, through the action of foreign missionaries, might appear phenomenologically to constitute a very different thing from conversion from within, inside a (partly) shared civilization and religious matrix. And a distinction has no doubt to be drawn between conversion understood as transformation and trans-valuation going from one level to another (and thus constituting a form of *metanoia*) and conversion understood as the relinquishing of one religion in favour of another one (*epistrophé*) and being a proselyte (literally 'one come over, a stranger').[249]

Finally, in relation to missionary activity and conversion, it is of interest to recall the case of the 'quarrel on rites' that arose with Christian missionaries in Ming and Ch'ing China (e.g. M. Ricci) concerning the extent to which local custom and ritual might usefully and appropriately be adopted by Catholics. Some missionaries, Jesuits in particular, regarded non-Christian customs as a reserve fit to be drawn upon in certain circumstances (cf. above p. 98, on *usus iustus*). A distinct, but not unrelated, problem has arisen in connexion with the use of Zen and Yoga techniques in Christian practice.

In summary, in addition to (i) the various EXOGENOUS and HISTORICALLY INDIAN (and the less numerous historically Chinese) components that were taken over, internalized and fully integrated into Tibetan civilization and the Buddhism of Tibet, and alongside (ii) the ENDOGENOUS but TYPOLOGICALLY INDIAN components developed by the Tibetans themselves when thinking along Indian lines, and which have here been

---

cography in the Indian and Buddhist cultural field (Munich, 1998), pp. 123–4.

249 Tib. *sgyur ba* 'change' is rendered as either 'convert' or 'translate' according to the context. And Tib. *'dul ba* = Skt. *vi-nī-* 'subdue, discipline, tame, train' has also been rendered as 'convert' in certain contexts. On the idea of conversion – Gk. *epistrophé* or *metanoia* (usually translated 'repentance') – see p. 53, n. 76 above. Buddhism is regarded as a missionary religion, unlike Hinduism which is not usually considered as such (although there exist records of the existence of Hinduism outside India, perhaps for the most part in the form of Indian emigrant communities and of travelling merchants).

termed INDIC, Tibetan Buddhism has also embraced (iii) elements that are indigenous to that land (and to Inner Asia). In the first two cases, the processes firstly of intercultural borrowing and then of intracultural elaboration that have been at work in Tibet might perhaps be described as two forms of ENCULTURATION. But in the second case – a remarkable convergence and synergy of the intercultural and intracultural, of the exogenous and the endogenous – it is no doubt preferable to speak of a process of original CREATIVE ELABORATION based on ways of thinking that are typologically Indian. In the third case, which also represents an intracultural process in Tibet, it is possible to speak of osmosis and absorption integrating endogenous elements.[250]

At all events, notwithstanding the real and very significant differences found to exist between these processes of either intercultural or intracultural integration, both the *laukika* : *lokottara* contrastive opposition – where the *laukika* level embraces a substratum partly shared with ambient religions and cultures – and the (not altogether unrelated) docetic emanation model, which constitute the two main topics studied in this monograph, may be identified as seminal ideological and hermeneutical paradigms that have informed and infused the above-mentioned religio-cultural processes, fitting elements of various origins into the Buddhist frame that has pervaded and structured most of Tibetan religion and culture throughout its history.

---

[250] This analysis does not take into account the still obscure issue of the possible existence of a culture partly shared between India and the area north of the Himalayan mountains in pre-Buddhist times (and alluded to above, p. 168 ff.).

Appendix II

The noetic and the conventional

The questions of taxonomy, structure and level that have been discussed in the present work arise in a particular form in the case of the entities known as *ḍākinī*s (Tib. *mkha' 'gro ma*). This is borne out by the fact that different kinds of *ḍākinī* are distinguished, a differentiation being made between ordinary *ḍākinī*s – as aerial faeries or ogresses – and a *jñāna-ḍākinī* (Tib. *ye šes mkha' 'gro ma*), '*ḍākinī* of Gnosis', that is, the particular type of *ḍākinī* who belongs to the noetic (or noumenal) world of the *sādhaka*'s yogic practice. In Indological secondary literature, the *ḍākinī* has frequently been defined as a (female) imp, goblin or witch, or again as a demoness. But this definition, justified though it may be for certain contexts, is hardly confirmed by the bulk of the relevant Buddhist sources.

Traditionally, in indigenous Sanskrit dictionaries, the word itself is explained through an etymology linking it with the root *ḍī-* 'move in the sky, fly'. This derivation then passed to the *sGra sbyor bam po gñis pa* (early ninth century), which refers back to the Dhātupāṭha entry *ḍī*(*ṅ*) *vihāyasā gatau* '[the root] *ḍī-* denotes movement through the sky';[251] and in this Tibetan lexicographical work *ḍākinī* is explained as 'the name for one who has attained miraculous power (*r̥ddhi*) such as moving through the sky having realized this through *mantra*' (*sṅags grub nam mkha' la 'gro ba la sogs pa rdzu 'phrul thob pa'i miṅ*). The *ḍākinī*s are linked in particular with Yoginītantras. The alternative form *ḍāginī* appears to be Prakritic. Morphologically comparable is the word *śākinī*, also defined in dictionaries as a demoness. Some semantically related words are *khasar-paṇa* and *khecara*/*khecarī* (Tib. *mkha' spyod ma*, the name of a tutelary deity, as in Tib. Nāro mkha' spyod ma, where *ḍākinī* appears as the Sanskrit equivalent). The word *ḍāka* (Tib. *mkha' 'gro*) – a rarer form attested for instance in the title *Ḍākārṇava*(*mahāyoginītantrarāja*) – appears as the masculine form of *ḍākinī*.[252] Through assonance, and the

---

[251] See the Pāṇinian *Dhātupāṭha* i.1017 (Class I: *bhvādi*) and iv.27 (Class IV: *dīvādi*).

[252] The words *ḍāka* and *ḍākinī* are found in the Māṃsabhakṣaṇa (p. 252) and Dhāraṇī

(supposed common) etymon *ḍī-*, there exists an association of the *ḍākinīs* with Uḍḍiyāṇa/Oḍḍiyāna/Udyāna (Tib. U rgyan/O rgyan), the land of miracles and of thaumaturges such as Padmasambhava.[253] In the *Kathāsaritsāgara*, one Ḍākineya – apparently a metronymic form signifying 'son of the Ḍākinī'– figures as the name of a gambler invested by a pair of demons.[254]

The Vajrayānist literature of Buddhism knows several forms of *ḍāka*. In Abhayākaragupta's *Niṣpannayogāvalī* (no. 24) there is the *maṇḍala* of the pentad composed of Vajraḍāka (with Nairātm[y]ā, emanated by Akṣobhya), Buddhaḍāka (with Locanā, emanated by Vairocana), Ratnaḍāka (with Māmakī, emanated by Ratnasambhava), Padmaḍāka (with Paṇḍarā, emanated by Amitābha), and Viśvadāka (with Tārā, emanated by Amoghasiddhi). Karmaḍāka (Tib. Las kyi mkha' 'gro) is also known, as is Jñānaḍāka (emanated by Vajrasattva).[255]

The *ḍākinīs* too are multiple.[256] Examples are Buddha°, Ghora°, Padma°, Ratna°, Vajra°, Viśva°, and Jñānaḍākinī (*Niṣpannayogāvalī*, no.

(pp. 261–2) chapters of the *Laṅkāvatārasūtra*. Concerning the *Ḍākārṇava* and the *Vajraḍāka* texts, see Hara Prasad Shāstri, *Descriptive catalogue of Sanscrit manuscripts in the Government Collection*, vol. i (Calcutta, 1917), pp. 89–110.

253 For Swāt, etc., see G. Tucci, *Travels of Tibetan pilgrims in the Swat Valley* (Calcutta, 1940); and 'On Swāt: the Dards and connected problems', *EW* 27 (1977), pp. 3–103.

254 On problems connected with the lexemes *ḍāka*, *ḍākinī*, *ḍāginī*, *ḍhākini*, and *śākinī*, see M. Mayrhofer's *Kurzgefaßtes etymologisches Wörterbuch des Altindischen*, i, p.461 and iii, pp. 321, 717, 718 (taking the words *ḍākini* and *śākini* to be probably rhyming echo-words), and R. Turner's *Comparative dictionary of the Indo-Aryan languages*, p. 311 (for the Middle and New Indo-Aryan forms), as well as W. Wüst, *PHMA* 3 (1957), pp. 38–46. (suggesting that ḍ- is non-Sanskritic in relation to Indo-Aryan *ś-*). The etymological derivation from the root *ḍī-* may be a hermeneutic (*nirukta*) one; it is not impossible that the words *ḍākinī* etc. are of non Indo-Aryan origin.

255 See, e.g., Abhayākaragupta, *Niṣpannayogāvalī* nos. 24–25. On the *ḍākas* and their iconography, see M.-T. de Mallmann, *Introduction à l'iconographie du tântrisme bouddhique* (Paris, 1975).

256 On the *ḍākinīs*, their iconography and their rituals, see M.-T. de Mallmann, *op. cit.*; A. Herrmann Pfandt, *Zur Stellung und Symbolik des Weiblichen im tantrischen Buddhismus* (Bonn, 1992); T. Skorupski, 'In praise of the Ḍākinīs', in: S. Karmay *et al.* (ed.), *Les habitants du toit du monde* (A. Macdonald Felicitation Volume, Nanterre, 1997), p. 309 f.; and L. Kuo, article 'Dakini' in: *Hōbōgirin* 8 (Paris-Tōkyō, 2003), pp. 1095–1106.

4 and *passim*). Padmasambhava's consort Ye šes mtsho rgyal may be described as a *ye šes mkha' 'gro ma* (= *jñānaḍākinī*). On the contrary, an 'ordinary', i.e. *laukika*, *ḍākinī* – a sort of ogress – requires to be tamed/ trained (*vi-nī-* = *'dul ba*) by Mahākala/Vairocana or by Vajrapāṇi,[257] a *topos* often met with and discussed earlier in the present study.

For the purposes of this investigation, the concepts of *jñānaḍāka* and *jñānaḍākinī* are of significance because the factor of *jñāna* 'gnosis' locates the entity in question on the noetic or noumenal, and therefore transmundane, level, in contradistinction to the ordinary level of the *laukika*. In Tibetan, a *ye šes mkha' 'gro ma* is in fact described as one who is *'jig rten las 'das pa*, i.e. as *lokottara* 'transmundane', and as Vajrayoginī (rDo rje rnal 'byor ma).

Consider now the entities known as the *ye šes pa* and *dam tshig pa*. The *ye šes pa* is defined as a *'jig rten las 'das pa'i lha*, i.e. as a *lokottara* deity. The correlative, and contrasted, concept is *dam tshig pa*, a word that designates the sacralized yogic practiser on the conventional, and 'microcosmic', level of the 'pledger' in Vajrayānist practice. The term *ye šes pa* is of course derived from *ye šes* = *jñāna*, 'gnosis' or ' noesis', and thus refers to a noetic/noumenal theophany or hierophany. And *dam tshig pa* is a derivative of *dam tshig* = *samaya*, 'convention, pledge', and it thus refers to the theophany realized in the *sādhaka* through yogic practice. In the course of Vajrayānist meditation and ritual, the *ye šes pa* – the noetic hierophany thought of as invited and precipitated (*'bab pa*) before the practiser-adept who visualizes him – is described as Jñānasattva (*ye šes sems dpa'*). And, as the vessel of this hierophany, the *dam tshig pa*, the sacralized visualizer located on the conventional (*sāmayika*) level of ritual and yogic practice, is described as Samayasattva (*dam tshig sems dpa'*).[258]

---

[257] See *Hōbōgirin* 8, p. 1100.

[258] The 'invitation' and the 'precipitation' or 'entry' of the noetic and noumenal hierophany (*ye šes pa 'jug pa* : *jñānasattvapraveśa*) on to the level of the practiser-yogin, and the process of self-identification with the noetic level of the transmundane divine – a special kind of self-deification and *theōsis* (cf. above, pp. 84–85) – form part of the *lha'i rnal 'byor* = *devatāyoga*. In addition to the *dam tshig sems dpa'* = *samayasattva* and the *ye šes sems dpa'* = *jñānasattva*, yogic procedure posits the *tiṅ ṅe 'dzin sems dpa'* = *samādhisattva* (correlatable with the *dharmakāya*) as its culmination. When yogically generated together (*cig car du*), the three are referred to as the *sems*

It would seem possible to discern here a certain parallelism – perhaps even some sort of isomorphism – between the two pairs *jñāna* : *samaya* and *lokottara* : *laukika* and the pair *paramārtha* (*-satya*) : *saṃvṛti*(*-satya*). At the same time it appears that these sets of concepts are not simply interchangeable (see below). Yet non-duality – *advaya*, as distinct from a monistic identity – does characterize the relation between the two terms of each of these pairs, if in different ways. In philosophical analysis, the truth/reality *of* the surface-level (*saṃvṛti*) is not simply identical with the *paramārtha*(*satya*); still, the truth/reality *about* the *samvṛti* is, in a sense, *paramārtha*, i.e. that state of reality where all things (*dharma*) – conventional and even ultimate – are Empty of self-existence (*svabhāvaśūnya*, *niḥsvabhāva*), 'originally extinguished' and tranquil (*ādiparinirvṛta*, *ādiśānta*, etc.). In this perspective, *saṃvṛtisatya* is transformed into what is termed *saṃvṛtimātra* (*kun rdzob tsam*) in the view of the Ārya.[259] The *paramārtha* may cancel, and so to say 'zero', the lower surface-level of *saṃvṛti*. But an utterance asserting non-substantiality (*niḥsvabhāvatā*, i.e. *śūnyatā*) has been declared *not* to destroy, to *make* non-substantial and Empty, the lower level: in reality this level *is*, already and always, non-substantial and Empty (*śūnya*) of self-existence.[260] In terms of Madhyamaka thought, what an utterance stating non-substantiality can be said to do is, then, to make known (*jñāpayati*) the fact that all factors of existence (*dharma*) *are* Empty, etc., a state of reality pertaining to the *paramārtha*.[261]

---

dpa' sum brtsegs. For the *ye šes pa* (correlatable with the *sambhogakāya*) and the *dam tshig pa* (correlatable with the *nirmāṇakāya*), see, e.g., the index s. uu. 'Being: Symbolic Being' and 'Being: Knowledge Being' in F. Lessing and A. Wayman, *Mkhas grub rje's Fundamentals of the Buddhist Tantra* (The Hague, 1968), esp. p. 162 n. 17 and p. 296 n. 29; and the index s.uu. 'wisdom-being' and 'pledge-being' in Dalai Lama XIV, J. Hopkins, *et al.*, *The Yoga of Tibet*: *The Great Exposition of Secret Mantra – 2 and 3, by Tsong-ka-pa* (London, 1981). The Sanskrit terms are found, e.g., in Candrakīrti's *Pradīpoddyotana* (ed. Chakravarti), p. 99.

[259] For the notions of *saṃvṛtimātra* and *saṃvṛtisatya*, see D. Seyfort Ruegg, *Two prolegomena to Madhyamaka philosophy* (Studies in Indian and Tibetan Madhyamaka thought, Part 2, Vienna, 2002), Index s.uu.

[260] See *Kāśyapaparivarta* § 63, with Nāgārjuna, *Vigrahavyāvartanīvṛtti* 64, and Candrakīrti, *Prasannapadā* xiii.8.

[261] See D. Seyfort Ruegg, Three *studies in Indian and Tibetan Madhyamaka philosophy* (Studies in Indian and Tibetan Madhyamaka thought, Part 1, Vienna, 2000), p. 208 f.

Here, for the *saṃvṛti*-level, *jñāna* 'gnosis' has so to speak a transformative function that raises the surface-level, by a sort of TRANSVALUATION, to the level of the *paramārtha*, even as a function of *jñāna* may be transformatively to raise the *laukika* to the *lokottara* level or to trans-valuate the *dam tshig pa* (: *sāmayika* or 'conventional') to the *ye šes pa* (noetic/noumenal) level. Perhaps the *lokottara* might be said to 'show', to 'point to', the ultimate level – the *pāramārthika* – without of course itself being the *niṣparyāya-paramārtha*.[262]

Hence, although the *lokottara* and the *paramārtha* are not identical or equatable, as the higher levels attained, thanks to the 'mesocosmic' and transformative cognitive function of *jñāna*, from the base of the *saṃvṛti* or of the 'microcosmic' *sāmayika-laukika*, the two could perhaps be thought of as nonetheless parallel and to a certain degree isomorphic. In Buddhist thought, this function of *jñāna* represents a 'gnôsis' (if not Gnosticism strictly speaking).

[262] See p. 91 above. For the *niṣparyāya-paramārtha* opposed to the (*sa*)*paryāya-paramārtha*, see D. Seyfort Ruegg, 'The *Svātantrika-Prāsaṅgika* distinction in the history of Madhyamaka thought', *IIJ* 49 (2006), p. 319 f.

Indices

Names

Abhinavagupta • 6, 112, 138
Afghanistan • 127, 128, 178
Amida • 38
Anavataptahrada (mTsho ma dros pa) • 173
Ardhanārīśvara • 59
Ārya-Śūra • 163
Aśoka • 5, 154
Aśvaghoṣa • 9, 12
Atiśa (Dīpaṃkaraśrījñāna) • 112, 127
Avalokiteśvara / Avalokiteśa • 7, 11, 13, 25, 31, 32, 33, 37, 46, 57, 101, 102, 122, 132, 165, 166, 169, 176
Bactria • 127, 171, 178
Bālāha • 122, 176
Bali (Indonesia) • 23, 47, 178
Bhairava • 58, 59, 80
Bhasmeśvara • 57
Bhāviveka (Bhavya) • 13, 14, 88, 117, 137, 140, 141
Brahmā / Brahmán • 13, 19, 24, 28, 31, 32, 33, 35, 39, 43, 54, 58, 59, 60, 63, 65, 67, 70, 72, 74, 75, 76, 77, 88, 92, 98, 99, 116, 138, 178
Bu ston (Rin chen grub) • 11, 12, 55, 63, 64, 65, 66, 88, 124, 166
Byaṅ bdag • 166
Byaṅ chub 'od (lHa btsun) • 127
Cakrasaṃvara • 80, 165, 173
Cambodia • 47, 178, 179
Caṇḍamahāroṣaṇa • 58
Caṇḍikā • 165
Candra • 19, 20, 31, 32, 33, 74, 92
Candragomin • 158
Chinnamastā • 110, 111
Chinnamuṇḍā • 110
Dharmottara • 112
Ekajaṭā • 110, 111
Gaṇapati • 25, 77
Gandhāra • 65, 127, 128
Gaṇendra • 123
Gaṇeśa • 25, 156
Garuḍa • 65, 101
Gauḍapāda • 139
Ge sar • 124, 175, 176, 177
Gilgit • 31, 32, 57, 58, 81
Grags pa rgyal mtshan (*sku žaṅ* of Ža lu) • 64, 166
Hanumant • 123, 124, 165
Hara • 12, 38, 53, 58, 77, 123, 184
Hari • 58, 71, 77, 101, 123, 141, 154
Haribhadra • 23, 24
Harihara • 59, 102
Harihariharivāhanodbhava-Lokeśvara • 101, 103
Hārītī • 27, 28, 65
Harṣa (King Harṣavardhana) • 154
Hayagrīva • 122, 176
Heruka/Hevajra • 58
Himālaya • 164
Hiraṇyagarbha • 43, 58, 60, 72
Indra • 14, 19, 23, 24, 33, 39, 53, 58, 63, 67, 71, 72, 74, 178
Japan • 18, 24, 25, 38, 39, 47, 52, 122, 136, 158, 159, 166
Java • 47, 178
Jayadeva • 121
Jayantabhaṭṭa • 97, 137, 138
Kailāsa (Gaṅs Ti se) • 73, 80, 81, 123, 165, 166, 173
Kālacakra • 25, 58, 77, 115, 116, 117, 118, 119, 121, 122, 123, 124, 125, 126, 140, 163, 166, 168, 174

Subjects

Selected book titles

Sanskrit key words

Pali key words

Tibetan key words

Japanese terms